£2

GGW

13/3.

DINING IN GRAND STYLE

PHOTOGRAPHY BY MICHAEL GRIMALDI

DINING IN GRAND STYLE

BY ELIZABETH SCHNEIDER

◆

WITH DIETER HANNIG

AND THE CHEFS OF HILTON INTERNATIONAL

DESIGN BY ANA ROGERS
PHOTOGRAPHS STYLED BY DIETER HANNIG

It is with much pride in their accomplishments that we dedicate this book to all the Hilton International chefs and their kitchen brigades.

John Jarvis
Chairman
Hilton International Co.

The publisher would like to acknowledge the tremendous support and cooperation of all the individuals whose contributions helped to realize this project. Of special note are Alan Gould and Maddy Cohen of Hilton International; Thorsons Publishers, Inc., staff members Leslie Colket, Estella Arias, and Jeanie Levitan; and the staff members of Thorsons Publishing Group in the United Kingdom.

Ehud C. Sperling, Publisher

British Library Cataloguing in Publication Data

Schneider, Elizabeth
Dining in grand style : with the chefs
of Hilton International.
1. Cookery   2. Entertaining
I. Title   II. Hannig, Dieter
641.5′68   TX739

ISBN 1-85336-001-5

*Equation is part of the Thorsons Publishing Group,
Wellingborough, Northamptonshire NN8 2RQ,
England*

Colour reproduction by Novacolour Ltd, Birmingham
Printed and bound in Italy by New Interlitho S.p.A., Milan

1 3 5 7 9 10 8 6 4 2

PAGES 2–3: **Stuffed Tofu with Prawns** (see page 264 for recipe) on an ornamental carrot net
PAGES 4–5: **A fleet of canapes from the Hilton International Wien**
PAGES 6–7: **Braised and Grilled Chicken in Coconut and Javanese Spices** (see page 312 for recipe) surrounded by chilli-peppers, cones of palm sugar, lemon grass stalks, candlenuts (kemiri), fresh turmeric, and wild lime leaves
PAGES 8–9: **Executive chef Albert Schnell (holding silver *cloche*) with his precision team in Toronto**

CONTENTS

THE AMERICAS

EUROPE

ASIA AND AUSTRALIA

Dining in Grand Style...

Once upon a time the good life revolved around hotels. At the heart of each great hotel were its dining rooms and ballroom, where fashionable society gathered. When chef Auguste Escoffier reigned at the Grand Hotel in Monte Carlo, then the Savoy, and the Carlton, the *haut monde* followed—taking their steamer trunks bursting with morning dresses, smoking jackets, tea gowns, and sundry supper finery. The days of a 'year abroad' would commence beneath down coverlets with a silver service of hot chocolate, discreetly delivered, and finish with a champagne soirée in the ballroom.

Dining in grand style is not simply a dream of yesteryear, for the old-style service and spacious and tranquil dining rooms of Hilton International are more in tune with Escoffier's era than the business bustle of the jet-age. The array of crystal and cutlery, the decorative napkin folds, the dazzling (not fussy) garnishes, and the low-key formality all suggest a past few have known—with all the modern conveniences. Today's luxury hotel is a haven from the speed of our times, whether it serves as an oasis for the accomplishment of business negotiations or for romantic idylls.

Worldwide...

The term 'hotel dining' has quite different meanings from one continent to another. In the Americas, particularly the United States, the words 'fine food' and 'hotel' have until recently been just about mutually exclusive; but a resurgence of quality dining in hotels is refreshingly apparent. In particular, local ingredients and cooking styles have come into their own, and restaurants that celebrate regional specialities have burgeoned. In the mid-seventies European-trained Albert Schnell, area chef for Hilton Canada, began featuring superb local produce—Manitoba wild rice, Alberta beef, Canadian apples and maple syrup—in elegant dinner menus in the hotels he supervised. At the outset of the '80s, a team at the American Harvest Restaurant in the Vista International Hotel in New York City pioneered the fine dining-room presentation of simplified traditional dishes, such as Martha's Vineyard Green Corn Pudding and Shaker Lemon Pie.

In contrast, fine dining has long been considered a province of hotels throughout Europe, which are *expected* to prepare the best food—even when measured against small restaurants run by big-name chefs—whether in Strasbourg, Brussels or Vienna and whether they serve 20 or 2,000 meals a day. Europe is the best known jousting ground for proving culinary prowess. Critics lie in wait to applaud, downgrade, bemoan, enshrine, and otherwise point out the virtues and vices of every morsel of food that enters a luxury dining room. And the European audience, parochial or cosmopolitan, amateur or professional, is composed of indefatigable judges. In this competitive atmosphere Hilton International hotels have flourished, winning kudos (and stars) from such travel arbiters as *Michelin*, recommendations of the highest order in restaurant handbooks, and a devoted local clientele wherever Hilton chefs hang their toques.

In Asia, food presentation in hotels is, simply, without equal. Every diner is visiting royalty. Graceful men and women attend. Roses and jasmine perfume the air. Drink

Messieurs Bergeret (left) and Dupont of the Hilton International Genève in the hotel's dining room, Le Cygne

and food preferences, and the names of each member of the party are recorded by the staff, it appears, from the moment of arrival. Torrents of carved fruit greet the early morning breakfaster or all-night discoer at the hotel's coffee shop. Ice sculptures and sprays of orchids vie for attention with the overflowing desserts displayed at even the simplest lunch buffet. The choice of cuisines is considerable throughout the Orient, and European-trained chefs and American cultural exports have recently expanded the repertoire. Businessmen zip between Tokyo and San Francisco, London and Hong Kong, and bring with them their East-West tastes and appetites. Yet traditional Oriental cuisines are still the focus in most Asian hotels. Venerable local dishes, exquisitely prepared, star in the Hilton International restaurants in Tokyo and Jakarta, Bangkok, Kuala Lumpur, Singapore and Taipei, among others, even as those same kitchens are transforming the riches of the East into a powerful new hybrid vocabulary.

To meet the multicultural requirements of contemporary guests (represented by as many local residents as worldly voyagers), each Hilton International hotel includes several restaurants—from coffee-shop casual to sparkling fine dining room. These proffer both internationally known classics and, most intriguing for the adventurous traveller, dishes that reflect the cooking of the country in which the hotel is located—both scrupulously researched authentic fare and chefs' original creations. The interpolation of local ingredients and use of regional handicrafts in the decor are key policies of the company, which educates staff members in the culture and cuisine of an area through an extensive culinary heritage programme. Whether the subject is speedily stir-fried noodles with Oriental vegetables in the Jakarta Hilton International's informal Peacock Café, or a complex chef's invention such as spiced smoked duck breast with a palette of sweet-hot Eastern vegetable salads in the elaborate Taman Sari Grill Room in the same hotel, aesthetics and flavours are sure to be Indonesian.

with the Chefs of Hilton International

It takes a special kind of executive chef to supervise the scope of these large hotels, to oversee the banquet and room service operations and as many as a half-dozen restaurants. For not only must he be superbly organized, able to direct others, imaginative, cost-conscious, healthy as a horse, and have the physical and emotional energy to keep up such a balancing act; he must be willing and able to assimilate the culture and customs of a foreign country in order to appreciate and understand his staff, the food and the local guests. He usually does this without the personal celebrity allotted to chefs whose names are synonymous with their own small restaurants. He is what might be called a chef of the old school, who apprentices in his early teens, works through the ranks, and whose life *becomes* the hotel kitchen. It is not unusual, for example, to find a 35-year-old chef who has spent 22 years in the business, working a strenuous 14 or so hours per day, six days per week. The drive and dedication needed to sustain such a role might be compared to that of a ballet dancer or competitive athlete—always in training, always ready to perform. Yet the chef's performance takes place backstage; it is the food that stars.

A chef's work is reinforced by every member of the food staff, maintained by kitchen teams that often work together for decades. He relies on his sous-chef(s) to handle the grand-scale fulfilment of each day's assignments and on his maître d' to report responses to a new dish on the menu; the waiter depends upon the maître d's familiarity with the clientele to guide him through the maze of personalities and individual preferences. Dining rooms and kitchens of this calibre are no place for transient actors, college students, or other part-timers, as is often the case in more casual restaurants. The roles are reserved for professionals who are devoted to the task. As in a fine theatre troupe, all parts, no matter how small, are pivotal to the performance.

About the Recipes

Although each of Hilton International's hotels offers unique dishes in its dining rooms, the recipes in this volume represent about one-quarter of its hotel kitchens in the Americas, Europe, and Asia. In order to create a broad and balanced selection of flavours—and to produce a book that is portable—a number of noteworthy restaurants have, of necessity, been left aside.

While this may be a geographical simplification, it nevertheless describes much of the scope of the food produced in the Hilton International kitchens, where culinary cross-fertilization is a fact of life: Oriental presentation deeply affected all of European Nouvelle Cuisine; European chefs working in Asia applied their Western techniques to the stimulating array of unfamiliar ingredients; concurrently, other European-trained cooks travelled westward and were captivated by the bounty of North America; while at the same time, the American Melting Pot was boiling over with newly found regional self-expression. The recipe for a dish created in the United States by a Swiss chef who has spent years in the Caribbean will be found in the Americas section, because that is where the chef, restaurant, and diners for whom the dish has been developed are located. Thus the recipes do not usually reflect any single national cuisine, but rather a multicultural approach to restaurant dining.

A meal in the fine dining room of a de luxe hotel is a special event. There, one celebrates—a fiftieth anniversary, a success in business, Christmas, the beginning of a new career, or falling in love. The atmosphere is far from the ordinary, but not so demanding that attention focuses on the surroundings, rather than the occasion. Diners dress up in order to feel festive and formal, to create an aura of timelessness, a magic landscape. Thus, for the most part, people come to enjoy 'non-home' cooking, to be pampered, to linger—to eat more and drink more than they do other evenings. Although dishes may appear simple, more often than not they will be intricate and rich. It is in a fine dining room that a chef can let his creative fancy run free, where exotic and unfamiliar ingredients are explored, where luxury reigns. This is party food.

Naturally, no one eats party food every night, nor would a home cook attempt to duplicate some of the specialities served in a Vista or Hilton International dining room—unless he or she had a kitchen staff of 15. Selected here are a range of particularly delicious and unusual recipes of varying degrees of simplicity and difficulty of preparation, all of which have been tested and adapted for successful reproduction by the home cook. Some are quickly made and inexpensive, some are time-consuming to prepare, many are gloriously rich, and some undeniably luxurious. All are to be enjoyed in a party mood, for that is what fine dining is about.

RECIPES BY CATEGORY

APPETIZERS

SALADS

SOUPS

VEGETABLES, GRAINS AND PASTA

SEAFOOD

MEAT AND POULTRY

DESSERTS

THE AMERICAS

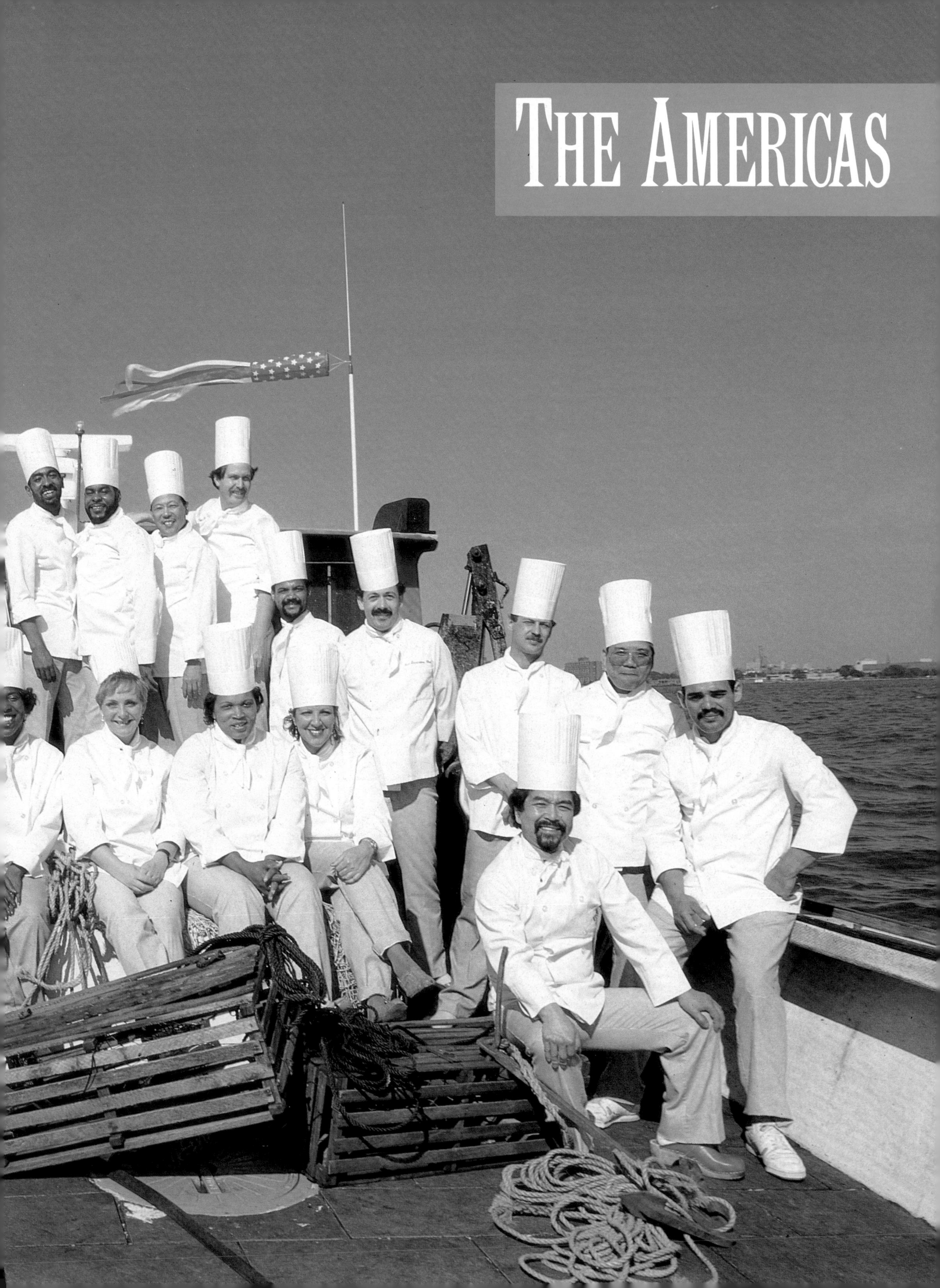

RECIPES

APPETIZERS

Smoked Salmon and Golden Caviar Crêpes with Salad Greens *(Canada)* 32
Snails in Black Bean Sauce on Tofu *(Hawaii, United States)* 34
Gravlax (Salmon Marinated with Dill and Pepper) *(Canada)* 35
Swordfish and Grapefruit *Escabeche (Puerto Rico, United States)* 37
Terrine of *Gravlax (United States)* 38
Barley 'Risotto' with Blue Cheese *(United States)* 40

SALADS

Avocado and Grapefruit Salad with Honey Vinaigrette *(Canada)* 41
Spinach, Quail Eggs and Livers in Raspberry-Walnut Vinaigrette *(Canada)* 41
Mangetout-Cucumber Salad *(United States)* 44
Pepper Slaw *(United States)* 45
Scallops, Cucumbers and Mushrooms in Basil-Peppercorn
Vinaigrette *(United States)* 47
Black Bean and Seafood Salad *(Puerto Rico, United States)* 48
Mussel Salad with Leeks *(Canada)* 49

SOUPS

Puréed Squash-*Apio* Soup with Crabmeat *(Puerto Rico, United States)* 55
Wine Soup with Peppered Cheese, Onions and Croûtons *(United States)* 56
Cold Beetroot Soup with Scallops *(United States)* 57
Wisconsin Diced Vegetable and Sorrel Soup *(United States)* 58
Carrot and Walnut Soup *(United States)* 59
Seven Greens and Mussel Gumbo *(United States)* 59
Cape Cod's Bookbinder Red Snapper Soup *(United States)* 62

VEGETABLE AND GRAIN DISHES

Martha's Vineyard Green Corn Pudding *(United States)* 67
Manitoba Wild Rice Croquettes *(Canada)* 68

PREVIOUS PAGE: **Executive chef Walter Plendner with members of the kitchen staff of the Vista Hotel in New York**

SEAFOOD

MEAT AND POULTRY

DESSERTS

The Food Research Center:
The Heart of the Story

When a delegation of Indonesian businessmen at the Vista International Hotel in Washington, D.C., wishes to treat their American associates to an authentic *rijstaffel,* the chef needs little time to find out how to prepare and serve the many parts of this traditional meal. The Texas businessmen staying at the Jakarta Hilton International and pining for a homestyle American barbecue can have their desire fulfilled easily. A Hilton chef in Nairobi who wishes to learn about the latest developments in vacuum-pouch cooking can become *au courant* at a moment's notice. Before a chef *garde-manger* (cold kitchen chef) moves from Strasbourg to the Caribbean, he can acquaint himself with the fruits and spices of the area, while a barman transferring from Chicago to Sydney can familiarize himself with Australian speciality drinks in no time flat. And the banquet for 4,000 that requires the same number of starched napkins to be folded artichoke-style will run more smoothly if new employees study up on the intricate creases with the help of Napkin Folding II.

What gives the Hilton International kitchen staff immediate access to these topics are the microfiches created by the Food Research Center in New York City. Through the magic of a tiny colour transparency, the Center has made it possible for all members of the food and beverage staff of Hilton International to obtain information about the subjects above and some 150 others. Each of the hotels is equipped with a microfiche reader (comparable to a small slide projector) that allows the operator to view the film at his own speed, either on a small personal-size screen or a large one, for class instruction. The goal of this microfiche system is not to create a uniform style or to dictate what is correct or incorrect, but to offer springboards off which kitchen teams can perform in ways that best suit them, given the limitations of each geographical/ cultural region. The recipes included in such films are points of departure for the chef, for Hilton International encourages the personal expression of its cooks, and even flights of fancy (a German chef constructed an entire Bavarian gingerbread village for Christmas at the Mayaguez Hilton in Puerto Rico, for example—to the delight of the staff, guests and locals).

The tiny Food Research Center quietly ticks along in an unglamorous subterranean maze beneath the shining silver towers of The World Trade Center at the Vista International Hotel. The microfiches, as well as an award-winning in-house quarterly trade magazine, are generated from this modest office. Begun in 1976 at the Queen Elizabeth Hotel in Montreal, the Center has since completed some 290 microfiches. Foremost is the collection of over 4,200 recipes from 43 countries—the result of Hilton International's 39 years in the hotel business, and a clear expression of the willingness of its chefs to share their wisdom and experience.

The microfiches are conceived, written and photographed through the Food Research Center. Subjects are determined by the proposals of company chefs and food and beverage managers, who submit annual suggestions for their preferences. About two-thirds of these are fulfilled on location (worldwide) by the director of the Food Research Center assisted by the individual hotel staffs; one-third is executed completely

Dieter Hannig of the Food Research Center—en route, as usual

at the Center, in its shining test kitchen. It takes a unique combination of culinary, photographic, teaching and diplomatic skills to be able to handle the job of director of the Food Research Center for Hilton International; but if anyone can live up to the challenge, it is energetic, experienced, charming Dieter Hannig, whose considerable stamina and organizational abilities have earned him medals both in hotel kitchens and on ski slopes worldwide.

Consider a morning in the life of the Food Research Center. As chambermaids who tend to the 829 rooms of the Vista New York chat and change in locker rooms alongside, as the remains of a wine-tasting for 500 are wheeled by for disposal and a group of new employees are guided through the corridor on a tour of the hotel's underpinnings, Hannig (the same fanciful chef responsible for the Caribbean cookie town) pulls out the microfiche on Atlantic Salmon Farming. With the film in the microfiche reader to check a fact for a press release to be used by the American Harvest Restaurant upstairs, he casts an eye over the supply of oranges needed to demonstrate a giant new juicer to the visiting food and beverage managers of 25 hotels attending a course at the Career Development Institute of Hilton International, farther down the hall. He hurries into the kitchen adjacent to his office to lower the heat on the duck stock that will be part of tomorrow's lunch for a departing executive, sets aside the muffins he is testing and will later photograph for a microfiche on American breakfast items, and smiles to welcome a cheesemaker from New Jersey who has arrived with samples of her excellent goat cheese. He then reviews the schedule for London, where he will be presenting a workshop on vacuum-pouch cooking that weekend, questioning a few points. His utterly unflappable secretary notes the changes, accepts a delivery of electrically heated copper chafing dishes to be evaluated, puts off a manufacturer of instant sauces who has just telephoned, and greets the troupe that squeezes into the kitchen for the juicer demonstration.

As is the case for most European chefs, training for Mr Hannig began early, away from home. From an apprenticeship begun at 13, he moved among fine hotels in

The Magical Microfiche: A 6 x 4-inch plastic-coated film containing 49 photos and 49 recipes or training lessons is Hilton International's primary communicating medium

The test kitchen of the Food Research Center

Germany and Switzerland. Divided between a career in the kitchen or on the ski slopes, the cooking side won out—although the athletic outlets are still numerous. Hannig became sous-chef of the Hilton International, Kensington, in 1974, then held various positions of authority throughout the company. It was during assignments in locales with little access to up-to-date culinary magazines and books that he became acutely aware of the need for transmitting information throughout the whole system on a regular basis. 'Many of our chefs do not have the opportunity to stay abreast of the new food trends and technical developments because of their geographical location,' he explains. 'In certain regions of the globe professional literature is rare or nonexistent. Microfiche projects judged superfluous by some constitute a precious work tool for others.'

Even on a small scale, Mr Hannig is a hands-on learner and educator, enthused by the challenge of the new. Faced with the unfamiliar task of testing recipes for a cookbook, he plunged in with gusto, so thoroughly adapting to the needs of a home cook that his colleagues at Vista suggested he exchange his chef's garb for a ruffled apron with roses. Teased continually about tiny whisks and spoonlets, he cheerfully continued to acquire a *batterie* of home-size utensils, the spoons and measuring jugs dwarfed to ridiculousness by the professional-scale equipment that surrounds the testing area. He became the part, rearranging sliced meat on platters to serve family-style, avoiding last-minute preparations, finding compromises that would not alter the integrity of a dish; in short, raising questions that simply do not enter into the vocabulary of a professional chef. What he does, he does wholeheartedly. He has visited almost all the hotels to understand the workings of the kitchens, staff and surroundings. His natural curiosity and intuition have given him a keen awareness of the strengths and weaknesses of the vast human network that makes up the Hilton International family—which has in him an effective, sympathetic central transmitter for its food and beverage communications system.

SMOKED SALMON AND GOLDEN CAVIAR CRÊPES WITH SALAD GREENS

CANADA

This is the work of Albert Schnell (executive chef of the Hilton International Toronto), who pays particular attention to the acquisition of the finest local ingredients. While he calls for both Canadian smoked salmon and Canadian golden caviar, fish from other waters would not be out of order. The luxurious appetizer is generously endowed with silky salmon in a cream mosaic twirled into pale crêpes. The spiral slices are embellished with a flurry of fashionable (and striking) salad leaves.

1 whole egg
1 egg yolk
Salt
100 ml (4 fl oz) single cream
40 g (1½ oz) plain flour
1 tablespoon melted butter, plus additional melted butter for the pan
100 g (4 oz) golden (salmon) caviar (or substitute red lumpfish roe)
225 ml (8 fl oz) sour cream
1 teaspoon finely chopped onion

About 1 teaspoon lemon juice
250–275 g (9–10 oz) smoked salmon, cut into paper-thin slices
1 teaspoon finely chopped shallot
1 tablespoon red wine vinegar
Pepper
50 ml (2 fl oz) walnut oil
Finely chopped tarragon and chives (or other herbs to suit)
32 assorted salad leaves, rinsed and dried (see Options)

1. Blend together the whole egg, egg yolk, a pinch of salt and cream in a mixing bowl. Mix in the flour. Add the butter. Strain through a fine sieve. Cover and let stand for 1 hour or longer.

2. Heat a 15 cm (6-inch) crêpe pan over moderate heat. Brush lightly with butter. In portions of 3 scant tablespoons each, ladle the batter into the pan; quickly tilt and shake to cover the bottom of the pan completely. Cook the crêpe for 30–45 seconds, until the top is dry; turn and cook for 15 seconds, until barely coloured. Set aside. When all of the batter is used, you should have 7 crêpes—one as security, or to eat.

3. Place the caviar in a small strainer and tap firmly until no more liquid drips off. Combine in a small bowl with ¾ of the sour cream. Add the onion and about ½ teaspoon lemon juice, or to taste. Spread the cooled crêpes with the remaining sour cream, smoothing with a flexible spatula. Top each with a neat layer of smoked salmon to cover completely. Spread the caviar-cream over this, leaving a margin around the rim. Gently and slowly roll into neat cylinders.

4. Place the crêpes on a platter, wrap tightly and refrigerate for 2–6 hours.

5. At serving time, cut each roll into 4 pieces on the diagonal, slicing slowly and carefully. Arrange 3 slices on each of 8 plates.

6. Combine the shallot, vinegar, ½ teaspoon lemon juice, and salt and pepper to taste in a small bowl. Whisk in the oil. Gently toss with the finely chopped herbs and salad leaves. Distribute on the plates.

Serving/Presentation: *Do not crowd the rolls. Serve on wide plates that play off the colour and drama of the arrangement.*

Advance preparation: *The crêpes can be made up to a day before serving. The salmon rolls can be prepared and refrigerated up to 6 hours ahead. If tightly covered, they even can be sliced in advance.*

Options: *Chicory, radicchio, little gem,* mâche *(corn salad), and oak leaf lettuce are colourful and tasty companions—choose all or some.*

8 SERVINGS AS AN APPETIZER

SNAILS IN BLACK BEAN SAUCE ON TOFU
(Escargots Dau See)
HAWAII, UNITED STATES

A striking departure from traditional snails in garlic butter—both in appearance and flavour: dark snails and salty black beans are spooned over white tofu rectangles accompanied with shining mangetout peas and cherry-red pepper strips. This unusual opener is a regular (in a restaurant filled with devoted regulars) at the deliciously gaudy Maile restaurant of the Kahala Hilton in Honolulu. Gold-trimmed presentation plates, the heaviest cut crystal, an ochre carpet studded with red Japanese medallions, and mammoth displays of bamboo, ginger flowers, cerise anthurium and polished maile leaves ('to Hawaii, what the laurel was to Rome') set the scene in what is among the most beautiful properties in the company.

---

400 g (14 oz) canned snails (about 36), preferably from France
450 g (1 lb) medium tofu
2 medium spring onions
3 tablespoons peanut oil
1 teaspoon finely chopped garlic
1 tablespoon finely chopped fresh ginger
2 tablespoons fermented (salted) black beans, chopped (see Note)
100 ml (4 fl oz) homemade (unsalted) chicken stock
50 ml (2 fl oz) oyster sauce (see Note)

About 2 teaspoons finely chopped fresh hot chilli-pepper (such as jalapeño, seeds removed)
¾ teaspoon sugar
1½ tablespoons Chinese rice wine (or substitute dry sherry)
1 teaspoon cornflour
36 mangetout peas, strings removed
1 large red pepper, seeds and ribs removed, cut into 5 x .5 cm (2 × ¼-inch) strips
Fresh coriander leaves

---

1. Preheat the oven to 200°C/400°F (gas mark 6). Drain the snails, reserving the liquid. Cut the tofu crosswise into 6 pieces. Place on a towel to drain. Cut the spring onions in fine slices, separating the white and green parts.

2. Heat 1 tablespoon of the oil in a medium saucepan over moderate heat. Stir in the garlic, ginger, and the white part of the spring onions. Stir for 1 minute to soften, but not colour.

3. Add the black beans, chicken stock, oyster sauce, 1 teaspoon chilli-pepper, and sugar; bring to a simmer. Blend together the rice wine and cornflour. Stir into the sauce and bring to a boil. Add the snails, 2 tablespoons of the reserved liquid, and the green part of the spring onions; remove from the heat.

4. Heat an ovenproof nonstick pan with 1 tablespoon of the oil. Place the tofu in the pan in a single layer, leaving some extra space. Set in the centre of the oven for 10 minutes.

5. Meanwhile, heat the remaining 1 tablespoon oil in a wide frying pan. Add the mangetout peas and red pepper and toss over moderate heat for 4–5 minutes, until they lose their raw crunch, but are still crisp. At the same time, warm the snails over low heat.

6. Arrange the tofu on 6 dishes; over this, spoon the snails and sauce. Arrange the vegetables alongside. Sprinkle with the remaining chilli-pepper and coriander to taste.

Note: *Salty, dried fermented black beans are available in Oriental shops, as is oyster sauce. Both will keep indefinitely in the refrigerator.*

6 SERVINGS AS A FIRST COURSE

Gravlax (Salmon Marinated with Dill and Pepper)

CANADA

While this version of the classic Scandinavian salt-cured salmon was developed by Albert Schnell, executive chef of the Hilton International Toronto, many variations are best-sellers in Hilton International hotels worldwide.

The firm, translucent slices of salmon are counterpoised by a sharp-sweet, herb-flecked sauce that is quite light in texture and holds its shape softly. This popular appetizer is appropriate year-round, particularly with iced aquavit and pumpernickel fingers.

700 g (1½ lb) salmon fillet (with skin)
60 g (2½ oz) coarse sea salt
85 g (3½ oz) sugar
1 tablespoon white peppercorns, crushed

1 small bunch fresh dill (reserve some for garnish)
1 tablespoon brandy
1 tablespoon light vegetable oil

1. With tweezers or fine pliers, pull out any small bones that may remain in the salmon fillet. Place the fish, skin side down, in a heavy plastic bag.

2. Combine the salt, sugar and peppercorns: rub over the fish. Turn over the fillet. Bruise the dill to release its aroma; spread over the fish. Drizzle the brandy and oil over this. Close the bag tightly and set it in a pan; place another pan on top and set a 1.5 kilo (3 lb) weight in this to press down the fish. Let stand at room temperature for 6 hours or so, turning occasionally.

(continued)

3. Refrigerate the *gravlax* for about 2 days, turning as convenient (preferably every 6–8 hours) then replacing the weight.

4. Shortly before serving, remove the fish from the bag and reserve the marinade. Scrape the seasoning mixture from the fish, and set the salmon on a work surface. Working at an extreme angle, cut into very thin, even slices, freeing each slice from the skin with a firm cut.

5. Arrange the slices petal-fashion on individual serving dishes. Place about 2 tablespoons Mustard-Dill Sauce (recipe follows) alongside and garnish with dill sprigs.

8–10 SERVINGS AS AN APPETIZER

Mustard-Dill Sauce for Gravlax

3 tablespoons sugar
1½ teaspoons dry mustard
3 tablespoons distilled white vinegar
1 tablespoon strained marinade from *Gravlax* (preceding recipe)
6 tablespoons mild prepared mustard

2 teaspoons sharp or Dijon-style mustard
About 225 ml (6 fl oz) sunflower oil (or another light vegetable oil)
2–3 tablespoons finely chopped dill leaves

1. Combine the sugar, dry mustard, vinegar and reserved marinade in a small nonaluminium bowl. Stir to blend. Add the mild and sharp prepared mustards.

2. Gradually whisk in the sunflower oil. Add the dill. Cover and refrigerate for at least 1 hour.

8–10 SERVINGS

SWORDFISH AND GRAPEFRUIT ESCABECHE

PUERTO RICO, UNITED STATES

This sunny yellow appetizer is perfect for parties, as it mellows and improves with keeping. Sweetly oniony, gently spiced, the modicum of olive oil and refreshing addition of grapefruit make this updated version of a traditional Caribbean recipe considerably lighter than its forebears. Its concentrated flavours and close textures are more attractive in small portions, as a first course, than as a main course, but escabeche is customarily offered in large servings.

500 g (1¼ lb) swordfish
About ¾ teaspoon salt
White pepper
5–6 tablespoons olive oil
¼ teaspoon turmeric
3 medium onions, halved and
 thinly sliced
2 medium yellow peppers, cored and
 cut lengthwise into thin slices
1 medium garlic clove, thinly sliced

1 teaspoon mixed pickling spices
½ teaspoon finely chopped thyme or
 lemon thyme
1 bay leaf, crumbled
3 medium-large grapefruit
3–4 tablespoons white wine vinegar
3 small heads of soft lettuce, rinsed
 and dried
1 red pepper, cut into fine julienne

1. Trim away the skin and dark centre area from the fish. Cut the flesh on the diagonal into 3 cm (1½-inch) square slices, each about 1 cm (½ inch) thick. Sprinkle with ½ teaspoon salt and white pepper to taste.

2. Heat 1½ tablespoons oil over moderate heat in a wide non-aluminium pan. Add half the fish and colour on both sides, just to cook through—about 2 minutes. Transfer to a wide dish. Heat 1 tablespoon oil and cook the remaining fish; add to the dish.

3. Blend 2 tablespoons oil with the turmeric. Add to the pan and reduce heat to low. Add the onions, peppers, garlic, pickling spices, thyme, and bay leaf. Cook for 5 minutes, until the vegetables are no longer raw, but still crisp.

4. Squeeze enough grapefruit to make 175 ml (6 fl oz) juice. Add to the vegetables, along with 3 tablespoons vinegar; simmer for 3 minutes. Pour over the fish, distributing evenly.

5. Let cool, then cover and refrigerate for at least 24 hours, or up to 3 days, turning occasionally. Season with salt, oil and vinegar to taste.

6. To serve, let the *escabeche* reach room temperature. Arrange the lettuce on 6 plates. Cut all the rind, pith and membrane from the 2 remaining grapefruit. Cut between the membranes to release the sections. Arrange them with the *escabeche* on the lettuce. Top with the red pepper julienne.

6 SERVINGS AS A FIRST COURSE

TERRINE OF GRAVLAX

UNITED STATES

Originated in European kitchens, this fine appetizer has been adapted by Leo Waldmeier, executive chef of The Drake hotel in Chicago. Opalescent strips of leek and rosy salmon meld in a mosaic of shining aspic. When cut, the colourful chessboard design is as charming and unpretentious as the straightforward flavours: salty salmon and fresh-sweet vegetables in a light, briny aspic.

2.25 litres (4 pints) fish stock (see
   recipe, page 326)
4 large leeks (about 1.4 kilos/3 lb)
6 g (¼ oz) unflavoured gelatine
8 long, narrow carrots (about 600 g/
   1¼ lb)

Gravlax (see recipe on page 35, but
   do not slice)
Mustard-Dill Sauce (see recipe on
   page 36)

1. Boil the stock until reduced to 400 ml (14 fl oz).

2. Meanwhile, have ready a narrow terrine mould (about 27.5 x 9 x 9 cm/11 × 3½ × 3½ inches). Trim the roots from the leeks. Remove several layers by cutting a lengthwise slit in each and unpeeling; when you have a smooth central core of leek about 1.25 cm (¾-inch) in diameter, stop removing the layers. Trim this core to the length of the mould. Discard dry or damaged outer layers of leek; trim the green from the remaining peeled-off layers. Place these and the 4 cores to soak in cold water.

3. When the stock has reduced, sprinkle the gelatine over it and stir to dissolve. Peel and trim the carrots. Drop them into a large pan of boiling salted water. Cook until tender (*no* crunch remaining or the terrine cannot be cut smoothly), about 8 minutes. Fish them out of the water and place in ice water to chill; drain and dry on kitchen paper.

4. Drop the 4 leek cores into the water; poach gently until tender, about 4–5 minutes. Lift these out, then refresh in ice water. Drain and dry thoroughly on kitchen paper, pressing to remove liquid. Turn the heat to high, drop the leek layers into the boiling water and boil until pliable, a minute or two. Refresh, drain, and dry.

5. Set the pot of stock in a pan of ice and water. Stir the aspic now and then until syrupy-thick.

6. Line one side of the terrine with the leek layers, arranging them so that they overlap slightly and one narrow edge is centred in the base of the terrine while the other hangs over the side. Continue around the terrine, overlapping the bottom slices slightly as you place them in the other side of the terrine. Trim the carrots as necessary to form a single band along each long side of the terrine.

7. Cut the skin from the *gravlax*. Slice the fillet lengthwise to form 4 equal strips, which should be more or less the same length as the terrine. Place one of these between the carrots. Ladle in enough almost-jelled aspic to just cover this layer. Set the terrine in ice water until the aspic sets.

8. Place a whole leek core lengthwise on top of each carrot band. Cover the salmon strip in the centre with trimmed lengths of carrot. Place a strip of salmon on top of each leek. Pour in chilled aspic to barely cover this layer, then set in ice water.

9. When the aspic has firmed, place another trimmed band of carrot along each side, a leek next to this, and a salmon strip in the centre. Pour in aspic to barely coat. Fold the leek ends over the top, trimming to meet neatly in the centre. Finish with a thin coat of aspic.

10. Chill for at least 6 hours, or up to 24. To unmould, dip in hot water, then run a knife gently around the edge to release the aspic. Invert onto a cutting board, rapping sharply. Immediately return to the refrigerator for a few minutes to fix any melting exterior aspic.

11. Cut gently into serving slices, sawing rather than pressing down on the loaf. Serve with Mustard-Dill Sauce alongside each slice.

Serving: *As an appetizer, offer one slice per person. For a cool, summer lunch, serve 2 slices, along with boiled new potatoes (with skins)—set at a distance from the cold aspic, or they'll melt it.*

14–16 SERVINGS AS AN APPETIZER; 8 AS A LUNCH MAIN COURSE

Barley 'Risotto' with Blue Cheese

UNITED STATES

Dieter Hannig, director of the Food Research Center, developed this unusual multinational first course in the style of the Italian rice speciality risotto when he was working on a microfiche about French cheeses. In the southern part of Germany, where he has lived, grains (particularly barley) are used with almost daily regularity. In this rather sumptuous treatment of an ingredient usually considered rustic, the chewy barley is enriched by the fermented flavour of the blue cheese, the undertone of wine, and a generous butter liaison. The pearly, cream-slicked grains are far too dense and rich to serve as anything but a first course, perhaps with a red wine from the Rhône Valley. Follow up with a main course of ham or cold veal roast and salad.

---

250 g (9 oz) barley
100 g (4 oz) butter
40 g (1½ oz) finely chopped shallots
1¼ teaspoons finely chopped garlic
100 ml (4 fl oz) dry white wine
50 ml (2 fl oz) double (or whipping) cream

100 g (4 oz) mild blue cheese, such as *Bleu d'Auvergne* (see Options), crumbled
Pepper
Watercress

---

1. Pour the barley into a generous amount of boiling salted water, stirring until it returns to a boil. Boil gently until tender, about ½ hour. Drain and rinse lightly.

2. Heat ¾ of the butter in a wide, deep casserole over moderate heat. Add the shallots and garlic and cook until softened, but not browned.

3. Add the barley and toss over high heat until the grains are coated. Add the wine and stir for a few minutes until most has evaporated. Add the cream and bring to a boil, stirring. Remove from the heat.

4. Stir in the cheese, then the remaining butter and add pepper to taste. Spoon into heated plates, garnish with watercress, and serve immediately (or the dish becomes gluey).

Options: *Any mild blue-veined cheese can be substituted for the* Bleu d'Auvergne, *if it is difficult to obtain:* Fourme d'Ambert, Pipo Crem', Gorgonzola. *The stronger blues—such as* Roquefort *and* Danish blue—*are too sharp.*

4 SERVINGS AS A FIRST COURSE

Avocado and Grapefruit Salad with Honey Vinaigrette
CANADA

When Albert Schnell, area chef for Hilton Canada, Inc., introduced this salad on the appetizer menu of the Beaver Club at the Queen Elizabeth hotel in 1976, it was a novelty. Now, similar recipes are popular throughout North America, but few have the delicate balance of this simple classic: the creamy dressing (both light textured and coloured—thanks to the sunflower oil) clings to the smooth avocado and juicy grapefruit without hiding the natural, low-key flavours.

1 tablespoon honey
¼ teaspoon salt
¼ teaspoon white pepper
3 tablespoons lemon juice
⅓ cup sunflower oil

2 medium grapefruit
2 medium avocados (preferably the dark, pebbly-skinned Haas variety)

1. In a blender or processor, mix the honey, salt, pepper and lemon juice to blend. With the motor running, gradually add the oil, processing until pale and creamy. Refrigerate until serving time.

2. Cut all rind, pith and membrane from the grapefruit. With a sharp knife cut between the interior membranes to free each section. Halve, stone, and peel the avocados; cut each half into 5 lengthwise slices.

3. Alternate overlapping slices of the avocado and grapefruit over 4 salad plates. Spoon dressing over each slice.

Note: *Although the dressing can be made in advance, do not cut the grapefruit much before serving, or it will liquefy the dressing. If you find it inconvenient to prepare this way, place the sliced fruit in a sieve until serving time.*

4 SERVINGS AS A SIDE DISH OR FIRST COURSE

Spinach, Quail Eggs and Livers in Raspberry-Walnut Vinaigrette
CANADA

Like all of Albert Schnell's recipes, this one is a thoughtful balance of colour, texture, temperature and taste. A mound of spinach ribbons crowned with white mushroom

(continued)

Spinach, Quail Eggs, and Livers in Raspberry-Walnut Vinaigrette

confetti, red-orange tomato dice, and glistening walnut bits is accented by halved ovals of quail egg. The walnut flavour blends with the gamey liver and earthy vegetables for a salad that is at once fresh and rich. The dish is suitable for light supper or lunch, perhaps preceded by a delicate cream soup; or served as a first course.

2 tablespoons raspberry vinegar
About ¼ teaspoon salt
White pepper
1 teaspoon finely chopped shallot
1 teaspoon lemon juice
½ teaspoon finely chopped fresh tarragon leaves, or ¼ teaspoon dried, crumbled
8 tablespoons walnut oil

350 g (12 oz) small-leaf spinach
6 quail eggs (see Note)
100 g (4 oz) medium button mushrooms, chopped (see Note)
2 medium tomatoes, peeled, seeded, and diced
50 g (2 oz) walnut halves, coarsely chopped
350 g (12 oz) (about 12 medium) chicken livers, cleaned and halved

1. In a small bowl, combine the vinegar, salt, pepper to taste, shallot, lemon juice and tarragon; stir to blend. Gradually whisk in 7 tablespoons of the walnut oil.

2. Dunk the spinach into a sink filled with cool water. Swish around, then lift out so the soil falls to the bottom. Repeat as necessary. Strip the stems from the leaves and discard them. Dry the leaves completely, preferably in a salad-dryer. Set aside 24 of the smallest; cut the remainder into thin strips.

3. Place the quail eggs in a small pan of simmering water and cook for 1½ minutes. Refresh momentarily in cold water, then peel carefully (their centres will be soft).

4. Mix the mushrooms and tomatoes with 2 tablespoons of dressing. Combine the spinach strips and walnuts; toss with 50 ml (2 fl oz) of the dressing. In another bowl, combine the whole leaves with 2 tablespoons of the dressing.

5. Arrange the whole leaves around 4 plates. Divide the strips into the centre of each, then top with mushrooms and tomatoes.

6. Sprinkle the livers with salt and pepper. Heat the remaining walnut oil over moderate heat in a small pan. Sear the livers to brown lightly on each side. Add the remaining dressing; toss the livers to just cook through.

7. Arrange the livers on the plates; garnish with the quail eggs, carefully halved. Serve warm.

Note: *If you cannot obtain quail eggs, substitute 2* hard-*boiled chicken eggs (these larger eggs cannot be neatly cut if soft-boiled), each sliced into 6 wedges.*
   If you prefer to have palest white mushrooms, peel them.

4 SERVINGS AS A MAIN COURSE; 6–8 AS A FIRST COURSE

Mangetout-Cucumber Salad

UNITED STATES

Low-calorie, nutritionally balanced recipes, such as the following, are the subject of a microfiche put out by the Food Research Center. Summery ribbons of mangetout peas and yellow pepper, cucumber crescents, and sweet rounds of water chestnuts are refreshingly dressed with lemon and ginger. Appealing crunchiness and simplicity make this a fine foil for barbecued and fried meat, fish, or poultry.

About 250 g (9 oz) fresh water chestnuts (see Note)
175 g (6 oz) mangetout peas
700 g (1½ lb) cucumber, peeled
1 yellow pepper, seeds and ribs removed, cut into fine julienne

2 tablespoons chopped onion
1 tablespoon grated fresh ginger
3 tablespoons safflower oil or another light vegetable oil
50 ml (2 fl oz) rice vinegar
Salt

---

1. Scrub the water chestnuts under running water. Peel as closely as possible, then drop into boiling salted water and boil for 7–8 minutes, until cooked through. Meanwhile, string the mangetout peas; cut the pods diagonally in half. Lift the water chestnuts from the pot with a slotted spoon and drop into ice water. Toss the peas into the water; boil until they just lose their raw crunch—a minute or so. Drain and add to the ice water.

2. When the vegetables are cooled, drain them. Cut the water chestnuts into thin coins. Pat the peas dry on kitchen paper. Quarter the cucumbers lengthwise, then scoop out the seeds. Slice crosswise into thin crescents. Combine in a bowl with the water chestnuts, peas and pepper.

3. Combine the onion, ginger, oil, vinegar and salt to taste. Toss together with the vegetables. Season to taste. Chill thoroughly, but no longer than 6–7 hours, or the cucumbers will give off too much liquid and the peas will discolour.

Note: *Fresh water chestnuts, available in Oriental groceries and some supermarkets, are sweet, crisp, and altogether delightful. In comparison, canned chestnuts are crunchy—and that's about it. However, if you cannot obtain the fresh, a 225 g (8 oz) can of whole peeled water chestnuts will do.*

4 SERVINGS AS A FIRST COURSE OR SIDE DISH

PEPPER SLAW

UNITED STATES

When the American Harvest Restaurant at the Vista International New York was planned, 1,500 well-loved typical American recipes competed for inclusion in the seasonally-adjusted menu. Among the final selections was this version of a recipe from James Beard, whose readers frequently requested that it be reprinted in his American newspaper columns.

It is a pleasant change from more traditional cole slaws, with its larger pieces, big crunch, and vivid colour. Serve it with hamburgers, steak, ham, and all kinds of barbecue.

---

60 ml (2½ fl oz) distilled white vinegar
½ teaspoon salt
Pepper
1 tablespoon Dijon-style mustard
2 teaspoons mustard seeds
2 teaspoons celery seeds
2 teaspoons sugar
100 ml (4 fl oz) light vegetable oil

600 g (1¼ lb) white cabbage
450 g (1 lb) green peppers (about 4
  medium), seeds and ribs removed
2 small carrots, cut into paper-thin
  slices
1 medium onion, halved and cut in
  paper-thin slices
1 celery stalk, cut into 1 cm (½-inch)
  dice

---

1. Combine the vinegar, salt, pepper to taste, mustard, mustard seeds, celery seeds and sugar in a bowl; whisk to blend. Slowly add the vegetable oil, whisking constantly.

2. Trim the cabbage; cut into 1.25 cm (¾-inch) slices, then cut these again to form squares; separate the layers. Cut the peppers into 1.25 cm (¾-inch) squares. Combine in a bowl with the carrots, onion and celery.

3. Pour the dressing over the vegetables and toss. Add seasoning to taste. Refrigerate for 3–6 hours. Season again before serving.

6 SERVINGS AS A SIDE DISH

SCALLOPS, CUCUMBERS AND MUSHROOMS IN BASIL-PEPPERCORN VINAIGRETTE

UNITED STATES

Crunchy cucumbers, soft scallops, zesty cress and fleshy raw mushrooms contrast and complement in a pale-hued salad touched with the keen pungency of green and pink peppercorns—the work of Franz Kranzfelder, award-winning senior sous-chef at The Drake hotel in Chicago.

50 ml (2 fl oz) white wine vinegar (preferably basil-flavoured)

½ teaspoon salt

175 ml (6 fl oz) olive oil

About 1½ teaspoons drained, water-packed green peppercorns, chopped

About 1 teaspoon dried pink peppercorns, crushed with a knife blade

1 hard-boiled egg, chopped

2 tablespoons very finely sliced basil leaves

1½ teaspoons finely chopped shallot

1 kilo (2 lb) scallops

225 ml (8 fl oz) boiling water mixed with ½ teaspoon salt

1 large cucumber

350 g (12 oz) small-medium mushrooms, peeled

1 bunch watercress, trimmed, rinsed, and dried

8 cherry tomatoes, halved

1. Make the dressing: blend together the vinegar and salt; slowly add the oil, whisk in. Stir in the green peppercorns, the pink peppercorns, the egg, basil and shallot. Mix well and set aside for at least 2 hours so that flavours blend.

2. Place the scallops in a saucepan in a single layer; pour over the boiling salted water; cover and return to a simmer. Remove from the heat, uncover, and let cool.

3. Cut the cucumber into fine julienne (do not peel); arrange in the centre of 4 large plates to make a circular bed in each.

4. Drain the scallops. Slice into thin rounds. Arrange over the cucumbers.

5. Trim the mushroom stems, slice the mushrooms and arrange in 4 heaps on each plate, around the cucumber.

6. Place heaps of watercress between the mushrooms. Decorate with cherry tomatoes. Divide the dressing evenly among the salads, stirring frequently and spooning slowly to coat all ingredients.

Advance preparation: *The salads can be arranged up to an hour in advance, as the scallops are particularly tasty at room temperature.*

4 SERVINGS AS A MAIN COURSE; 6–8 AS A FIRST COURSE

TOP: **Terrine of Gravlax (see page 38 for recipe) with Mustard-Dill Sauce (see page 36 for recipe)** BOTTOM: **A slightly modified version of Scallops, Cucumbers and Mushrooms in Basil-Peppercorn Vinaigrette**

BLACK BEAN AND SEAFOOD SALAD

PUERTO RICO, UNITED STATES

When Dieter Hannig was executive chef at the Hilton International Mayaguez, he served special dinners in a dining room off the kitchen called The Chef's Table. There, local products were the focus and culinary invention the expected mode. An example of such an approach is this salad based on the ubiquitous black beans—in a new guise.

175 g (6 oz) dried black beans
1 medium onion
2 cloves
1 bay leaf
450 g (1 lb) cleaned squid (or 600 g/
    1¼ lb uncleaned; see page 324)
8 Dublin Bay prawns in the shell
    (about 450 g/1 lb), raw if possible
3 plum tomatoes, peeled and
    chopped
1 large green pepper, seeded and cut
    into small dice

1 tender celery stalk, finely chopped
1 small onion, chopped
2 tablespoons chopped fresh corian-
    der
¼ teaspoon salt
½ teaspoon black pepper
1 tablespoon lime juice
2 tablespoons sherry vinegar
1 tablespoon finely chopped garlic
2 tablespoons olive oil
4 coriander sprigs

1. Rinse and pick over the beans. Soak overnight in cold water, covered.

2. Drain the beans and combine with 1 litre (2 pints) water in a saucepan. Bring to a boil; lower the heat, then return to a boil, skimming. Make an incision in the onion and insert the cloves and bay leaf. Add to the beans; cook, covered, over low heat until just tender. (Timing can vary considerably, but 45–60 minutes is usual. Check often after 30 minutes of cooking.) Cool, uncovered, then strain off any liquid.

3. Meanwhile, slice the squid mantles into thin rings. Divide the tentacles into man-ageable mouthfuls, if necessary. Drop into a pan of boiling salted water. Barely simmer for 2 minutes, or until just cooked through. Drop the raw prawns into another pan of boiling salted water; return to a simmer and remove from the heat. Drain, then peel and devein. Omit the cooking if raw prawns are unobtainable.

4. Combine the beans, squid, tomatoes, pepper, celery, chopped onion and coriander in a large bowl and blend gently.

5. Combine the salt, pepper, lime juice, sherry vinegar, garlic and olive oil in a small bowl; mix well. Pour over the salad and toss gently. Marinate for 1 hour or so. Taste for seasoning. Divide the salad onto serving plates. Slice the prawns lengthwise and set around the salad. Garnish with coriander sprigs.

Advance preparation: *The salad can be refrigerated for 24 hours, but the flavours will be more pronounced.*
Options: *At the Hilton International Mayaguez grilled prawns were served instead of the cold poached ones, and the dish was served with deep-fried plantain slices* (tostones) *and corn sticks* (surullitos).

4 SERVINGS AS A MAIN COURSE; 6–8 AS A FIRST COURSE

Mussel Salad with Leeks

CANADA

Lightly cooked leek strips and full-flavoured mussels are bound here with a pale yellow mayonnaise-like dressing made from reduced cooking juices. Shreds of celery and acid tomato slivers balance harmoniously, thanks to chef Albert Schnell. The portions suggested will do nicely as a main course for lunch. Gauge about 20 medium-large mussels per person, or 25 smaller ones.

2 large shallots, finely chopped
175 ml (6 fl oz) dry white wine
About 2.5 kilos (5 lb) cultivated mussels (see page 324)
2 medium leeks (about 450 g/1 lb), trimmed, halved lengthwise, and well washed
2 tablespoons olive oil
¼ teaspoon saffron threads
100 ml (4 fl oz) double (or whipping) cream

2 heads of soft lettuce, rinsed and dried
Salt and pepper
Lemon juice
1 tomato, peeled
50 g (2 oz) thin julienne of tender celery sticks
1 teaspoon finely chopped fresh tarragon (see Options)

1. Combine the shallots and wine in a wide non-aluminium pan and bring to a boil. Add the mussels, cover, and cook, shaking the pot occasionally, over moderately high heat just until opened, about 2 minutes. Lift out the mussels and let them cool briefly, then remove from the shells, placing mussels in a large bowl.

2. Strain the cooking liquor through doubled, dampened muslin, pouring slowly to avoid sand that may lurk in the bottom. Pour into a saucepan.

3. Cut the leeks into fine julienne about 6 cm (2½-inches) long. Add to the pan. Bring to a full boil, reduce the heat, and cook on low for 5 minutes, or until just tender.

4. With a slotted spoon, transfer the leeks to the bowl with the mussels. Add the olive oil, saffron and cream to the poaching liquid in the pan; boil, stirring, until reduced to 225 ml (8 fl oz).

5. Pour over the mussels and leeks, mix, and leave to cool. Cover and refrigerate for several hours or up to 1 day.

6. Arrange the lettuce leaves on a large serving platter. Season the mussel mixture, adding salt (taste carefully: mussels can be very salty), pepper and lemon juice to taste. Arrange over the lettuce leaves. Quarter the tomato; cut out and discard the interior. Slice the tomato shell into thin julienne. Arrange these and the celery over the mussels. Sprinkle with tarragon; serve.

Options: If fresh tarragon is difficult to find, substitute thyme, basil or parsley. A dash of Pernod or Ricard adds a lively Mediterranean lift.

4 SERVINGS AS A MAIN COURSE; 6–8 AS A FIRST COURSE

Conquistadores con Canapés, Bar Mitzvahs con Brio at the Caribe Hilton International— Where It All Began

Chef August Schreiner receiving the morning's catch PREVIOUS PAGE: **A photographic session on location.**

Difficult as it may be to believe, there was little tourism in Puerto Rico until relatively recently. The 18 acres of Atlantic ocean-front that embrace the complex of buildings that make up the Caribe Hilton International (and include the only virtually private beach in Puerto Rico) went begging for years. When local businessmen could not be encouraged to build a first-class tourist hotel in the area, the president of the Puerto Rican Industrial Development Company turned to the United States for investors. There was just one interested party, who replied in Spanish: Conrad N. Hilton. The rest, as they say, is history, for thus began the operation of the first hotel by the company that has since become Hilton International. A resounding success since its first day in 1949, it has remained the foremost resort on the island, attended by a devoted following of local residents and mainland guests who are moving into their third generation.

The staff and much of the menu are doing the same. Foods favoured in the fine dining room, La Rotisserie, have not changed dramatically since the opening: roast prime ribs or rack of lamb, spit-roasted poultry, and grilled steaks and lamb chops are in the forefront. Warm, chatty Miguel Marquez, the maître d', has greeted diners there for 35 years (as have five of the waiters). Handsome Roberto Pagan, red-kerchiefed and dressed in starched white, has manned the open grills of the dining room for 21 years (a relatively short time for a member of this staff), keeping up with the demands of a regular audience ('Roberto, remember that I want the end-cut,' or 'I'll be in for dinner at 8 o'clock tomorrow with company; 12 kosher chickens, nice and dark, with crispy potatoes—you know, the way I like them'). Daily, William Otero has confected 13 types of pastry for 29 years—with Napoleons, rum balls and *coquitos* (toasty, super-sweet coconut squares with a fudge-like texture) the most popular items. Hector Torres, the affable bar manager, heads a staff of 35, whose members represent over 700 years of service to the hotel. Seventy-year-old Ramon (Monchito) Marrero, who invented the celebrated piña colada at the Caribe, has supervised the assembly of what is now a daily average of at least 300 of the rum, coconut cream and pineapple juice drinks. Expressive Epifanio Rivera (Riverita), who began in 1949, explained, gesticulating, that 'if you don't feel it, you can't work in a hotel. It involves your family, your mind, everyone. New boys coming in—they don't love the life the way we do.' In fact, about 35 per cent of the food and beverage staff has been on board for at least 20 years, giving the large and ever-growing Caribe a surprisingly homely quality.

Francisco (Pancho) Gonzales, the methodical, dignified chef *garde-manger·* (cold kitchen chef) 'began as a cold meat man when the hotel opened and is still the absolute best and fastest in the business,' praised August Schreiner (Augusto to all), the electrically charged, much-loved executive chef, who works at lightning pace himself (and speaks at the same, alternating English, Spanish, and German). 'Just last week Pancho prepared 10,000 canapés in eight hours; someone else would need two days for the job,' praises Chef Augusto. The party for which Pancho set up the canapés was for 3,000 guests (who polished off 6,000 piña coladas). Riverita was responsible, among other things, for the preparation of 10,000 *empanadillas de carne* (fried meat-filled turnovers), 1,000 lb of blood sausage, and a farm-full of pigs for barbecue.

Every event seems larger than life in this buzzing extension of the San Juan social community. The day's activity calendar in the lobby lists seminars for an international bank, cooking classes, a local dance troupe's show, a lecture on chromosome abnormality, junior executives' society cocktails, a bar mitzvah—and more. Doctors in grey suits brush past bikini-garbed sun-worshippers en route to poolside; beruffled wedding parties pour into a banquet room recently vacated by the manufacturers of a new soft drink. An average year tallies 50 weddings; 125 cocktail parties, 75 dinners, and 80 lunches (all for more than 400); 70 poolside barbecues; 150 grand-scale birthday parties; 85 theme events (Caribbean Night, Conquistador Night, and suchlike); 75 food society gourmet dinners; 16 mammoth bar mitzvahs; and 200-plus miscellaneous events, including conventions of 1,200 for a week at a time. (Among the more complex, a 10-day kosher convention required a total overhaul of equipment, replacement of all cooking and cleaning utensils, removal of all existing foodstuffs, new china, and the fulfilment of 40 more requirements, plus a grocery list of near-200 kosher items).

For a recent party, the garden, usually studded with sleepy peacocks, was transformed into a Taino (local Indian) village. Thatched huts overflowed with salads of conch, squid, corn and pepper, and green bananas; chilled shellfish displays; Caribbean lamb stew with root vegetables and coconut; fried plantains with *chorizo* (spicy sausage), mini corn sticks, and crab turnovers. Accompanied by the omnipresent *chirrup* sound of tiny *coquis* (tree frogs), guests crossed a torch-lined causeway to San Jeronimo, the small fort adjoining the grounds. With surf pounding and an escort of *conquistadores*

A traditional country-style feast at the Caribe Hilton International

playing a trumpet fanfare, they entered the 350-year-old structure, where they perched on cannons and turrets to consume *paella,* spicy shrimps and crayfish (heaped in an old fishing boat), barbecued sausages, kebabs, and on and on. For the finale, a large ballroom inside the hotel had been transformed into an 18th-century version of the Port of San Juan, so that guests could plunder the cargo wagons of pastries, fruits, cheeses and breads. (Of course, the whole affair could have fallen on the same day as a Wine Society dinner for 12, consisting of three autumn terrines, duck consommé perfumed with tarragon, scallops in orange butter, saddle of rabbit with mustard, spiced granita, noisettes of venison in port, cèpe-stuffed crêpes, Alpine cheeses, chestnut charlottes, coffee and petits fours, with eight noteworthy wines and spirits.)

This type of hoopla is, naturally, additional to the routine of La Rotisserie, where à la carte lunch and dinner are served daily; the Caribe Terrace, a large, open-air restaurant, where breakfast, lunch, and dinner buffets (a different theme and decor each night) are offered; El Cafe, where you can snack anytime; the Caribar Cocktail Lounge; Juliana Discotheque; the Club Caribe; the vast bar; and, of course, room service. A romantic, octagonal restaurant, El Batey del Pescador, has recently opened among the palms at the beach-side to serve grilled Caribbean lobster, grilled scallops and their roe, buttery soft-shell crabs, and fish and more fish. Cooking classes, private dinners at the Chef's Table, and various outside catering jobs help keep Chef Augusto and his brigade from sitting idle and twiddling their fingers between courses.

Puréed Squash-*Apio* Soup with Crabmeat

PUERTO RICO, UNITED STATES

A favourite of August Schreiner, executive chef of the Caribe Hilton International, the delicacy of this golden purée is punctuated by a blast of finely chopped fresh ginger added at the last moment. Although the tuber known as apio *(or* arracacha) *is used in Puerto Rico, celeriac (also called celery root) is an excellent substitute. This very popular first course is served with alternative garnishes, most frequently lobster medallions, though for a simple meal, a sprinkle of fresh coriander will do. The light soup can also be enjoyed chilled (you may want to thin it with a little single cream or stock) or reheated.*

---

40 g (1½ oz) butter

800 g (1¾ lb *calabazo* or butternut squash, peeled, seeded, and cut into 4 cm (1½-inch) chunks (see Note)

175 g (6 oz) carrots, peeled and cut thin

450 g (1 lb) *apio* or celeriac, peeled and thin-sliced

1 bay leaf

About 1 litre (2 pints) chicken stock

About 100 ml (4 fl oz) double (or whipping) cream

1½ teaspoons very finely chopped peeled fresh ginger

About ¾ teaspoon Worcestershire sauce

Salt

About ¼ teaspoon white pepper

175 g (6 oz) lump crabmeat, carefully picked over

Fresh coriander sprigs

---

1. Heat the butter in a saucepan. Add the squash, carrots, and *apio;* stir occasionally over moderate heat for about 5 minutes.

2. Add the bay leaf and stock; bring to a boil. Cover and simmer until tender, about 20 minutes. Uncover and boil for 5 minutes. Let cool for about 30 minutes. Remove the bay leaf.

3. Purée in batches in a blender or processor until smooth. Add the cream, or to taste. Heat through over low heat. Add the ginger, Worcestershire sauce and salt and white pepper to taste. Adjust the thickness by adding more cream or stock, if necessary.

4. Divide into 6 soup cups. Top with crab and coriander sprigs.

Note: *Called Pumpkin Soup on the hotel's menu, the vegetable of choice is the orange-fleshed, fairly large* calabazo, *also known by a variety of local names, including West Indian pumpkin. The fine-grained, medium-sweet, fairly large squash (often sold by the slice) is similar in taste and texture to butternut squash, which substitutes perfectly if there is no West Indian market in your neighbourhood.*

6 SERVINGS AS A FIRST COURSE

Wine Soup with Peppered Cheese, Onions and Croûtons

UNITED STATES

Assembling the ingredients that remained after preparing a microfiche on the subject of French cheeses, Dieter Hannig, director of the Food Research Center, came up with this intense, peppery-winy cold country brew. There is an Alpine feeling to this rich, strong soup, which is best served in small portions. It is delightful as a restorative après-ski, with no other accoutrements, or as a first course.

---

75 g (3 oz) butter
4 medium onions, thin-sliced
225 ml (8 fl oz) chicken broth
8 fairly thin slices from a narrow loaf
of French bread (*baguette*)

300 ml (½ pint) dry white wine (see
Note)
100 g (4 oz) *crottin poivre* cheese
(see Note), grated
Salt and pepper
Finely chopped parsley

---

1. Preheat the oven to 200°C/400°F (gas mark 6). Melt 60 g (2½ oz) butter in a large, heavy-based saucepan; stir in the onions. Cook over moderately low heat, stirring often, until soft and translucent but not browned, about 10 minutes. Add the broth. Scrape into a blender or processor and purée thoroughly.

2. Meanwhile, place the bread slices in a single layer on a baking sheet; bake until golden, about 10 minutes.

3. Return the onion mixture to the saucepan. Add the wine and bring to a simmer. Remove from the heat; gradually stir in the cheese. Season with salt and pepper to taste.

4. To serve, ladle soup into 4 small bowls; top with the warm toast. Cut the remaining butter into 8 pieces and set a dab on each croûton. Sprinkle with parsley and serve at once.

Note: *Wine is the flavour here. Use a dry, full-bodied white, preferably French. Avoid fruity, semi-dry wines.*

Crottin poivre is a firm, cylindrical cheese made of cow's or sheep's milk and coated with a distinctively grooved black wax. It originates in the Auvergne, home of a number of zesty, rustic cheeses. Shot through with whole peppercorns, its pungent bite is considerable, although the cheese is nutty and not aggressively strong. Its high salt content pleasantly balances the brisk pepper.

Advance preparation: *Most soups to which cheese is added cannot be made ahead—but this one can. The slightly granular texture and appearance of the finished soup do not change when reheated.*

4 SERVINGS AS A FIRST COURSE

COLD BEETROOT SOUP WITH SCALLOPS

UNITED STATES

Brunch, that leisurely late-morning meal for weekends and holidays, is a well-established American pastime, yet virtually unknown in the rest of the world. After receiving many requests from abroad, Dieter Hannig developed a microfiche on the subject for use among chefs—particularly those outside the United States.

This updated version of a Slavic classic is substantial, but light-tasting, an unusual offering for a spring-to-summer brunch. Shocking-pink soup thick with maroon beetroot shreds, scallops, ribbons of ham and cucumbers is seasoned with snippets of spring onion and dill and served refreshingly chilled.

10–12 small beetroot, (about 1 kilo/2 lb, weighed with 5 cm/2-inch tops)
1.75 litres (3 pints) chicken stock, skimmed of all fat
450 g (1 lb) scallops
225–250 g (8–9 oz) sliced ham, trimmed of fat, then cut into thin julienne

2 small cucumbers
3 medium, thin-sliced spring onions
2–3 tablespoons red wine vinegar
3–4 tablespoons lemon juice
300 ml (½ pint) sour cream
About 2 tablespoons finely chopped dill plus 6 small sprigs for garnish
Salt and pepper

---

1. Scrub the beetroot and drop them, unpeeled, into boiling salted water. Boil, uncovered, until very tender when pierced with a skewer; timing varies, but 20 minutes is average. Drain, cool slightly, then slip off the skins and stems. Cut in thin slices, then thin strips.

2. Bring 350 ml (12 fl oz) stock to a simmer in a small saucepan. Add the scallops and keep under a simmer until barely cooked, about 2 minutes. Cool in the stock, then refrigerate.

3. Peel, halve, and seed the cucumbers. Cut each half lengthwise in half again, then cut across into thin slices. Combine in a bowl with the beetroot, ham, spring onions, 2 tablespoons vinegar, and 3 tablespoons lemon juice. Whisk together the sour cream and 2 tablespoons dill. Gradually whisk in the remaining stock. Strain the poaching liquid from the scallops and add it to the bowl. Cut the scallops in thin slices and add to the soup.

4. Chill thoroughly. Season to taste with additional salt, pepper, vinegar, lemon juice, and dill. Divide the soup between the serving bowls, then garnish with dill sprigs.

Serving: *Buckwheat waffles make an interesting accompaniment.*
Advance preparation: *Although the soup should be made long enough in advance to chill and blend the flavours, a few hours will suffice. More than that and the cucumbers exude too much liquid and the solids will turn a rather livid pink.*

6 SERVINGS AS A MAIN COURSE; 10 AS A FIRST COURSE

Wisconsin Diced Vegetable and Sorrel Soup

UNITED STATES

A fresh first course for any time of the year, this soup is served at the American Harvest Restaurant. Based on a recipe from the Wisconsin County Cookbook and Journal *by Edward Harris Heth (1956), this subtle combination of soft-cooked diced vegetables in broth tastes sweetish at first, then tart and grassy from the acid sorrel.*

2 medium leeks (about 450 g/1 lb), dark green tops and roots removed
40 g (1½ oz) butter
1 medium-large onion, chopped
2 medium turnips, peeled and cut into .5 cm (¼-inch) dice
2 medium carrots, peeled and cut into .5 cm (¼-inch) dice

1 small wedge of cabbage, cut into .5 cm (¼-inch) squares
2 litres (3¼ pints) chicken stock
200 g (7 oz) fresh sorrel
1 tablespoon finely sliced basil
½ teaspoon finely chopped fresh marjoram
Salt and pepper

1. Quarter the leeks lengthwise. Wash meticulously, then cut into .5 cm (¼-inch) chunks. Heat the butter in a large, heavy pan. Stir in the leeks and onion; cook over moderate heat until translucent, but not browned, about 5 minutes.

2. Add the turnips, carrots, and cabbage; cook for 4–5 minutes, stirring now and then. Add the chicken stock. Simmer, partly covered, for 20 minutes.

3. Meanwhile, strip off and discard the sorrel stems. Cut the leaves into thin strips, using a stainless-steel knife.

4. Add the sorrel, basil, marjoram, salt and pepper to taste to the soup. Simmer, uncovered, for 3 minutes and serve hot.

8 SERVINGS AS A FIRST COURSE

CARROT AND WALNUT SOUP

UNITED STATES

Lightly sweet and thick, with a natural vegetable taste (not spiced as this type of soup often is), this purée is the kind usually associated with family celebrations (particularly Thanksgiving), for it seems to please all ages. The walnuts lend depth, meatiness, and a curry-yellow colour. Another from the American Harvest Restaurant, where the seasons are marked by a menu that features such autumnal pleasures as this.

30 g (1 oz) butter
1 very small onion, chopped
450 g (1 lb) carrots (weighed without tops), sliced
50 g (2 oz) walnuts, chopped
About 900 ml (1½ pints) chicken stock

225 ml (8 fl oz) double (or whipping) cream
Salt and pepper
Garnish
50 g (2 oz) walnuts
About 1½ tablespoons thin-sliced chives

1. Melt the butter in a saucepan over moderate heat. Add the onion and stir for a few minutes until translucent, but not browned. Add the carrots and cook for 2–3 minutes, stirring often. Add the chopped walnuts and 600 ml (1 pint) stock. Bring to a boil, stirring from time to time. Simmer the soup gently, covered, for 30 minutes.

2. Purée in a food processor until smooth. Return to the saucepan with the remaining stock and the cream. Bring to a simmer. Add salt and pepper to taste. Add more stock, if needed, to obtain the desired consistency.

3. Divide the soup among heated bowls or cups. Place the walnuts for garnish in a rotary cheese grater and grind over the soup. Garnish with chives.

6 SERVINGS AS A FIRST COURSE

SEVEN GREENS AND MUSSEL GUMBO

UNITED STATES

Served at Vista's Greenhouse Restaurant, an airy glass enclosure set amid the soaring skyscrapers of the World Trade Center in New York City, this rough-textured soup is hot and herbal, smoky and briny, rich in the flavour of good bitter greens—and as backcountry as the setting is urban.

Although the tremendous quantity of greens requires considerable cleaning and chopping time, the soup is straightforward to cook, and improves if made in advance.

(continued)

Seven Greens and Mussel Gumbo

100 g (4 oz) butter
275 g (10 oz) chopped onions
1 tablespoon finely chopped garlic
225 ml (8 fl oz) dry white wine
36 cultivated mussels, rinsed and
    cleaned (see page 324)
225 g (8 oz) precooked garlic sau-
    sage, such as *andouille* or *kiel-
    basa*, coarsely chopped
100 g (4 oz) chopped celery
225 g (8 oz) chopped green peppers
About 2½ teaspoons salt
¼–1 teaspoon cayenne pepper (see
    Note)
1½ teaspoons paprika
¼ teaspoon crushed red pepper
    (pepper flakes)

1 teaspoon dried thyme
½ teaspoon dried oregano
1 teaspoon dried basil
2 bay leaves, crumbled
50 g (2 oz) coarsely chopped parsley
1 bunch watercress, stems removed,
    chopped
4 very green large cos lettuce leaves,
    cut into wide slices
450 g (1 lb) spinach, stems removed,
    leaves rinsed and cut into
    wide slices
6 outer leaves chicory or escarole, cut
into wide slices
1 bunch spring onions, chopped
4 outside leaves iceberg lettuce,
    cut into wide slices
1 tablespoon filé powder (see Note)

1. Melt all but 15 g (½ oz) of butter in a large pot over moderate heat. Add half the onions and all the garlic; stir until softened. Add the wine and an equal amount of water. Add the mussels. Cover and bring to a boil; the mussels should open up. Lift out the mussels. Shell and reserve them, along with the cooking liquid.

2. Heat the remaining butter in a soup pot. Add the sausage and fry for a few minutes to render some fat. Add the remaining onions and the celery and peppers. Cook over moderate heat until soft. Add 2 teaspoons salt, ground red pepper, paprika, pepper flakes, thyme, oregano, basil and bay leaves; stir. Add the parsley, watercress, cos, spinach, chicory, spring onions, and iceberg lettuce (you may want to add them gradually, pushing in each green as the others reduce in volume).

3. Add the reserved cooking liquid and 900 ml (2½ pints) water. Simmer, uncovered, for 30 minutes.

4. In a food processor, purée the gumbo in batches to a rather coarse texture. Return to the pot; heat through. Remove 1 cup of the mixture and stir in the filé powder. Return mixture to pot and heat again until thoroughly warmed through, but not boiling.

Note: *Lovers of fiery food may want to go for the full teaspoon of ground red pepper, but delicate palates should begin with ¼ teaspoon. You can always add more later.*

Filé powder, made of dried, ground sassafras leaves, contributes a unique herbal flavour to soups; at the same time it adds thickness and a slightly slippery texture. It should not be boiled, as it may become sticky and ropy. Rather, simply heat through to bind and flavour the gumbo. It is not easy to find in Britain, but is well worth seeking out for an authentic dish.

If you're in no mood to tackle seven varieties of greens, a lesser quantity will be as delicious, if different.

6–7 SERVINGS AS A MAIN COURSE

Cape Cod's Bookbinder Red Snapper Soup

UNITED STATES

During cold weather, Chicagoans come to The Drake hotel to down this by the boatload, along with overflowing baskets of rolls and crackers. It is a buttery, thick American-style soup that brings out the goodness of seafood: no Mediterranean seasoning, no cream or egg finishing—just mild vegetables and fish. The soup is served in the hotel's extremely popular Cape Cod Room, in fact a cosy clutch of rooms, decorated with nautical Americana—ancient cauldrons, a gargantuan crab, a stuffed swordfish, brass sconces that may have travelled the seven seas, copper and pewter ware from New England.

The recipe on which the sturdy pottage is based comes from Bookbinder's Seafood House in Philadelphia. The original version, a soup special to that area and to southern New Jersey, has quite a different snapper as its featured ingredient—snapping turtle.

Stock
Head and bones from filleted red snapper (below)
About 700 g (1½ lb) additional fish bones and head(s)
2 onions, quartered
2 celery sticks with leaves, sliced
1 large carrot, sliced
1 bay leaf
Soup Assembly
200 g (7 oz) butter
1 small carrot, chopped
3 small celery sticks, chopped
2 medium onions, chopped

1 medium garlic clove, finely chopped
1 bay leaf
15 white peppercorns, crushed
½ teaspoon dried thyme
150 g (5 oz) plain flour
75 g (3 oz) tomato purée
About 1.5 kilos (3–3½ lb) red snapper, filleted and skinned (head and bones used in stock)
About 100 ml (4 fl oz) dry sherry
Salt and pepper
Optional: medium-dry sherry for finishing the soup (see Note)

1. Make the stock: Rinse the fish bones and heads and combine in a stockpot with all of the other stock ingredients and 4 litres (7 pints) water. Bring to a simmer, skimming. Simmer gently for 20 minutes. Ladle through a sieve and set aside (you should have about 3.5 litres/6 pints).

2. Assemble the soup: Melt all but 25 g (1 oz) of the butter in a large heavy pot; add the chopped carrot, half the celery, half the onions and the garlic; stir over moderate heat for 2 minutes. Add the bay leaf, peppercorns, thyme and flour: stir for another few minutes.

3. Blend together the tomato purée with 225 ml (8 fl oz) of the stock. Add this, then the remaining stock to the pot. Whisk over high heat until the soup boils. Lower the heat and simmer, uncovered, for 20 minutes, skimming occasionally.

4. Meanwhile, cut the snapper fillets into 1 cm (½-inch) squares. Heat the remaining butter in a wide frying pan. Add the remaining onion and celery; stir over moderate heat for a few minutes, to just soften. Add the fish and stir for about 1 minute; add the dry sherry and toss for another minute.

5. Add the mixture to the soup. Simmer for about 15 minutes, until thickened and savoury. Season with salt and pepper; taste for additional sherry.

Note: *At The Drake, miniature carafes of medium-dry sherry are offered to the diners so that they can adjust the sherry to taste.*

Imported red snapper is usually available frozen from good fishmongers, larger supermarkets and many oriental markets.

Advance preparation: *Although at The Drake this soup is never kept beyond the day it is made, we found it to be mellow and delicious after 24–48 hours in the refrigerator.*

6–7 SERVINGS AS A MAIN COURSE; 12 SERVINGS AS A FIRST COURSE

A shellfish extravaganza in the Cape Cod Room of The Drake

The American Harvest Restaurant: Regional Bounty, Traditional Food in a Fine Dining Room

The timing was on target. By the end of the '70s it was no longer necessary for diners in-the-know to prefer minestrone to mixed vegetable soup, or *tarte Tatin* to apple pie à la mode. American food was coming out of the shadows into the California (Florida, New Mexico, etc.) sunshine. At Hilton International, what began as research for an American Bicentennial celebration to be held in its hotels became the basis for the American Harvest Restaurant at the Vista hotel in New York City—the company's first entry into the U.S. market after 32 successful years managing 89 hotels elsewhere on the globe. Thus began the formidable task of creating a menu which could represent all regions of a country with more ethnic groups than any other, and present a panorama of dishes to highlight the abundance of its fields, forests, ponds, streams, and oceans at their seasonal best.

The result is a menu unique to each month: buttered fiddlehead ferns and sesame-fried soft-shell crabs appear in May; June's tart of wild American morels or creamed, minted green peas might follow; Wisconsin vegetable and sorrel soup, blueberry cream puffs and raspberry summer pudding denote July; sunny Martha's Vineyard green corn pudding means August; tomatoes and sweet onions with basil dressing belong to September; while a pumpkin cheesecake, Ozark Apple Pudding, and apple pies, cobblers, and compotes leave no doubt that October is upon us.

The small group that developed the restaurant concept arrived at these and more than 300 other exemplary American recipes after five years of ploughing through cookbooks, periodicals and historical documents. In typical American fashion, the backgrounds of the principal players were diverse—the food consultant, chefs, and key Hilton International executives hailing from the Midwest, Austria, France, Germany, Britain, Holland, Pennsylvania, and New York. Journeying back and forth between Montreal (where the Food Research Center was located at the time) and New York, members of the team cooked, sampled, and rated some 1,500 home recipes. Seventy potato dishes from almond-studded to walnut-crusted were candidates; 110 chicken recipes from batter-fried to stewed with dumplings were in the running at the start of the competition; 75 cookies from apricot bars to wagon wheels were tasted—as were comparable quantities in some 50-odd categories ranging from soup to nuts. Given the possible scenarios, it seems amazing that the internecine skirmishes were so few and that the 'learning process' prevailed. For a trial clam-bake, for example, executive chef Walter Plendner (born in Austria) served the largest steamer clams he could find, not realizing that they were to be broth-dunked and eaten whole, as clam-bake etiquette dictates. French pastry chef Alain Roby, who trained at the celebrated Pâtisserie Lenôtre, kept turning out perfect tiny *tartelettes* and petits fours, balking at the American preference for voluminous desserts. After a crash course in American taste, the steamers were appropriately petite, the Shaker lemon pies and walnut chiffon cakes full-blown, and many such peculiarities set in their proper perspectives. But with comments, scores and ultimate agreement required for each recipe, the final 350 choices were hard-won.

All this attention is focused on a restaurant that is a quiet, 90-seat oasis in the centre of New York's hectic financial district, where the Vista was the first major hotel to be built in 145 years. Prior to its opening, there were few (or no, depending on your definition) truly American up-market restaurants in the city. The American Harvest embraces a quintet of intimate-feeling dining areas that suggest a modern melding of townhouse, Shaker barn and Southern colonial home (a curious environment for the 'power breakfasts' and corporate lunches that are frequently held there). Tiny geometric shapes dot the pastel silk upholstery, a dark oak table holds baskets of the season's harvest, and spongeware pottery and stencilled cups grace a pale, antique wooden breakfront. Conservative, tasteful, the decor is in keeping with the fresh, simple food, which is presented attractively, with relatively little embellishment. Salt, pepper and butter are the main seasonings for the wide palette of honest American vegetables and generous helpings of fresh fish and meat. Handsome glassware and soft-hued napery, a sprinkle of parsley on the thick squash purée, a crumble of nuts on the pumpkin cheesecake are sufficient decoration.

As much of the United States leaps to create a glamorous new hybrid cuisine, the American Harvest seems a safe place to savour the past—modified ever so slightly to fit the tastes of a broad spectrum of contemporary diners who are happy with tradition, updated. This is accomplished not only with monthly menus that salute its culinary heritage, but with annual celebrations that single out the cooking of groups of Americans who have had abiding influences—the Shakers, Pennsylvania Dutch and American Indians, for example. It is a place for some to feel nostalgic, for some to feel at home, for others to learn about their heritage, and to dignify simple American fare.

MARTHA'S VINEYARD GREEN CORN PUDDING

UNITED STATES

Sweet corn is a fairly recent agricultural development. Before it became common, 'green corn', well sugared, was the vegetable that appeared in preparations such as this one. 'Green corn' is the term for fresh (not dried) field corn or 'critter corn', the starchy grain that is used for animal feed or ground into meal.

A favourite old-fashioned summer dish at the American Harvest Restaurant, this pudding has a memorably intense flavour that depends entirely on the quality of corn itself—so choose only the very freshest. A bit messy and time-consuming to prepare, you must be a real corn-lover to appreciate the goodness of this delicacy.

The recipe on which the pudding is based is attributed to Mrs Charles L. Foote of West Tisbury, Massachusetts, on the island of Martha's Vineyard. The original, which appears in The Yankee Cookbook *by Imogene Wolcott, was 'dry enough to be cut into squares' after 2–3 hours baking. The American Harvest adaptation is tender and baked in individual dishes for less than half an hour.*

---

12 ears of fresh sweetcorn, preferably white, husks and silk removed (see Note)
2 eggs

½ teaspoon salt
2 tablespoons melted butter
225 ml (8 fl oz) milk

---

1. Preheat the oven to 180°C/350°F (gas mark 4). With a sharp knife cut lengthwise through the centre of each row of kernels. With the dull side of a butter knife, press and rub the kernels to extract their pulp. *Do not* scrape the kernels from the cob.

2. Blend together the eggs, salt, and butter in a mixing bowl. Add the corn. Add the milk.

3. Divide the mixture evenly among eight 175 ml (6 fl oz) buttered ramekins, cocottes, or custard cups, stirring the mixture so that the corn is equally distributed as you spoon it. Set the cups on a baking sheet in the centre of the oven.

4. Bake for 20–25 minutes, until the centres are barely set. Serve hot, warm, or lukewarm.

Note: *The yield will vary considerably with the size and freshness of the kernels, from 8 to 16 ears being required. Buy a few extra ears of corn and measure as you scrape the pulp from the cobs.*

The custard can also be baked in a shallow 1 litre (2 pint) dish for 25 minutes or so.

Serving: *Enjoy this delightful dish for breakfast or brunch along with ham or smoked chicken or turkey. Or offer it as an appetizer, with a pat of butter, as is done at the American Harvest Restaurant.*

8 SERVINGS AS A SIDE DISH OR FIRST COURSE

MANITOBA WILD RICE CROQUETTES

CANADA

Albert Schnell features the ingredients of Canada in most of his menus. Manitoba is home to deep-brown wild rice, the seed of a native American grass. The crunchy crumb-coating of these croquettes breaks open to reveal chewy grains bound with creamy béchamel.

---

200 g (7 oz) wild rice
75 g (3 oz) butter
30 g (1¼ oz) plain flour
600 ml (1 pint) milk
3 tablespoons finely chopped shallots
100 g (4 oz) finely chopped ham
¼ teaspoon mace
½ teaspoon salt

¼ teaspoon pepper
2 tablespoons finely chopped parsley
For coating and frying
60 g (2½ oz) plain flour
3 eggs, beaten
300 g (10 oz) fine dry white bread
   crumbs
Light vegetable oil for deep frying

---

1. Combine the rice and 825 ml (28 fl oz) water in a small, heavy saucepan and bring to a rolling boil over high heat, stirring. Turn heat to its lowest point and cover the pan. Cook until firm-textured but not hard; this can vary from 25 minutes to 1 hour, depending upon the rice. Add water if necessary. Cool the rice, then chill.

2. In a small pan, heat 50 g (2 oz) butter; stir in the flour. Cook for 30 seconds over low heat; add all the milk and bring to a boil, stirring, then simmer for 5 minutes, stirring often.

3. Melt the remaining butter in a medium frying pan. Add the shallots and ham; stir over low heat for 2 minutes. Add the rice; stir for 3–4 minutes. Add the white sauce, mace, salt and pepper. Add the parsley. Let the mixture cool.

4. Line a baking sheet with greaseproof paper. Using a pastry bag with a 2 cm (¾-inch) plain tube, pipe mixture in long strips onto the sheet. Freeze until firm. Wrap strips tightly; freeze.

5. When ready to coat and fry the croquettes, preheat the oven to 110°C/225°F (gas mark ¼). Cut the frozen strips into 5 cm (2-inch) lengths (you can fry as small a batch as suits the meal: just reduce the coating ingredients to suit). Dust the still-firm croquettes with flour, then coat completely with beaten egg. Roll in the crumbs, making sure there are no bare spots. Set on a sheet of greaseproof paper.

6. Heat 5 cm (2 inches) of oil to 170°C/325°F in a wide, heavy frying pan or deep fat fryer. Fry the croquettes in batches until golden brown, but not dark—about 3 minutes. Place on a kitchen-paper-covered dish in the warm oven until all are ready. Serve hot.

Serving: *The croquettes, which are neat to eat as finger-food, can also be offered as an hors d'oeuvre.*
Advance preparation: *Uncoated croquettes can be frozen for months, then crumbed and fried as you like. Or they can be prepared through Step 5, then refrigerated for up to a day (uncovered) before frying.*

56 SMALL CROQUETTES

WOODSY BUCKWHEAT

UNITED STATES

An updated variation of an old-world favourite, kasha (roasted buckwheat grains) and mushrooms, from Dieter Hannig—a lively New-World chef with training in the classical school. Earthy and wild-flavoured, the fluffy grains of buckwheat are generously laced with chewy black Chinese mushrooms and morels and punctuated with the fruitiness of sun-dried tomatoes. Serve as a light main course or roast accompaniment.

16 medium-size dried morels
16 dried Chinese black mushrooms (shiitake)
1 tablespoon olive oil
30 g (1 oz) butter
3 tablespoons chopped shallots
1 teaspoon finely chopped garlic

50 g (2 oz) sun-dried tomatoes, chopped
350 ml (12 fl oz) chicken stock
1 egg, beaten
225 g (8 oz) roasted buckwheat grains
2 small spring onions, trimmed and sliced thin

1. Combine 450 ml (¾ pint) water, the morels, Chinese mushrooms and olive oil in a saucepan. Bring to a boil, then remove from the heat and let cool. Lift out the mushrooms; strain the remaining liquid slowly through several layers of dampened muslin to remove any soil or sand. (You should have about 100 ml/4 fl oz.)

2. Quarter the morels, rinsing if necessary. Trim off the black mushroom stems and reserve for stock-making. Quarter the caps.

3. Heat the butter in a frying pan over moderately high heat. Add the shallots, garlic, and mushrooms; toss for 3 minutes. Lower the heat; add the tomatoes, stir for 2 minutes longer. Add the chicken stock and mushroom liquid and bring to a boil.

4. Meanwhile, heat another pan over moderate heat. Mix together the egg and buckwheat to coat well. Add the mixture and flatten and stir the grains in the hot pan for 3–4 minutes, until they are dried and separated.

5. Being careful to avoid splatters, add the grains to the hot stock. Cover and cook over lowest heat for 10 minutes. Remove from the heat and let stand 5–20 minutes before serving, sprinkled with the spring onions.

Advance preparation: *If the mushrooms are soaked in advance, the dish can be quickly assembled.*

4 MAIN COURSE SERVINGS; OR 6 AS A SIDE DISH

A VEGETARIAN THANKSGIVING FEAST

UNITED STATES

Although this recipe looks formidable, it yields a full meal, will take less time to prepare than a traditional American Thanksgiving dinner, can be done in substantial part a day in advance—and provides a colourful, bountiful feast for vegetable lovers (vegetarians or not). It would also serve as a very special Christmas lunch for a vegetarian family.

Adapted from a prize-winning creation of Franz Kranzfelder, senior sous-chef at The Drake hotel in Chicago, it is a merry medley: bread dumpling slices marbled with chestnuts and figs are served with a cranberry red-wine sauce; maple-glazed sweet potatoes are embellished with sultanas and pecan halves; porcelain-pretty striped sweet dumpling squash are heaped with a nutmeg-perfumed carrot purée, arranged with crescents of acorn squash topped with coins of courgette, and set around a tumble of baby ears of corn.

Cranberry-Wine Sauce
350 g (12 oz) fresh cranberries, sorted and rinsed
300 ml (½ pint) dry red wine
85 g (3½ oz) sugar
¼ teaspoon ground cinnamon

Chestnut-Fig Bread Dumplings
225 g (8 oz) fresh chestnuts
450 g (1 lb) day-old hard rolls (6–8 medium size)
2 tablespoons vegetable oil
75 g (3 oz) diced onion
2 celery sticks, diced
1 egg, beaten, to blend (see Note)
8–9 dried figs, cut in 1 cm (½-inch) dice
1½ teaspoons finely chopped fresh sage
About ¼ teaspoon salt
¼ teaspoon pepper
¼ teaspoon nutmeg

Carrot Purée with Nutmeg
900 g (2 lb) large carrots (weighed without tops), peeled and sliced .5 cm (¼ inch) thick
½ teaspoon nutmeg
½ teaspoon salt
40 g (1½ oz) butter

Vegetables
3 medium-large sweet potatoes (about 300 g/10 oz each), peeled and halved lengthwise
6 sweet dumpling squash (about 175 g/6 oz each)
Salt and pepper
1 acorn squash (about 700 g/1½ lb)
175 g (6 oz) pure maple syrup
40 g (1½ oz) butter
75 g (3 oz) sultanas
75 g (3 oz) pecan halves
2 medium courgettes, sliced thin
Two 400 g (15-oz) cans baby corn-on-the-cob, drained

1. Preheat the oven to 220°C/425°F (gas mark 7). Combine the cranberries, red wine, sugar and cinnamon in a medium non-aluminium saucepan. Bring to a boil, stirring occasionally. Boil about 2 minutes, until most of the skins pop. Pass through the medium disk of a food mill. Cool the sauce, cover, and refrigerate.

2. Make the dumplings: Cut a cross through the tip of each chestnut. Bake in a pan in the centre of the oven for 10 minutes. While still hot, remove the shells and husks. Cut into 1 cm (½-inch) dice.

3. Halve and slice the rolls; soak in 1 litre (2 pints) cold water for 15 minutes or more, tossing occasionally. Meanwhile, heat the oil in a medium pan. Add the onion; stir for 3 minutes. Add the celery; stir until tender, but still crunchy.

4. Squeeze the water from the rolls. Combine in a mixing bowl with the chestnuts, onions and celery, beaten egg, figs, sage, and salt, pepper and nutmeg to taste. Squeeze and knead to blend thoroughly. Divide the mixture into 4 parts. Roll each to form a cylinder about 6 cm (2½-inches) in diameter. Roll each in a length of plastic wrap. Twist the ends tightly, then fold underneath each roll. Refrigerate for about 24 hours.

5. Make the carrot purée: Combine the carrots, nutmeg, salt and butter with 350 ml (12 fl oz) water in a saucepan over high heat. Simmer, covered, for about 15 minutes, until soft. Uncover and boil briefly, if necessary, until almost no liquid remains. Transfer to a food processor; blend to a smooth purée. Cool, cover and refrigerate.

6. Drop the sweet potatoes into boiling, salted water. Boil until tender, 15–20 minutes. Lift out carefully with a slotted spoon; cool. Cut crosswise into 1 cm (½-inch) slices. Arrange in a single layer in a 20 × 27.5 cm (8 × 11-inch) baking dish. Cool, cover and refrigerate.

7. *About 40 minutes before you plan to serve dinner:* Preheat the oven to 190°C/375°F (gas mark 5). Cut out the stem ends of the sweet dumpling squash (or halve larger ones); scoop out the seeds. Season to taste. Set in a baking pan; add in water to just cover the bottom of the pan. Cover tightly with foil. Halve the acorn squash; scoop out seeds and fibres; then cut each half lengthwise in thirds. Place in a baking dish, sprinkle with salt and pepper, add water to barely cover the bottom of the dish. Cover tightly with foil. Bake both types of squash until just tender, 25–40 minutes (check frequently). Remove from the oven but leave the oven on; let the squash stand, covered, while you complete the meal.

8. While the squash bake, finish the sweet potatoes: Combine the maple syrup, 15 g (½ oz) of the butter, the sultanas, and pecans in a small pan and bring to a boil. Pour over the potatoes. As soon as the squash is removed from the oven, set the potatoes in the centre; bake for 15 minutes, until browned and bubbling.

9. At the same time, set the dumpling logs on a steamer rack over boiling water. Cover tightly; steam for 10 minutes. Remove and let stand for 5 minutes.

10. Meanwhile, attend to these simultaneously: Heat 2 very large pans over high heat; add 15 g (½ oz) of butter to each. Toss the courgettes in one until just tender, about 2 minutes. In the other, toss the corn until slightly coloured, about the same amount of time. Warm both the carrot purée and the cranberry sauce (which should be thick, but pourable; add red wine if it is too dense).

11. Tip juices out of the sweet dumpling squash; arrange around the edge of a very large, heated platter. Divide carrot purée into them. Place acorn squash between the dumpling squash. Heap corn in the centre of the platter. Spoon the courgettes onto the acorn squash. (The platter can wait for 10 minutes in the turned-off oven.)

12. Unwrap the dumpling logs; cut each into 6 diagonal slices. Arrange in a warm dish; serve with the cranberry sauce alongside.

Advance preparation: *Steps 1–6 can be accomplished a day in advance.*

6 SERVINGS

The Drake: Great Expectations
Fulfilled—and the Role of the Roll

In the Chef's Office of The Drake hotel, a place for brainstorming and conferring

T he 67-year-old brick oven of The Drake Hotel in Chicago, Illinois, United States of America, is delivered of at least 8,000 golden, light-textured rolls (cheese, caraway-rye, sesame, onion, and so on) each day. Once a year the oven must be cooled, cleaned and refired. During this three-day period the management is invariably alerted to the complaints of regular diners who object to the 'imports', and there may even be an empty table (an unheard-of occurrence at this popular meeting place) from a *regular* regular who may not wish to dine in such dire conditions.

A staff of life for Chicagoans, a monument (recognized officially as an historical landmark), a place of substance: The Drake is an elegant *grande dame* who will have no truck with 'glitz' or short-cuts. It offers deep comfort, a gracious pace; walnut-panelled, mirrored lifts with salmon and pale-green seats are operated by polite, efficient 'elevator ladies'. Though discreetly (and beautifully and expensively) refurbished, the massive building has retained its special personality. It would be wise to do so, or the clientele—many of whom request the same spacious rooms and suites year after year—would mutiny. The American Association of Railway Surgeons has held its annual dinner at The Drake for 51 years; the Arden Shore Home for Boys for 50. Staff members go back 35, 40, and 50 years. (And the fancy powder room—still so-called in this liberated age—is rated the finest in Chicago.)

If radical changes were made in its menus, there would probably be a revolt by the diners, who daily overflow the 54-year-old Cape Cod Room, the bright Oak Terrace and the Club International, a private association of 3,500. Executive chef Leo Waldmeier, without tampering with the revered dishes, has honed the style of the food and techniques of the cooks. In fact, in his brief tenure he has so sharpened the edge that the team has pulled in 27 medals and six trophies in national culinary competitions during the last four years. From a raised, glass-windowed office in a kitchen built before the days of property sold by the square foot, Waldmeier surveys an area the size of three tennis courts—including a pastry area that would engulf many modern main kitchens, soup tanks that would hide an ox, and vats of sauces.

Excellence on a grand scale is expected—and expectations are met, in full Midwestern style. Portions are hearty, food is piping hot, impeccably fresh, and cooked exactly as ordered. Fish is flown in daily from both coasts, coffee is strong and just-brewed, orange juice is always the real thing, and leftover soups are discarded every evening (Bookbinder's Red Snapper Soup, a dense, mahogany, pottage brimming with fish chunks is consumed at the rate of 35 gallons a day). For the most part (though Waldmeier and staff have introduced some eloquent exceptions), the menu is American at its finest—simple and straightforward: What you see is what you get. When a family looks forward to the sparkling fresh local whitefish or sweet crabmeat cakes, all members will depart the cosy Cape Cod Room beaming, satisfied. Blonde and blue-eyed debutantes relaxing in the sunny Oak Terrace after a morning of shopping at Chicago's equivalent of Harrods tuck into the utterly simple chicken salad (chunks of tender meat in a light mayonnaise with a touch of celery) and are never disappointed. An elegant couple finishing their pre-theatre dinner with the custardy rice pudding with sultanas (25 years on the menu) will be as pleased with it as was the late Mrs Maurice L. Rothschild, who lived at The Drake for 58 years, until her death at the age of 102 in 1980. A businessman entertaining European clients in the Club International can be justly proud of the Dover Sole Meunière, the well-aged sirloin, or the day's specials—oyster stew with linguine and yellow pepper sauce or lamb fillet with Burgundy and onion ragoût.

People are comfortable at The Drake. There, one feels special, but easy. It seems to instil devotion for generations. An example among many is the tap dancer who met her husband-to-be in the Camellia House (now The Drake Room), where he was a drummer in the 1930s. They married and honeymooned at The Drake, conceived their first child there—and named him Drake. Camille was their second. They recently celebrated their 40th anniversary—in The Drake Room.

'We like a hotel that has poise and yet is not stilted; that offers luxury without ostentation, convenience without conscious effort, and calm with its activity. We like a hotel that will charm and make you feel that you belong to its family,' wrote a couple in 1925. In 1986 one letter of praise was from a widow with seven grandchildren: 'I have stayed at The Drake since 1943 during World War II when I was on my honeymoon. I . . . have the pleasure of bringing [my grandchildren] (one at a time!) to Chicago for special little trips for fun and sightseeing. . . . I feel as safe there as in a friend's home.' The same month a young woman extolled the present management and explains that 'I have been coming to The Drake for 30 years—first with my parents and now as an adult.' Another: 'this weekend is the gift of our five daughters. They were wise in selecting The Drake for our 25th wedding anniversary.' Chances are good that the couple's grandchildren will celebrate life's passages in the same place—with a toast in the Cape Cod Room.

CRAB CAKES WITH LIGHT MUSTARD SAUCE

UNITED STATES

Large pieces of sweet crab are melded with mashed potato and egg yolk, seasoned with a generous quantity of pepper and Tabasco, dredged in soft crumbs, pan-fried, then served with a creamy mustard sauce. At The Drake hotel's bustling Cape Cod Room (a series of dim, cosy rooms that feel like an old inn and overflow with nautical antiques and good cheer) these are a best-selling item.

---

1 medium all-purpose potato, peeled
  (about 175 g/6 oz)
About ¼ teaspoon Tabasco sauce
3 egg yolks
450 g (1 lb) lump crabmeat, carefully
  picked over and slightly flaked
75 g (3 oz) soft white bread crumbs
3 tablespoons finely chopped red
  pepper (see Note)
½ teaspoon salt
¼ teaspoon pepper

Mustard Sauce
225 ml (8 fl oz) dry white wine
1–1½ teaspoons dry mustard
15 g (½ oz) butter
3 tablespoons finely chopped shallots
225 ml (8 fl oz) fish stock
100 ml (4 fl oz) cup dry vermouth
225 ml (8 fl oz) heavy (or whipping)
  cream

55 g (2 oz) clarified butter for frying

---

1. Boil the potato until soft, about 25 minutes. Mash with a fork and let cool completely.

2. Blend the Tabasco and egg yolks. Combine with the crab, one-third of the crumbs, the red pepper, salt, and ground pepper. Mix well. Form into 8 cakes about 2.5 cm (1 inch) thick and 7 cm (3 inches) in diameter.

3. Prepare the sauce: Blend together 2 tablespoons of the wine with 1 teaspoon dry mustard and set aside. Melt the butter in a small pan over moderately low heat. Add the shallots and stir for about 2 minutes, until softened. Add the remaining white wine, the fish stock, and dry vermouth. Boil to reduce to 225 ml (8 fl oz)—about 15 minutes.

4. Add the cream; boil again to reduce to about 225 ml (8 fl oz), or the desired consistency. Add the mustard mixture. Taste and stir in additional dry mustard, as desired (first dissolving in water), and salt. Strain.

5. Dredge the cakes in the remaining bread crumbs. Heat the clarified butter in a wide frying pan over low heat. Fry the cakes for 6 minutes on each side. Raise the heat to moderate; fry for 1 minute longer on each side, until golden. Heat the sauce; pour into a warm sauceboat. Serve alongside.

Note: *Both red and green peppers are used at the Cape Cod Room, 1½ tablespoons of each.*
Advance preparation: *The crab cakes can be fried until light golden, cooled, then covered and refrigerated. Heat through in a hot oven, 200°C/400°F (gas mark 6), to serve. The sauce can be cooled, covered, then refrigerated. Reheat over low heat, adding a little white wine or fish stock to restore the consistency.*

4 SERVINGS AS A MAIN COURSE; 8 AS A FIRST COURSE

SCALLOPS IN LIME AND GREEN PEPPERCORN SAUCE
UNITED STATES

White rounds of scallops sprinkled with fine strands of pungent lime zest blend in a thin buttery sauce sharpened by green peppercorns. To prepare this special served in the Cape Cod Room at The Drake, cook the scallops over the highest heat in the widest pan available—or they will exude too much juice and wind up stewed instead of sautéed.

---

700 g (1½ lb) sea scallops
1½ teaspoons drained, rinsed, water-packed green peppercorns
Salt and white pepper

1½ teaspoons very fine julienne-cut lime rind
60 g (2½ oz) butter
2 tablespoons lime juice
1 teaspoon coarsely grated lime rind

---

1. Slice the larger scallops horizontally in half; leave smaller ones whole. Finely chop (or crush) 1 teaspoon of the peppercorns. Sprinkle the scallops with the salt and white pepper. Drop the lime julienne into boiling water, return to a boil, then drain.

2. Heat a wide frying pan (30 cm/12 inches or so) over moderate heat. Add two-thirds of the butter; as it stops foaming spread the scallops in the pan in a single layer. Turn the heat to high and cook for 1 minute. Flip over the scallops and cook 1 minute longer.

3. Add the lime juice, grated rind, and finely chopped peppercorns. Toss for a moment. Cut the remaining butter into bits and add all at once. Off the heat stir to melt. Season to taste.

4. Scoop into a warm serving dish, sprinkle with the lime julienne and the ½ teaspoon whole peppercorns. Serve at once.

Serving: *The Drake offers a cornucopia of bright vegetables: asparagus tips, shiitake, green beans, mangetout peas, baby carrots, and tiny potatoes boiled with saffron. For a simple meal, steamed pink potatoes do well.*

4 SERVINGS AS A MAIN COURSE

LEFT: **Scallops in Lime and Green Peppercorn Sauce (see page 75 for recipe)**
RIGHT: **Crab Cakes with Light Mustard Sauce (see page 74 for recipe)**

SALMON STRUDEL

UNITED STATES

This is chef Leo Waldmeier's adaptation of the Russian kulebiaka *(or* coulibiac)*, simplified by the use of filo instead of brioche. He offers it at The Drake's Cape Cod Room as a menu special, or for banquets, where it is often accompanied with a beurre blanc or basil cream sauce. Rich salmon is centred in a coating of chopped, dill-seasoned millet, eggs, and mushrooms, then rolled in a buttery filo pastry. Extremely moist and rich, the strudel is tender and juicy enough not to require a sauce, should you prefer.*

---

50 g (2 oz) hulled millet (available in health food stores)

32 g (1¼ oz) rice noodles (see Note)

400 g (14-oz) skinned salmon fillet

50 ml (2 fl oz) dry white wine

2 hard-cooked eggs, chopped fine

100 g (4 oz) mushrooms, trimmed, cleaned, and chopped fine

2 tablespoons finely chopped dill

1–2 tablespoons lemon juice

½ teaspoon salt

¼ teaspoon pepper

At least 7 sheets filo or strudel dough 30 x 18 cm (12 x 7 inches) (see Note)

75 g (3 oz) melted butter

1 egg yolk blended with 1 tablespoon water

Optional sauce: About 225 ml (8 fl oz) sour cream, mixed with lemon juice, dill, and salt and pepper to taste

---

1. Preheat the oven to 200°C/400°F (gas mark 6). Drop the millet into a pot of boiling salted water; boil for 20 minutes, or until tender, but not soft. Rinse, drain, and spread on a plate to dry. Boil the rice noodles for 3 minutes in salted water. Drain, rinse, dry, then finely chop.

2. Remove any stray bones from the salmon with narrow pliers or tweezers. Halve the fish lengthwise. Pour the wine into a baking dish or pan to hold the fillets closely, then set them in the pan. Set in the centre of the oven and bake until half-cooked, 6–8 minutes, depending on the thickness. With a spatula, transfer to a plate to cool. Reduce the oven temperature to 190°C/375°F (gas mark 5).

3. Combine the millet, rice noodles, chopped eggs, mushrooms, dill, 1 tablespoon lemon juice, and the salt and pepper. Add additional seasoning to taste, overflavouring slightly.

4. Spread one leaf of filo or strudel on a clean, dry tea towel, a long side towards you. Brush with the melted butter to coat completely. Continue layering and buttering until five of the leaves are used. Spread 100 g (4 oz) filling on the fifth layer to cover evenly.

5. Place two more buttered sheets on the stack. Form a rectangle with the remaining filling, leaving a 5–7 cm (2–3-inch) margin all around. Match up one salmon fillet with the lower left corner of the stuffing rectangle, placing the narrow tip of the fillet inwards. Place the other fillet along the right hand corner so that its narrow end overlaps the other fillet. Fold over the short edges of filo where they meet the filling, then the long sides. Butter these folded leaves. Begin rolling from the long side close to you (do not roll very tightly) using the towel to shape a neat cylinder.

6. Place seam side down on a buttered baking sheet. Brush with the egg wash. Bake in the centre of the oven for 20–25 minutes, until nicely browned.

7. Let stand for about 15 minutes before slicing with a serrated knife. Serve with or without sour cream sauce alongside.

Note: *Rice noodles, also called rice flour noodles,* mi fun, *long rice, and Chinese vermicelli are widely available in Oriental shops; if you prefer, use the clear cellophane noodles (also called glass noodles, silver noodles, or bean threads). Both noodles serve as a textural substitute for the sturgeon spinal marrow* (viziga) *that is used at The Drake. Obviously, if you have access to this delicacy, it is to be preferred. Prepare by boiling for 6–8 hours until it can be easily crushed or broken with your fingers. Wash with cold water, then clean off the white particles, keeping only the shiny, clear mass. Chop fine with a heavy knife.*

Filo or strudel pastry is available in 400 g (14 oz) packets containing 13–14 sheets of pastry approx. 48 x 28 cm (19 x 11 inches). Trim seven of the sheets to the required measure, and have a few extra sheets on hand in case of tearing.

4 SERVINGS AS A MAIN COURSE; 8 AS A FIRST COURSE

SALMON WITH MUSSELS IN WATERCRESS SAUCE

CANADA

Albert Schnell of the Hilton International Toronto makes use of salmon from British Columbia and local shellfish in this updated version of an haute cuisine classic. Tender fillets of pale salmon garnished with plump mussels bathe in pools of buttery watercress sauce (the blanching and puréeing remove all bite, but retain the brilliant green colour). Halved, the recipe makes an elegant first course.

2 bunches watercress (about 275 g/
   10 oz total weight), all stems
   removed (except 12 small sprigs
   reserved for garnish)
115 ml (4½ fl oz) dry white wine
3 tablespoons dry vermouth
2 tablespoons finely chopped shallots
24 mussels (about 450 g/1 lb),
   scrubbed and beards removed
   (see page 324)

175 ml (6 fl oz) double (or whipping)
   cream
Pinch dried tarragon
150 g (5 oz) cold butter, cut into
   1 cm (½-inch) dice
About 1 teaspoon lemon juice
Salt and pepper
15 g (½ oz) melted butter
12 skinned salmon fillets (about 50 g/
   2 oz each)

1. Drop the watercress into a pan of boiling, salted water; return to a full boil. Drain, then chill in iced water. Drain again. Purée thoroughly in a processor or blender.

2. Combine all but 1 tablespoon of the wine, the vermouth, and shallots in a wide non-aluminium pan; bring to a boil. Add the mussels; cover tightly and bring to a boil over high heat. Remove from the heat as soon as the mussels open, about 2 minutes.

3. Strain the liquid through a dampened muslin-lined sieve. You should have about 100 ml (4 fl oz); if more, boil to reduce to this amount. Remove the mussels from their shells; set aside in a small non-aluminium pan with 2 tablespoons of the stock.

4. Preheat the grill. Add the cream and tarragon to the stock; boil to reduce to 100 ml (4 fl oz). Off heat, whisk a piece of butter into the sauce. Continue to add bits of butter, whisking just until the last is nearly incorporated. Set the pan over very low heat now and then to keep the butter melting, but not long enough to turn it oily. The sauce should be a creamy suspension. Add lemon juice, salt, and pepper to taste. Blend in the watercress. Set the saucepan in a frying pan of barely simmering water to keep warm.

5. Blend the remaining 1 tablespoon wine with the melted butter. Brush a wide flame-proof serving dish with half this mixture. Arrange the fillets in a single layer in the dish; brush with the remaining stock-butter mixture. Sprinkle with salt and pepper.

6. Set as close to the heating element as possible. Grill until barely cooked through, 2–2½ minutes. Reheat the mussels at the same time.

7. Divide the sauce (see Option) among 6 *barely* warmed serving plates, tilting to distribute neatly. Arrange the salmon on top of the sauce, garnish with the reserved cress sprigs and mussels. Serve at once.

Option: *If you have a continental-style electric hand-blender, place it directly in the saucepan and whiz to create a lovely froth, as the chef does.*

6 SERVINGS AS A MAIN COURSE

BAKED SEA BASS WITH CARAWAY

UNITED STATES

When Kazuhito Endo was sous-chef of the Vista International in New York, he created this simple and attractive dish, and a number of other low-calorie, low-sodium main courses for the changing menus, which regularly feature light, healthy specials.

Slivers of chicory and tomato, dressed with a light curry vinaigrette touched with tarragon, form an unusual backdrop for the caraway-topped sea bass fillets, decorated with their natural motif of black netting. Surprisingly big flavour and satisfying texture make this dish a success with dieters—as well as other customers. If you prefer salt, add to taste—but the natural bitter-sweetness of the chicory and the punch of curry and caraway will be sufficient seasoning for most.

½ teaspoon curry powder
50 ml (2 fl oz) tarragon vinegar
100 ml (4 fl oz) light vegetable oil
Lemon juice
Four 150 g (5-oz) sea bass fillets with skin (for this you'll need two bass, each weighing 550–700 g/1¼–1½ lb)

2 teaspoons caraway seeds
450 g (1 lb) small heads of chicory, halved, cored, and cut crosswise into thin slices
1 medium tomato, peeled, seeded, and cut into thin strips
Fresh tarragon leaves or chervil sprigs

---

1. Preheat the grill. Blend together the curry powder and vinegar in a small bowl. Beat in the oil gradually, then add lemon juice to taste.

2. Place the fillets, flesh side down, on an oiled grill pan rack. Score the skin diagonally every 3 cm (1½-inches) or so. Sprinkle with the caraway. Set the pan under the grill at the middle level. Cook for about 5 minutes, until just opaque throughout.

3. Meanwhile, toss together the chicory, tomato, and tarragon leaves with the dressing. Arrange on 4 serving plates.

4. Arrange a fillet on each salad; serve at once.

Serving: *This dish should be served as soon as the fish emerges from the grill to enjoy the contrast of the juicy-firm hot sea bass and the cool, crisp salad.*

4 SERVINGS AS A MAIN COURSE

SHELLFISH WITH RICE, HAM, MUSHROOMS AND BRANDY
'El Pescador'
PUERTO RICO, UNITED STATES

El Pescador *is a mild seafood and rice dish that has been featured in the main dining room of the Caribe Hilton International since 1956. Prepared at the table, the simple flavours (reminiscent of paella) and generous amount of luxury shellfish please guests of all ages and backgrounds.*

4 crawfish tails (fresh, or frozen, defrosted; 225–275 g/8–10 oz each)
12 medium-large prawns in the shell
225 g (8 oz) long-grain white rice
¼–½ teaspoon saffron threads
75 g (3 oz) blanched (or frozen,
defrosted) peas
1 whole large canned pimiento, cut
into fine dice
30 g (1 oz) butter
50 g (2 oz) salt pork, cut into 1 cm
(½-inch) dice
50 g (2 oz) cooked ham, cut into
1 cm (½-inch) dice

2 teaspoons finely chopped garlic
1 medium green pepper, cut into 5
mm (¼-inch) dice (see Note)
75 g (3 oz) small mushrooms, thin-
sliced
1 medium tomato, peeled, seeded,
and cut into 1 cm (½-inch) dice
Finely chopped coriander leaves
60 ml (2½ fl oz) brandy, preferably
Spanish
225 ml (8 fl oz) chicken stock
Salt and pepper
8 cooked king crab claws for garnish
(optional)

1. Place the crawfish tails in a frying pan of boiling salted water to cover. Simmer for 3 minutes. Add the prawns and simmer for another minute. Drain and cool until you can remove the shells. Devein the prawns; cut the crawfish into 1 cm (½-inch) slices.

2. Meanwhile, combine the rice and saffron with 400 ml (14 fl oz) water in a small saucepan. Bring to a boil, stirring. Turn the heat to its lowest point, cover, and cook for 20 minutes. Remove from the heat; let stand, covered, 15–30 minutes, as convenient. Stir in the peas and pimiento.

3. Heat the butter in a very wide frying pan. Add the salt pork; cook over moderately high heat until lightly coloured, about 1 minute. Add the ham and toss. Add the garlic and toss for 30 seconds. Add the green pepper, mushrooms, tomato, and coriander. Toss for 2 minutes.

4. Add the brandy and ignite, shaking the pan. Add the stock; boil for 1 minute. Add the seafood; return to a boil, tossing.

5. Add the rice mixture; toss for about 2 minutes, to heat through. Add salt and pepper to taste. Heap onto a serving plate and garnish with the crab claws, if desired.

Note: *The tiny, distinctively aromatic sweet chilli-peppers known as* ajies dulces *add an inimitable flavour to the dish when it is prepared in Puerto Rico. If they are available, substitute for one-third of the green pepper.*
Advance preparation: *The components for the dish can be prepared through Step 2 a day ahead, then cooled, covered, and refrigerated.*
Options: El Pescador *has been prepared at the Mayaguez Hilton International with cooked* gandules *(pigeon peas) instead of green peas for a more Puerto Rican flavour. For those who like a stronger ocean taste, substitute fish stock for the chicken, and add the seafood raw, increasing the cooking time slightly to almost cook through, rather than simply heat.*

4 SERVINGS AS A MAIN COURSE

MONKFISH CHILLI

UNITED STATES

This culinary hybrid from executive chef Walter Plendner of the Vista International Hotel in New York City is a product of both the Deep South and the Southwest. It was created as a result of the Cajun foodfest at the hotel's Greenhouse restaurant, undertaken in collaboration with the popular Louisiana restaurateur-chef-celebrity, Paul Prudhomme.

Completely original, this unusual mixture may astound chilli 'purists' but pleases a large number of diners who order it regularly at the Vista's elegant American Harvest Restaurant. The firm-fleshed fish holds its shape, the red and green pepper dice add colour and texture, the beans soften, thickening the sauce—which is richly hot-sweet.

2 tablespoons vegetable oil
2 medium onions, cut into
    1 cm (½-inch) dice
2 medium green peppers, ribbed,
    seeded, and cut into
    1 cm (½-inch) dice
2 medium red peppers, ribbed,
    seeded, and cut into 1 cm (½-
    inch) dice
1 teaspoon salt
½ teaspoon ground cumin
¼ teaspoon ground cayenne pepper
¼ teaspoon crushed red pepper
    (pepper flakes)
½ teaspoon dried thyme

½ teaspoon dried oregano
½ teaspoon dried basil
3 bay leaves, crumbled
½ teaspoon dried marjoram
1 kilo (2 lb) monkfish, cut into 3.5
    cm/ (1½-inch) dice
50 g (2 oz) pure mild chilli powder
    (see Note)
6 tablespoons tomato purée
3 large tomatoes, peeled and diced
750 ml (1¼ pints) fish stock (see
    page 326)
700 g (1½ lb) cooked drained red
    kidney beans

1. Heat the oil in a wide casserole or deep frying pan about 28 cm (11 inches) in diameter. Cook the onions over moderately low heat until soft and translucent, about 10 minutes. Add the red and green peppers and toss for 1 minute.

2. Blend together the salt, cumin, ground cayenne, crushed red pepper, thyme, oregano, basil, bay leaves, and marjoram. Add to the pan; cook for 5 minutes, stirring occasionally.

3. Add the fish and chilli powder; stir over moderate heat until the fish whitens on the outside. Add the tomato purée and stir gently for 2 minutes. Add the tomatoes and fish stock; bring to a boil. Add the kidney beans and return to the boil. Simmer for 5 minutes. Cool, then cover and refrigerate.

4. To serve, reheat over low heat, stirring gently so as not to break up the beans or fish.

Note: *A powder of ground whole chilli-peppers—and nothing else—is vastly superior to any of the commercial spice mixtures. It is available in many supermarkets and in stores that stock Mexican ingredients. If you must use the combination of spices called 'chilli powder', buy the one with the shortest list of ingredients on the label.*

Serving: *This is a casual, easy party dish that keeps well on a hot tray. Accompany with unsweetened cornbread, a salad of bitterish greens and citrus, and plenty of chilled lager.*

Advance preparation: *Like most stewy dishes, this one improves with reheating, the flavours becoming more mellowed and balanced.*

8 SERVINGS AS A MAIN COURSE

STUFFED HALIBUT STEAMED IN COS
WITH CAVIAR BEURRE BLANC

UNITED STATES

Franz Kranzfelder, senior sous-chef at The Drake hotel (but a very young man, indeed), invented this dish for the American 1985 National Restaurant Association competition— and won a gold medal for the 'Most Original Piece of the Show'. The delicate flavour and texture of snowy halibut are maintained by brief steaming in a stylish cloak of cos. The sea-sweet fish in a pool of butter sauce is sparked by lustrous salmon eggs.

2 halibut steaks (each about 350 g/12 oz), cut about 3 cm (1½) inches thick
1 medium-large head of cos lettuce (about 450 g/1 lb)
Salt and pepper
1 medium-large tomato, peeled, seeded, and diced

75–100 g (3–4 oz) mushrooms, cut into fine dice
1 tablespoon finely chopped parsley
1 tablespoon finely chopped shallot
100 ml (4 fl oz) dry white wine
175 g (6 oz) cold butter, cut into 24 pieces
75 g (3 oz) salted salmon eggs

1. Divide each halibut steak into 2 natural sections by cutting out the bone. Remove the skin from each section. Cut a pocket into the long flat side of each piece.

2. Remove 10 large leaves from the cos. Drop them into a wide frying pan of boiling salted water; return to a boil. Drain, refresh in ice water, then spread flat between towels to dry.

3. Sprinkle the fish with salt and pepper. Combine the tomato, mushrooms, and parsley in a bowl. Add salt and pepper to taste. Place each halibut slice on 2 overlapping lettuce leaves. Divide the filling evenly in the pockets, stuffing generously. Enclose each piece of fish in the lettuce, wrapping neatly and firmly.

4. Boil the shallot, white wine, and a sprinkling of salt and pepper in a small non-aluminium pan until reduced to a scant 2 tablespoons; set aside momentarily.

5. Arrange the fish packets on a buttered steamer rack. Set the rack inside the steamer over boiling water; cover. Steam for 11–12 minutes, until the fillets are just opaque throughout.

6. Meanwhile, heat the wine reduction. Off the heat, whisk in 1 piece of butter. When it has nearly melted, whisk in another. Over lowest heat, continue adding butter, one piece at a time, incorporating another just as the last almost melts. Remove the pan from the heat occasionally so that the butter does not become oily. Maintain a pale, creamy suspension. Remove from the heat and stir in the salmon roe. Season to taste.

7. As soon as the fish is cooked, set the packets on a cutting board. Cut in half or into 2 cm (¾-inch) crosswise slices. Arrange at once on individual serving plates; spoon 3 tablespoons of the sauce alongside each. Serve immediately.

Presentation and serving: *The colourful halved packets or slices and rich sauce need no more than rice as an accompaniment.*
Advance preparation: *The stuffed, wrapped fish packets can be prepared hours ahead of cooking time and refrigerated.*
Options: *The steamed fish makes a lovely first course or salad when chilled and served with a light mustard vinaigrette.*

4 SERVINGS AS A MAIN COURSE

Red Snapper Fillets with Coriander Sauce
VENEZUELA

Silvery red snapper patterned with its distinctive rosy netting is imbued with the vivid aroma of fresh coriander, the parsley of South America, in this simple presentation from Frank Muller, executive chef of the Caracas Hilton International. The fish is steamed on a thick bed of the herb, then the fragrant cooking liquid is strained, slightly reduced, and finished with butter and feathery coriander leaves.

The success of the deliciously pure ensemble depends entirely upon the beauty and freshness of the fish—and a sense of timing: The fish must not be overcooked. The simple savour is best underscored by no more than steamed baby potatoes and a cool Chablis or Meursault.

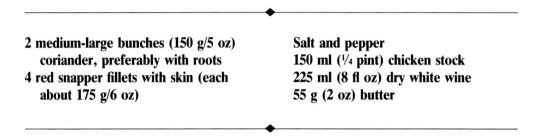

2 medium-large bunches (150 g/5 oz) coriander, preferably with roots
4 red snapper fillets with skin (each about 175 g/6 oz)

Salt and pepper
150 ml (¼ pint) chicken stock
225 ml (8 fl oz) dry white wine
55 g (2 oz) butter

1. Turn the oven to its lowest heat. Strip 25 g (1 oz) coriander leaves from their stems. Rinse and dry the leaves and reserve for the sauce. Dunk the remaining leaves and stems in several changes of water to remove all traces of sand and soil.

2. Halve the fish crosswise, on the diagonal, to make 8 more-or-less equal pieces. Sprinkle with salt and pepper. Set 4 serving plates in the warm oven.

3. Combine the coriander stems and leaves, chicken stock, and white wine in a wide non-aluminium pan large enough to hold the fish in a single layer. Bring to a boil, covered.

4. Place the snapper fillets skin side up on the coriander; return to a boil. Cover the pan and cook over low heat until not quite cooked through—about 2 minutes. With a spatula carefully transfer the fillets to the plates in the oven.

5. Strain the cooking liquid into a non-aluminium saucepan; boil to reduce to about 175 ml (6 fl oz). Turn off the heat and stir in the butter, a little at a time. Add the reserved coriander leaves and salt and pepper to taste. Spoon the sauce over the fillets and serve at once.

4 SERVINGS

Fricassée of Poussins with Wine Vinegar Sauce

(Fricassée de Poussins au Vinaigre de Vin)

CANADA

A fine, traditional French family dish as refined by Albert Schnell, area executive chef for Hilton Canada, Inc.—no small realm. The golden-brown cream sauce, tomato-flecked, is poured over the hens in old-fashioned fricassée style. Because the generous quantity of savoury sauce is natural and liquid, not thickened, noodles suit perfectly.

---

4 *poussins* (baby chickens) (about
   700 g/1½ lb each)
1 teaspoon salt
¼ teaspoon pepper
60 g (2½ oz) butter
2 tablespoons vegetable oil
8 unpeeled garlic cloves
75 ml (2½ fl oz) white wine vinegar
2 teaspoons Dijon mustard

1 teaspoon tomato purée
225 ml (8 fl oz) dry white wine
50 ml (2 fl oz) Armagnac or brandy
150 ml (¼ pint) double (or whipping) cream
2 large tomatoes, peeled, seeded,
   and diced
About 2 teaspoons finely chopped
   chervil or parsley

---

1. Preheat oven to 190°C/375°F (gas mark 5). Remove loose fat deposits from the *poussins*. Cut off the wing tips; cut out the backbones; wrap and freeze for stock-making. Cut each *poussin* in quarters (see Note). Sprinkle with the salt and pepper.

2. Heat 22 g (¾ oz) butter and 1 tablespoon oil in a wide frying pan over moderate heat. Brown half the pieces lightly on both sides, then transfer to a roasting pan. Add 22 g (¾ oz) more butter and the remaining 1 tablespoon oil to the frying pan; add the remaining pieces and the garlic cloves to the pan. Brown these, then add to the roasting pan. Drain the fat from the frying pan, but do not wash it.

3. Set the *poussins,* uncovered, in the oven. Roast until the juices just run clear, about 20 minutes. Remove the garlic from the pan; slip off the skins, mash the garlic with the side of a knife blade and reserve. Pour the vinegar into the pan in which the *poussins* were browned. Scrape and stir over moderate heat to loosen all the brown bits. Pour over the birds, then set over moderate heat; boil for a few minutes, until the vinegar and juices have thickened. Transfer the *poussins* to a platter in the turned-off oven.

(continued)

4. Set the roasting pan over moderate heat; add the mustard and tomato purée and stir to blend. Add the wine and Armagnac and mix well (see Note). Boil for about 5 minutes, stirring, to reduce to 175 ml (6 fl oz). Strain; return to the pan along with the mashed garlic and cream. Season with salt and pepper. Bring to a boil, whisking. Off the heat, stir in the remaining butter.

5. Sprinkle the birds with the tomato dice. Pour the sauce over all. Sprinkle with chervil or parsley and serve.

Note: *For a more refined presentation, remove the breast bones and hip (pelvic) bones from the quartered birds. Do not take out the bones from drumstick, second joint, and wing, which give the birds their shape.*

If you prefer a completely smooth sauce, add the mashed garlic at the same time as the wine, rather than at the end.

6 SERVINGS AS A MAIN COURSE

Sauerkraut-Stuffed Duck Breasts with Sweet Red Pepper Sauce
UNITED STATES

A fine example of traditional cuisine, updated and refined by Dieter Hannig, who remembers a heavy, fatty (albeit delicious) version of this dish from his childhood and years of apprenticeship in Germany. In this elegant transformation, duck breasts (their skin and fat removed, cubed and crisped) are stuffed with a small quantity of sauerkraut, onion, grated potato and the browned fat cubes, then briefly roasted and served with a bright, fresh red pepper sauce.

4 boneless duck breast halves with skin attached

2 small onions, sliced

450 g (1 lb) sauerkraut, drained and rinsed

225 ml (8 fl oz) dry white wine

1 teaspoon sugar

½ small bay leaf

1 small potato (about 75 g/3 oz)

Salt and pepper

2 large red peppers

50 g (2 oz) butter

40 g (1½ oz) finely chopped shallots

225 ml (8 fl oz) chicken stock

1. Carefully remove the fat and skin layer from the duck breasts without cutting into the flesh. Wrap and refrigerate the meat.

2. Cut the fat into small cubes. Spread these in a 20–23 cm (8–9-inch) frying pan and cook over moderately low heat, stirring often, until the fat is rendered and the cubes are brown and crisp. With a slotted spoon, transfer the pieces to a dish.

3. Pour out all but 3 tablespoons fat from the pan. Add the onions and cook over moderately low heat for about 5 minutes, until tender but not browned. Add the sauerkraut, wine, sugar and bay leaf. Bring to a boil, stirring. Reduce the heat and simmer, covered, for 20 minutes. Shred the potato on the fine blade of a food processor or hand grater. Stir into the sauerkraut. Simmer for 2 minutes. Add salt and pepper to taste. Blend in the duck fat cubes. Let cool.

4. Meanwhile, grill the peppers directly in a gas flame until blistered and blackened almost all over. (Alternatively, you can cook the peppers as close as possible to the heating element of a grill.) Wrap in a damp tea towel and let stand for 5–10 minutes. Slip off the skin, scraping off stubborn bits with a knife. Halve the peppers; remove the ribs and seeds; cut the flesh into small pieces.

5. Melt a quarter of the butter over moderately low heat in a small saucepan. Add the shallots and stir for 2 minutes. Add the peppers and stir for another 2 minutes. Add the chicken stock and bring to a boil, stirring. Reduce heat to low, cover, and simmer for 10 minutes.

6. Preheat the oven to 200°C/400°F (gas mark 6). Pour the contents of the saucepan into a food processor. Purée to a fine consistency (you should have about 350 ml (12 fl oz). Scoop back into the saucepan and simmer to reduce to about 225 ml (8 fl oz). Season.

7. Cut a horizontal lengthwise pocket in each breast, being careful not to pierce through the sides. Divide the stuffing evenly among the 4 breast pieces, packing tightly. Secure with a toothpick or string, if necessary. Heat 25 g (1 oz) butter in an ovenproof frying pan over moderate heat. Brown the duck lightly on both sides. Set in the oven for 5 minutes (medium-rare) or 7 minutes (medium). Let stand for 5–10 minutes.

8. Heat the pepper sauce over low heat. Stir in the remaining butter. Divide between 4 warmed plates. Cut each breast in 6 long slices and arrange around the sauce.

Advance preparation: *The final cooking of the lean, meaty breasts requires less than 10 minutes, making for easy—and smokeless—entertaining. The sauce and stuffing can be made ahead, cooled, and refrigerated. Or if you prefer, the duck breasts can be filled with the chilled stuffing, then wrapped and refrigerated for up to 2 days.*

4 SERVINGS AS A MAIN COURSE

Beef Tenderloin with Fresh Goat Cheese Sauce

CANADA

When chef Albert Schnell of the Hilton International Toronto first served these plump rounds of fillet napped with a cocoa-coloured sauce (accompanied by Manitoba Wild Rice Croquettes, page 68), it was for a chefs' convention at the time when interest in regional specialities was just burgeoning. The beef was from the province of Alberta and the tart, fresh cheese from Quebec. Although there were just a handful at the time, now there are 160 goat farmers in that province.

The sauce is not a creamy one, as might be expected, but rather a winy-meaty gloss lightened and sharpened by the acid goat's cheese.

---

4 beef fillet steaks (150–175 g/5–6 oz each), trimmed and tied
Salt and pepper
1 tablespoon light vegetable oil
2 tablespoons Armagnac or brandy
25 g (1 oz) butter
2 teaspoons finely chopped shallot
150 ml (¼ pint) dry red wine

225 ml (8 fl oz) brown veal stock or beef stock (see Step 1 of Beef Steaks with Mustard Cream, page 292)
50 g (2 oz) fresh (not aged) white goat cheese, crumbled
Lemon juice
1 teaspoon finely snipped chives

---

1. Preheat the oven to it lowest heat. Season the beef with salt and pepper. Heat the oil in a medium frying pan over moderate heat; brown the meat on both sides, cooking to the desired degree of doneness (about 4 minutes for medium-rare). Pour out the fat. Add the Armagnac; light it, shaking the pan until the flames die out. Transfer the beef to a platter and set in the warm oven. (Set 4 plates in the oven to warm as well.)

2. Add the butter to the pan; stir in the shallot. Cook over moderately low heat until softened, but not browned, about 2 minutes. Add the red wine and boil over high heat until almost syrupy—about 5 minutes. Add the stock and boil to reduce to about 100 ml (4 fl oz).

3. Off the heat, stir in three-quarters of the cheese, and salt, pepper and lemon juice to taste.

4. Spoon about 2 tablespoons sauce on each round of beef. Arrange the remaining cheese in small dabs on these. Garnish with the chives. Serve at once, on heated plates.

4 SERVINGS AS A MAIN COURSE

Executive chef Albert Schnell selects fresh goat cheese from a local supplier

STUFFED POT-ROASTED BEEF, PUERTO RICAN-STYLE
(Carne Mechada)

PUERTO RICO, UNITED STATES

There are probably three or four versions of this dish for each of the Spanish-influenced Caribbean countries, and a few more in Central America. Garlicky, but mellow, this fancified pot roast in russet gravy has a salty-smoky Puerto Rican flavour, but is lighter than the version prepared at the Caribe Hilton International. You might serve the beef with potatoes, plain rice, yellow rice—or try cornmeal mush for a delicious side dish.

Seasoning mixture

1 medium onion, chopped

1 medium green pepper (see Note), cored, seeded and chopped

25 g (1 oz) fresh coriander leaves

3 large garlic cloves, finely chopped

1 teaspoon salt

Pot roast and sauce

1.7 kilo (3½-lb) top flank roast, tied

100 g (4-oz) end-cut cooked ham, cut into 2 cm (¾-inch) strips (see Note)

75 g (3 oz) belly of pork, rind removed, cut into 2 cm (¾-inch) wide strips

2 medium onions, cut into 2.5 (1-inch) chunks

75–100 g (3–4 oz) piece rindless bacon, cut into 2 cm (¾-inch) wide strips

4 tablespoons vegetable oil

1 large carrot, cut into 1 cm (½-inch) pieces

1 large celery stick, cut 1 cm (½-inch) wide

¼ cup tomato purée

2 large tomatoes, coarsely chopped

350 ml (12 fl oz) dry red wine

2 bay leaves

1 whole large canned pimiento, cut into 5 mm (¼-inch) dice

2 tablespoons finely chopped parsley

1. Preheat the oven to 180°C/350°F (gas mark 4). Combine the ingredients for the seasoning mixture on a chopping surface. Chop with a large knife until they become almost a paste.

2. Insert a long knife into one end of the beef and saw gently to make a 5 cm (2-inch) wide slit that extends to the centre of the meat; do the same from the other side to meet in the middle. Rub 1 tablespoon of the seasoning mixture into each end of the opening. Stuff in the strips of ham, pork, and bacon to form a tight, neat core. Rub a few tablespoons more seasoning on the meat.

3. Heat 2 tablespoons of the oil in a large, heavy flameproof casserole. Brown the meat well on all sides; transfer to a dish. Scrape out the solids and pour out the fat. Add the remaining 2 tablespoons oil and place over moderately high heat. Add the remaining seasoning paste and stir for a few seconds. Add the carrot, onion, and celery slices; stir for a few minutes to colour lightly. Add the tomato purée; stir for 2 minutes on moderate heat. Add the tomatoes and wine and stir.

4. Add the meat. Add enough water to almost cover the meat. Add the bay leaves. Bring to a boil. Cover and set in the oven. Simmer until tender, about 2½ hours. Uncover and simmer for 30 minutes longer. Turn the heat down to its lowest setting.

5. Transfer the meat to a platter, cover with foil, and place in the oven. Strain the sauce. Skim off the fat. Boil in a saucepan to reduce to a medium consistency, about 450 ml (¾ pint). Add the pimiento and parsley and bring to a boil.

6. Cut the meat in about 12 slices. Arrange on a platter, spoon over a generous quantity of sauce, and serve the remainder in a heated sauceboat.

Note: *In Puerto Rico the tiny, distinctively aromatic sweet chillis called* ajies dulces *are part of the seasoning mixture. If available, add enough to make about 3 tablespoons, finely chopped.*

An end-cut is called for simply so that you get a small quantity if purchasing ham just for the recipe.

Advance preparation: *The meat can be cooled, covered, and refrigerated and the sauce refrigerated separately. To heat, slice the meat, cover with sauce, and place in a moderate oven until heated through.*

Options: *You can serve the sauce chunky also: simply skim the unstrained mixture, then boil to reduce to the desired consistency. For a more Caribbean flavour, substitute coriander for the parsley used in the sauce.*

6–8 SERVINGS

CORNCAKE TOPPED WITH LAMB, GOAT CHEESE AND MUSHROOMS
UNITED STATES

A golden custardy corncake is topped with slices of pink lamb, pale goat's cheese, and tomato and mushroom dice. An unusual dish of equally weighted, solid flavours, this rather labour-intensive presentation will be a delight for lovers of lamb and rich food—from Dieter Hannig, director of the Food Research Center.

Although the intense lamb jus *(essence), a must in fine dining rooms, will add complexity and distinction to the dish, you might skip it if short of time or inclination.*

Lamb jus
Lamb bones and trimmings from rib roast of lamb (see below), bones and trimmings chopped or sawed into small pieces, and fat discarded (see Note)
1 medium carrot, sliced
1 stick celery, sliced
1 small garlic clove, crushed
1 medium onion, chopped
2 tablespoons tomato purée
¼ teaspoon dried thyme
¼ teaspoon dried rosemary
1 bay leaf
8 peppercorns, bruised
100 ml (4 fl oz) dry white wine
Cornmeal cake, lamb, and garnish
240 g (8½ oz) yellow cornmeal
500 ml (18 fl oz) milk
75 g (3 oz) butter

½ teaspoon salt
⅛ teaspoon nutmeg
50 g (about 2 oz) grated Parmesan cheese
1 egg yolk
2 tablespoons chopped onion
½ teaspoon finely chopped garlic
100 g (4 oz) mushrooms, thin-sliced
1 medium tomato, peeled, seeded, and diced
1 rack of lamb (8 ribs—about 1.2 kilos/2½ lb), meat removed in one long cylinder (see Note)
Pepper
1 tablespoon olive oil
160 g (5½-oz) cylinder (2 cm/1½-inch diameter) fresh soft goat cheese, cut into 8 slices
Basil sprigs for garnish

---

1. Prepare the lamb *jus:* Preheat the oven to 220°C/425°F (gas mark 7). Place the lamb bones and trimmings in a deep roasting pan or wide saucepan with an ovenproof handle. Roast in the preheated oven for 30 minutes; drain the fat. Roast for another 30 minutes until well browned; drain again. Add the carrot, celery, garlic, onion, and tomato purée; roast for 15 minutes longer.

2. On the top of the stove, add the thyme, rosemary, bay leaf, and peppercorns. Add the wine and bring slowly to a boil, stirring. Add 850 ml (1½ pints) water. Barely simmer, partly covered, for 1½ hours. Strain. Boil to reduce to 100 ml (4 fl oz).

3. Blend together the cornmeal and 450 ml (¾ pint) water. In a heavy saucepan, combine the milk, two-thirds of the butter, the salt and nutmeg; bring to a boil, stirring. Add the cornmeal mixture, stirring constantly. Reduce the heat and simmer, stirring, for about 3 minutes.

4. Remove from the heat and stir a moment to cool; stir in the Parmesan cheese, then the egg yolk. Pour into a buttered round 28 cm/11-inch pan (or set a similar-sized flan ring on a sheet of buttered foil and fold in the edges to improvise a pan; set on a baking sheet). Smooth with a spatula before the cornmeal begins to cool.

5. Melt the remaining butter in a frying pan; add the chopped onion and stir over low heat for 2 minutes; add the garlic and stir over moderate heat for 1 minute. Add the mushrooms; toss for a few minutes to cook through. Add the tomato; toss over high heat for 30 seconds. Set aside.

6. Thirty minutes before serving, set the corncake in a preheated 190°C/375°F (gas mark 5) oven. Sprinkle the lamb with salt and pepper. Heat the olive oil in a flameproof casserole. Sear on all sides; pour off the fat. Set in the oven with the corncake (which will have baked for about 10 minutes). Roast the lamb for 8 minutes, or until the internal temperature reaches 60°C/125°F for rare meat. Set aside, covered, while you finish the corncake.

7. When the cake has baked 30 minutes and is lightly golden, remove it from the oven; slide onto a heatproof serving dish. With a sharp knife, lightly score the surface into 8 wedges. Place an equal quantity of the mushroom mixture onto each wedge, positioning it toward the wide end. Set a round of cheese on this. Return the cake to the oven until the cheese begins to melt, about 5 minutes.

8. Meanwhile, reheat the lamb *jus*. Slice the rack into 16 pieces. Place 2 pieces on each wedge of the cornmeal cake. Set a sprig of basil in the centre and serve at once, with a spoonful of the lamb essence alongside each serving.

Note: *Have the butcher remove the rack and saw the bones for you, unless you're equipped with heavy-duty tools to hack the bones into small pieces.*
Serving and presentation: *Although the corncake slices are not large, the components are very rich and filling. You might serve a salad beforehand, as a first course, and fresh fruit afterwards.*
Advance preparation: *The unbaked corncake and lamb* jus *can be made up to 2 days ahead.*

8 SERVINGS AS A MAIN COURSE

Albert Schnell of the Hilton International Toronto: Discipline and Details, or Mignardises for Multitudes

Albert Schnell, executive chef of the Hilton International Toronto and area chef of Hilton Canada, Inc.

I magine the task of running a hotel where 4,500 can lunch together in a convention centre, where any one of a possible thousand hotel guests can order a dainty repast or hearty meal from the room service menu—at any moment, day and night—and where a sunny restaurant accommodates 250 at dinner and lunch—with a good 35 dishes making up the buffet service. Meanwhile, an airy coffee shop adjacent to the svelte, spacious lobby seats about 300 from early breakfast to midnight snack-time, a bar offers drinks and nibbles to as many as 200 suave sippers, and one hundred elegant lounge lizards may decorate the tailored sofas of the lobby, ordering an espresso or sandwich, Cognac or orange juice. Imagine that in an evening, the tall-backed club-style chairs of the fine dining room embrace up to 140 diners, while a private room adjoining the restaurant sets the scene for thematic gastronomic *tours de force* that private club members gather to enjoy.

And imagine that beneath the polished floors and ornate Chinese carpets, beneath a lobby bubbling gently with French, English, German, Italian and Japanese, is a vast labyrinth of chilly storerooms into which pour quantities of the highest quality ingredients, from woodsy-wild chanterelles to loquats, pheasants to fresh foie gras, tins of saffron and other sweet spices. Figure that during one week 115 cooks of the combined restaurants typically make use of 4,100 eggs—and the same number of pounds of chicken—1,300 pounds of butter, 275 pounds of chocolate, 350 quarts of cream, 700 pounds of onions, 500 of carrots, at least 300 pounds of lobster, and about 175 prime ribs of beef (each weighing about 15 pounds). And, finally, imagine that the 2,020 various food items required are specified by one man, the same man responsible for the quality of every dish that leaves the kitchens, whether a cheeseburger or an elixir of ringneck pheasant with morels under a puff pastry crust.

Albert Schnell—imposing, quietly authoritative, with a smile that is as ingenuous as it is mischievous—orchestrates (with help from his all-seeing sous-chefs, Tadashi Katoh and Daniel Lamy) such extravaganzas every day. A firm, disciplined man, his many years at the mammoth Queen Elizabeth in Montreal and the Harbour Castle in Toronto and a concurrent 20 years as the Area Chef for Hilton Canada, Inc., make him one of the very few executive chefs who could possibly be equal to the task of coordinating not merely the workings of a giant hotel, but all of Hilton International's kitchen operations in Canada.

Despite these overwhelming responsibilities, Schnell's attention to detail is such that he might well be garnishing each portion himself (the Swiss-born chef began as a pastry apprentice and has earned awards in this exacting culinary realm). Before each menu is drawn up, he will specify which plates must be used for each course, where the food should be placed, how the napkins must be decoratively folded under the bowl of pheasant consomme, how many doilies should grace the dessert saucer, the colour of the rose petals to be frozen in ice bowls to hold sorbet, and just how far the pool of raspberry purée should extend into the outer rim of crème anglaise on the plate. He is deeply engaged in each undertaking; it is a personal affair to him each time a meal is set out, whether for four or 4,000. He thinks that if the finest food is served at a huge event, many more diners will leave better educated, aware of the refinements. Teaching is of the utmost importance to him, and he has trained, honed, and contributed to the success of students who take his message worldwide, wherever fine dining flourishes.

Schnell's gala dinners, whether for the prime minister of Japan, Queen Elizabeth, or the Opera Ball, are tailored to fit the occasion: the concept of an entire meal, from the typeface of the menu to the shape of the tray for the after-dinner sweets, is his medium. For the prime minister, for example, he included a number of local ingredients to introduce the best of Canada: Brome Lake duck, Manitoba wild rice, the fine beef of Alberta, spring vegetables from the Okanogan Valley. At the same time he welcomed the Japanese guests with *La terrine de saumon des Maritimes escortée de sushi aux crevettes,* sesame seeds on the cheese straws, and a ragout of shiitake. The dinner for the queen finished appropriately with *La couronne glacée aux pêches de Niagara accompagnée de mignardises* (a selection of tiny pastries and bonbons)—for 2,100. The whimsical took over at the Opera Ball when Schnell served such creations as Noisettes of Lamb under a Veil of Seven Herbs with Love-Apples (Salome-inspired), followed by Carmelite Salad on Oakleaf Lettuce and Rose Petals Sprinkled with Virgin Olive Oil (The Dialogue of the Carmelites).

It was not surprising that shortly after we returned home from visiting this chef who has an eye for the whole picture and the finest detail, he sent a gracious, personal note and enclosed a meticulous recipe for a dessert that had been a favourite during our sampling, the fresh, sweet-scented Pear Soufflé which follows.

PEAR SOUFFLÉ WITH VANILLA PEAR SAUCE

CANADA

A meal in the Toronto Hilton International proceeded as follows: crêpes with golden caviar filling; pigeon breast sautéd with herbs and garnished with asparagus, endive and mâche in rose petal vinaigrette; duckling consommé with quail egg yolk; ragoût of minute morsels of crayfish tail, salmon, and frogs' legs in a beurre blanc with leeks; and spinach with sultanas. This was followed by a pear soufflé of sheer perfection. Only years of honing and experimenting from chef Albert Schnell (whose career began as a pâtissier) *could have produced such a refined, satiny, and beautiful soufflé. The result is worth every moment of the undeniably lengthy preparation.*

Soufflé Base
225 ml (8 fl oz) milk
½ vanilla pod, halved lengthwise
58 g (2⅓ oz) granulated sugar
31 g (1¼ oz) plain flour
Pinch of salt
4 egg yolks

Vanilla Sauce
½ vanilla pod, halved lengthwise
175 ml (6 fl oz) double (or whipping) cream
2 tablespoons granulated sugar
2 egg yolks

Assembly
About 900 g (2 lb) canned pears in heavy syrup (11–12 halves), drained
4–5 tablespoons *eau-de-vie de poire* (clear pear brandy)
Melted butter
Granulated sugar for coating the moulds
4 egg yolks, at room temperature
5 tablespoons granulated sugar
5 egg whites, at room temperature
Icing sugar

---

1. Prepare the soufflé base: Combine the milk and vanilla pod in a heavy, medium-size saucepan and bring to a simmer, stirring. Combine the sugar, flour, and salt in a mixing bowl. Blend in the yolks with an electric mixer. Slowly pour half the hot milk into the egg mixture, beating on low speed. Scrape into the remaining milk, stirring to blend. Stir over moderate heat until thick and pasty. Remove the vanilla pod and scrape the beans into the pan. Scoop into a small bowl; set a piece of cling-film on the surface and cool.

2. Prepare the vanilla sauce: Bring the vanilla pod and cream to a boil over low heat in a small pan; cover and reserve. Combine the sugar and egg yolks in a small bowl and whip with an electric mixer until thick and pale, the texture of soft meringue. Pour the cream into this mixture, beating on low speed. In a clean saucepan, stir the sauce over lowest heat until it just barely thickens and tiny wisps of steam begin to puff out. Immediately strain into a bowl set in a pan of ice water to stop the cooking. Once lukewarm, remove from the ice.

(continued)

FOOLPROOF COCOA SOUFFLÉ

PUERTO RICO, UNITED STATES

It is no wonder that in high season as many as 160 portions of this dessert are served each night at the Caribe Hilton International. You have to try this to believe it: an utterly unflappable soufflé that is easy, impressive, and can be made almost completely in advance. Smooth-crowned, its sugar-crisped sides rise high, and its bittersweet centre, reminiscent of a light steamed pudding, remains tender. Do not forgo the ice cream which perfectly complements the barely sweet, rather firm soufflé with its cool softness and sweetness.

---

30 g (1 oz) melted butter
Sugar for coating the moulds
50 g (2 oz) cold butter
150 g (5 oz) plus 3 tablespoons sugar
75 g (3 oz) bread flour (high-gluten flour)

40 g (1½ oz) unsweetened cocoa powder
450 ml (¾ pint) milk
7 eggs, separated and at room temperature
Vanilla ice cream

---

1. Paint 10 ramekins (individual soufflé dishes) about 8.75 cm (3½-inches) in diameter and 4.5 cm (1¾ inches) high with the melted butter; coat generously with sugar. Preheat the oven to 200°C/400°F (gas mark 6) with the rack set in the centre.

2. Combine the cold butter, 150 g (5 oz) sugar, the flour, and cocoa in a processor or blender; whirl to form a crumbly mixture.

3. Bring the milk to a boil in a medium saucepan, stirring. Whisk in the cocoa mixture. Return to a boil, stirring. Scoop into a mixing bowl, then whisk in the egg yolks, one at a time.

4. Combine the egg whites and the remaining 3 tablespoons sugar in a mixing bowl. With an electric beater, whip until soft, not stiff, peaks form. Stir one-third of the whites into the warm cocoa mixture to blend completely. Gently fold in the remainder.

5. Set the moulds on a folded tea towel in a roasting pan. Pour in boiling water to reach halfway up the sides of the moulds. Set in the centre of the oven and bake for 17–20 minutes, until the centre no longer seems liquid—but not until baked firm.

6. Serve at once, with the ice cream.

Note: *Although the service is simpler and more attractive and the soufflés hold their shape better if made individually, you can prepare the dessert in a 1.75 litre (3 pint) soufflé dish by making the following adjustments: Use 156 g (5¼ oz) plus 2 tablespoons sugar in the soufflé mixture combined in the processor. Set the dessert on the lower rack of the oven, rather than in the centre. Bake for about 40 minutes. Presented this way, you'll have about 6 servings.*

Advance preparation: *The soufflé mixture can be prepared and portioned 3–4 hours ahead, then left at room temperature (preferably cool) to pop into the oven as the main course dishes are cleared away.*

10 SERVINGS

APPLE TIMBALES ROUGEMONT WITH MAPLE SYRUP AND VANILLA SAUCE

CANADA

Rougemont is the centre of apple production in Canada, and Quebec of maple syrup. Executive chef Albert Schnell chose these native ingredients to reinterpret the classic upside-down tarte Tatin *in individual presentation. Neatly petalled apple slices, sweetened with caramely maple syrup, are inverted on a pastry crust and surrounded with thick vanilla sauce.*

Pastry
80 g (3¼ oz) plain flour
⅛ teaspoon salt
60 g (2½ oz) chilled butter, cut into bits
About 3 tablespoons iced water
Vanilla Sauce
¼ large vanilla bean pod, halved
  lengthwise
175 ml (6 fl oz) double (or whipping)
  cream

2 tablespoons sugar
2 egg yolks
Filling
40 g (1½ oz) pecans
4 medium-small Golden Delicious
  apples
2 tablespoons lemon juice
25 g (1 oz) butter
¼ teaspoon ground cinnamon
250 g (9 oz) pure maple syrup

1. Make the pastry: Blend the flour and salt in a bowl. Rub in the butter until it resembles porridge oats. Gradually sprinkle on the water, tossing with a fork until the dough can be massed together easily into a ball. Form a flat round, wrap, refrigerate for 1 hour or longer.

2. Preheat the oven to 150°C/300°F (gas mark 2). Prepare the vanilla sauce: Bring the vanilla pod and cream to a simmer over low heat in a small pan; cover and reserve. Combine the sugar and egg yolks in a small bowl and beat until pale and thick, similar to the texture of soft meringue. Pour half the cream into this mixture, whisking briskly. Pour the egg mixture into the remaining cream.

3. Set over low heat and stir constantly until the cream just barely begins to thicken and tiny wisps of steam begin to puff out. Immediately strain into a bowl set in a pan of ice water to stop the cooking. Stir now and then as the sauce cools. Refrigerate.

4. Make the filling: Spread the pecans in a cake tin and roast for 10 minutes in the oven. Remove and cool. Increase the oven temperature to 200°C/400°F (gas mark 6). Peel, quarter, and core the apples; toss with the lemon juice. Cut each quarter into 3 lengthwise wedges. Heat a quarter of the butter in a 27 cm (9-inch) non-stick frying pan. Sauté half the wedges over moderate heat until pale gold on both sides. Sprinkle with half the cinnamon; transfer to a plate. Repeat with another quarter of the butter and the remaining apples and cinnamon.

5. Chop the roasted nuts; reserve ½ tablespoon. Chop 12 of the apple wedges and mix with the remaining nuts.

6. Boil the maple syrup in a small saucepan until it is reduced to 175 ml (6 fl oz). Add the remaining butter and remove from the heat. Place 1 tablespoon of the syrup in each of 4 individual straight-sided ramekins or soufflé moulds about 8.75 cm (3¾-inches) in diameter and 4 cm (1¾-inches) high (or slightly larger).

7. Place 3 of the sautéed apple wedges overlapping against the dish to leave a hole in the centre. Arrange 3 more over these, petal-like then another 3 on top of them. Fill the other 3 moulds the same way. Stuff the chopped mixture into the centre holes, filling tightly. Spoon maple syrup into this section.

8. On a lightly floured work surface, roll out the pastry to form a circle large enough to cut 4 circles that will just fit within the rim of each dish. Place a round of pastry in each dish on top of the apples, but do not press down the edge.

9. Bake in the upper level of the hot oven for 20 minutes, until the dough is golden brown. Place on a rack; cool to lukewarm (see Serving).

10. To serve: divide the vanilla sauce onto 4 large serving plates, then tilt to distribute. Unmould each timbale onto a fish slice, then set carefully in the centre of each pool. Sprinkle with the reserved nuts.

Serving: *The amount of juice that accumulates as the timbales bake can vary enormously. If there seems to be a large quantity after the desserts have cooled, pour some off before unmoulding so that the sauce is not diluted or the pastry softened by the liquid.*
Advance preparation: *The sauce can be prepared completely in advance. The timbales can be completed through Step 8. Add 5 minutes to the baking time if refrigerated first.*

4 SERVINGS

SHAKER LEMON PIE

UNITED STATES

During the late eighteenth and early nineteenth centuries, communities of the religious society that came to be known as Shakers were established throughout the United States. These self-sufficient groups were renowned for their beautiful handicrafts and simple, good cooking—particularly baking. The American Harvest Restaurant in New York's Vista Hotel has featured the food of the Shakers, drawing inspiration from many of the settlements. The following easy and unusual lemon pie—one of 35 pie recipes in The Best of Shaker Cooking *by Amy Bess Miller and Persis Fuller (Collier Books, 1976)— is based on a recipe from North Union Shaker Village in Ohio.*

A powerful lemon-rind aroma leaps through the cross-cut centre of the sugar-glazed crust. The flavour is surprisingly complex and vivid for a filling that has but three ingredients. Bittersweet, pungent, brimming with sunny slices of fruit with its peel, this is for devoted lemon-lovers only. Plan a day ahead for this dessert, as the fruit must be macerated for 24 hours.

3 lemons, preferably thin-skinned
200 g (7 oz) plus 1 teaspoon sugar
250 g (9 oz) plain flour
½ teaspoon salt
175 g (6 oz) chilled, unsalted butter, cut into small bits

5–6 tablespoons cold milk
3 eggs
1 egg beaten with 1 tablespoon water and a pinch of salt for egg wash

1. Cut the lemons into paper-thin slices, removing seeds as you go (you should have 340 g (12 oz). Combine in a mixing bowl with 200 g (7 oz) of the sugar. Cover and let stand at room temperature for about 24 hours.
2. Whisk together the flour and salt in a mixing bowl. Rub in the butter until the mixture resembles fine breadcrumbs. Sprinkle in the milk 1 tablespoon at a time, tossing the flour mixture to incorporate evenly. Press the dough together gently to form a ball; if the pieces separate, add a few more drops of milk. Form the dough into 2 rounds. Wrap each in plastic and refrigerate for at least 1 hour.

(continued)

3. Preheat the oven to 230°C/450°F (gas mark 8). Roll out one piece of pastry on a lightly floured board to form a 27.5 cm (11-inch) circle; trim with scissors to form an even round. Fold the dough in quarters, place the centre point in the middle of a 23 cm (9-inch) pie dish, then unfold gently, easing into the dish.

4. Roll the remaining dough to form a circle 1 cm (½ inch) larger than the dish rim; trim neatly. Cut an X in the centre.

5. Beat the eggs to blend; stir into the lemon and sugar mixture, stirring to dissolve any remaining sugar. Pour into the shell; distribute the slices with a fork. Paint the exposed rim of pastry with the egg wash; lay the top crust on this, pressing lightly. Fold the overhanging pastry over this. Press, then seal with the tines of a fork. Paint the crust lightly with the egg wash. Fold open the corners of the X to make a square. Sprinkle the crust evenly with the remaining 1 teaspoon sugar.

6. Set on the lowest rack of the hot oven. Bake for 15 minutes. Reduce the heat to 180°C/350°F (gas mark 4) and bake for about 20 minutes longer, until well browned. Cool on a rack.

Option: *For a milder, slightly more tender and sweet variation, substitute 3 halved, thin-sliced oranges for the lemons.*

6–8 SERVINGS

CALVADOS SORBET

UNITED STATES

Fruity and flowery, this golden ice is clean and fresh, but has plenty of character—and alcohol. It is particularly suited to rich autumnal meals, those based on game or pork, for example. Although it is possible to prepare this in other ways, the ice cream makers that contain their own freezing elements are the surest routes to a fine-textured, light dessert. This comes from a series of microfiches devoted to frozen desserts that was developed by the Food Research Center.

155–200 g (5¼–7 oz) sugar (see
  Option)
825 ml (28 fl oz) apple cider, chilled
175 ml (6 fl oz) Calvados or other
  apple brandy

2–3 tablespoons lemon juice
1 egg white

1. Combine the sugar and 450 ml (¾ pint) water in a small pan; swirl over high heat until the syrup boils, then lower the heat, cover, and simmer for 2 minutes. Cool and chill.

2. Combine the cooled syrup, cider, and Calvados. Add the lemon juice to taste. Stir 1 cup of the mixture into the egg white. Blend well, but do not beat until foamy; pour this into the cider mixture.

3. Pour into the container of an ice cream maker. Freeze according to the manufacturer's instructions. Scrape into a freezer container, cover tightly, and freeze for at least 6 hours or up to a week.

4. To serve, soften slightly in the refrigerator.

Option: *If you like a strong Calvados flavour and tart edge to the sorbet, use the smaller amount of sugar. If you prefer a more traditional sweetness, use the larger quantity.*

ABOUT 1.75 LITRES/3 PINTS

CRANBERRY-APPLE SORBET

UNITED STATES

If you enjoy serving a palate refresher during a rich meal, this tart fruity sorbet, made with the minimum quantity of sugar, does a brisk job. For a ruby-pink, fine-textured dessert, use the maximum amount of sugar and offer the sorbet in tulipe *biscuit cups or decorated with fancy-cut apple slivers.*

350 g (12 oz) cranberries, rinsed and picked over

450 ml (¾ pint) apple juice
155–200 g (5¼–7 oz) sugar (see Note)

1. Combine the cranberries, juice, sugar, and 600 ml (1 pint) water in a non-aluminium saucepan. Bring to a simmer; cook for a few minutes until all of the berry skins pop. Set the pan in iced water to cool.

2. Purée the berries and liquid in a food processor until not quite smooth, then press through a fine sieve. (Or simply press through the fine disc of a non-aluminium food mill.)

3. Pour the mixture into the container of an ice cream maker. Freeze according to the manufacturer's instructions. Scoop into a container and freeze for 6 hours or up to a week.

4. Let the sorbet soften slightly in the refrigerator before serving.

Note: *Since berries may vary in ripeness and acidity, taste and add more sugar if necessary after you've puréed the fruit.*

ABOUT 1.5 LITRES/2½ PINTS

AMERICAN HARVEST PUMPKIN CHEESECAKE

UNITED STATES

A best-seller at the Vista New York's fine dining room, this oozingly rich cake is for devoted cream-cheese lovers. The spice blend tints the cake a pale beige (rather than the orangy colour you might expect) and adds subdued undertones to the pumpkin, which lightens the texture of the dense cheese.

Amusingly, the recipe, which evolved from one published in the December, 1979 issue of Gourmet *magazine ('Cheesecake Creations' by Margaret H. Koehler), was later requested from the restaurant by editors of the same magazine.*

---

8 gingernut biscuits
15 g (½ oz) melted butter
975 g (2 lb 3 oz) cream cheese, at
   room temperature
250 g (9 oz) sugar
5 eggs
1½ teaspoons grated orange zest
1½ teaspoons grated lemon zest
450 g (1-lb) can pumpkin purée
¼ teaspoon ground cinnamon

½ teaspoon nutmeg
2 teaspoons ground anise
1 teaspoon ground cloves
2 teaspoons ground coriander
50 ml (2 fl oz) double (or whipping)
   cream
50 ml (2 fl oz) sour cream
3 tablespoons Bourbon whisky
100 g (4 oz) walnuts, chopped
   medium-fine

---

1. Preheat the oven to 180°C/350°F (gas mark 4). Process the gingernuts in a processor or blender to form fine crumbs. Paint a cake tin about 25 cm (10 inches) in diameter and 8 cm (3¼-inches) deep with the melted butter. Coat evenly with the crumbs.

2. Cut the cheese into small chunks. In a large bowl, whisk until creamy; gradually beat in the sugar and work until very soft, with no lumps remaining. On low speed, add the eggs, one at a time. Beat in the grated zests, pumpkin, cinnamon, nutmeg, anise, cloves, and coriander. Add the cream, sour cream, and Bourbon. Beat to blend.

3. Pour the cheese mixture into the tin; sprinkle evenly with the nuts. Place in a roasting pan; pour in boiling water to reach halfway up the sides. Set in the centre of the moderate oven and bake for 1½ hours.

4. Set on a rack to cool completely. Refrigerate for at least 8 hours, or up to 2 days.

5. To unmould, dip the tin into very hot water for about 30 seconds. Run a knife carefully around the edge. Invert the cake onto a board, then invert onto a serving plate, so the nuts are on top. To serve, dip a wide cake knife in hot water to cut each slice (which may not be perfectly neat, as the cake is quite soft).

12–14 SERVINGS

HAZELNUT RICE PUDDING

UNITED STATES

The Vista Hotel won first prize in a competition in search of the best rice pudding in New York City with a dessert of creamy white rice flecked with wild rice and bound with richly perfumed ground hazelnuts (adapted below). The prize tied in neatly with an American Indian food festival that was held shortly thereafter at Vista's American Harvest Restaurant and which featured the distinctive native grain.

75 g (3 oz) hazelnuts	75 g (3 oz) raisins
68 g (2¾ oz) wild rice	85 g (3½ oz) lightly packed
85 g (3½ oz) long-grain white rice	dark brown sugar
500 ml (18 fl oz) milk	Whipped cream
Pinch of salt	50 g (2 oz) grated semisweet
	chocolate

1. Preheat the oven to 190°C/375°F (gas mark 5). Toast the hazelnuts in a pan in the hot oven for 10 minutes, until the husks split and the nuts are lightly browned. While still warm, rub together vigorously in a tea towel to remove as many husks as possible.

2. Combine the wild rice and 450 ml (¾ pint) water in a small, heavy saucepan; bring to a boil, stirring. Cover and cook over low heat until tender, but not mushy, testing occasionally. Timing can vary considerably, from 25 minutes to 1 hour. Drain and cool.

3. Meanwhile, combine the white rice in a small, heavy pan with the milk and salt. Bring to a boil, stirring. Cook over very lowest heat, uncovered, until the rice is almost tender and the milk is thickened and creamy, about 20 minutes; stir often. Add the raisins and cook 5 minutes longer, stirring frequently. Remove from the heat.

4. Combine the nuts and brown sugar in a processor; whirl to a fine texture. Add 60 ml (2 fl oz) water and whiz to a purée. Add another 60 ml (2 fl oz) water and continue processing until smooth. Stir this mixture into the white rice, blending well. Add the wild rice and mix thoroughly.

5. Cool to room temperature, stirring now and then. Spoon into 8 parfait or champagne glasses. Refrigerate until serving time (or ½ hour prior, for the most flavour and texture).

6. To serve, decorate with whipped cream rosettes and sprinkle the grated chocolate over all.

8 SERVINGS

RECIPES

APPETIZERS

Cornmeal Squares with Blue Cheese, Tomatoes and Basil *(Switzerland)* 120
Prawns on Leaf Salad with Fluffy Mustard
Mayonnaise *(United Kingdom)* 122
Mussels with Fennel in Saffron Butter *(Italy)* 123
Fish Fillets with Asparagus in Herb Sauce *(Austria)* 124
Poached Salmon with Sherry Cream and Tomato Parfait *(Germany)* 126

SALADS

Fennel Salad with Apples and Walnuts *(Switzerland)* 132
Farmer's Kale Salad *(Switzerland)* 133
Spinach, Bacon and Egg Salad *(Belgium)* 135
Fillets of Sole with Sautéed Apples and Salad Greens *(France)* 137
Salad of Chicory with Poached Egg and Bacon *(France)* 138

SOUPS

Alsatian Beer Soup *(France)* 139
Forest Mushroom Broth *(United Kingdom)* 140

VEGETABLES, GRAINS AND PASTA

'Ratatouille' with Mint *(Switzerland)* 144
Potato Dumplings, Alsatian-Style *(France)* 145
Potato Pancakes with Cheese and Caraway *(Switzerland)* 147
Risotto with Mint *(Italy)* 148
Spinach Noodles with Mandarin Cream Sauce *(Italy)* 149
Spinach and Carrot Tofu Cakes in Tomato Sauce *(Switzerland)* 150
Vegetable Strudel with Herbal Cream *(Austria)* 152

PREVIOUS PAGE: **Chef Eduard Mitsche, of the Hilton International Wien, displaying a selection of pastry in front of a monument to Johann Strauss in the beautiful Wiener Stadtpark adjacent to the hotel**

SEAFOOD

Lobster, Red Snapper, Scallops and Sole with
Vegetable Strands in Light Stock *(Austria)* 156
Fish Terrine with Basil *(Belgium)* 158
Fish Fillets in Red Wine Butter Sauce *(Germany)* 160
Brochettes of Monkfish and Salmon with Lime *(Switzerland)* 161
Sea Bass Fillets with Artichokes and Coriander *(Switzerland)* 165
Monkfish Fillet with Fennel and Red Onion *(United Kingdom)* 166

MEAT AND POULTRY

Lamb with Minted Red Wine Sauce and
Mustard Seeds *(United Kingdom)* 171
Sweetbreads with Honey Sauce and Melon *(Belgium)* 172
Veal Medallions with Apples and Walnuts *(Switzerland)* 174
Pigeon and Chicory with Salad Greens *(France)* 176
Duck in Two Acts: Crackling Salad and Sliced Duck with
Spring Vegetables in Broth *(United Kingdom)* 178
Poussins with Green Beans in Hazelnut Dressing *(Austria)* 183
Chicken Breasts with Red Pepper Sauce *(Switzerland)* 184
Chicken Breasts Stuffed with Liver in
Light Basil Cream Sauce *(United Kingdom)* 186
Rabbit and Chicory in Cream with Walnut Dressing *(France)* 187

DESSERTS

Layered Orange and Chocolate Parfait with Pear Sauce *(Belgium)* 192
Frozen Poppy Seed and Cinnamon Parfait with Rum Dates *(Austria)* 194
Honey-Ginger Ice Cream with Papaya and Mango *(Austria)* 196
Ice Cream with Melon and Jasmine Tea Sabayon *(Germany)* 197
Champagne Sorbet with Campari *(Switzerland)* 198
Engadine Nut Pie *(Switzerland)* 199
Flambéed Blackberries with Pernod and Ice Cream *Switzerland)* 200
Gâteau Devidal (Chocolate Mousse Cake) *(Switzerland)* 203
Thurgau Apple Cake *(Switzerland)* 204
Baked Apple Custard with Caramel Pepper Sauce *(Germany)* 206
Dialogue of Fruit Purées *(Austria)* 207
Prune Terrine with Sabayon Cream *(Switzerland)* 208
Berries Perfumed with Kümmel *(France)* 212

CORNMEAL SQUARES WITH BLUE CHEESE, TOMATOES AND BASIL

SWITZERLAND

Ticino is the Italian canton of Switzerland, and the source of this savoury appetizer that is served by chef Franz Kuhne at the casual Café de la Marine Suisse in the Hilton International Basel.

The butter-bright yellow squares of cornmeal porridge (polenta in Italian cuisine) are topped with tomato wedges and tangy blue-veined cheese in abundance (Gorgonzola being the Italian choice). The snippets of fragrant green basil are no longer strictly Italian, but part of a storehouse that is common to most fine restaurants in much of the world.

---

225 ml (8 fl oz) milk
50 g (2 oz) butter
¼ teaspoon salt
¼ teaspoon grated nutmeg
100 g (4 oz) fine-to-medium ground yellow cornmeal
1 egg yolk

100 g (4 oz) crumbled blue-veined cheese (see Options)
½ teaspoon finely chopped garlic
4 tomatoes (about 450 g/1 lb), peeled, seeded, and each cut into 12 wedges
2 tablespoons chopped basil leaves
Pepper

---

1. In a small, heavy saucepan, combine the milk, half the butter, the salt, and nutmeg; bring to a boil. Combine the cornmeal with 225 ml (8 fl oz) water. Add to the milk mixture, stirring constantly.

2. Bring to a boil; lower the heat and stir for 5 minutes. Off the heat, stir in the egg yolk. Spread on a baking sheet to form an 18 cm (7-inch) square. Let cool for 30 minutes or so, until rather firm. Meanwhile, preheat the oven to 220°C/425°F (gas mark 7).

3. Cut the cooled cornmeal into 16 squares. Scatter the blue cheese on top, then press it down. Set in the hot oven and bake for 7–8 minutes, until bubbly. Meanwhile, heat the remaining butter in a medium frying pan. Stir in the garlic; add the tomatoes, basil, and salt and pepper to taste. Sauté over moderate heat just to warm through.

4. Place 4 corn cakes on each of 4 serving plates; arrange the tomatoes in the centre.

Serving and presentation: *For a pretty effect you can also arrange the tomatoes directly on the cornmeal squares. An icy white wine from Northern Italy, such as a Riesling or Pinot Bianco from the Alto Adige, would do beautifully with this—as would a Fendant from Switzerland, if it is available.*

Advance preparation: *All but the tomato mixture can be prepared up to a day in advance. Simply slip the corn-cheese squares into the oven to heat while you assemble this savoury topping.*

Options: *Any number of blue-veined cheeses will suit this dish: Danish blue, French bleu d'Auvergne, Italian Gorgonzola. Or try one of a number of Swiss toppings: snails, sausage, wild mushrooms, or tomato-herb sauce.*

4 SERVINGS AS A FIRST COURSE

PRAWNS ON LEAF SALAD WITH FLUFFY MUSTARD MAYONNAISE

UNITED KINGDOM

Chef Graham Cadman, who confesses he is not by preference 'a banquet person', was relieved and delighted when he came up with this appealing appetizer for a party of 400 at the Gatwick Hilton International. A new twist on a prawn cocktail: prawns are bathed in an ivory cream in which blanched mustard seeds pop like caviar as you bite them.

1 tablespoon plus ¼ teaspoon salt
16 very large prawns in the shell
   (about 800 g/1¾ lb; see Serving)
1 egg yolk
1½ teaspoons Dijon mustard
1 teaspoon white wine vinegar
50 ml (2 fl oz) light vegetable oil
50 ml (2 fl oz) light olive oil

2 teaspoons lemon juice
White pepper
1 tablespoon mustard seeds
50 ml (2 fl oz) double (or whipping) cream
1 medium head of soft lettuce (about 4 oz), cored, rinsed, and dried
1 bunch lamb's lettuce (about 50 g/ 2 oz), trimmed, rinsed, and dried

1. Bring 750 ml (1¼ pints) water and 1 tablespoon of the salt to a boil; add the prawns. Cover and bring to a simmer over highest heat. Remove from the heat, uncover, and let cool in the liquid for 30 minutes.

2. Meanwhile, in a small mixing bowl, whisk together the egg yolk, mustard, the remaining ¼ teaspoon salt, and vinegar. Very gradually whisk in the vegetable oil, a tiny bit at a time, until completely incorporated. Add the olive oil in larger quantities, beating continually. Add the lemon juice. Season with white pepper.

3. Drop the mustard seeds into boiling water to cover generously. Boil for 20 seconds. Drain and rinse in cold water. Add to the mayonnaise. Whip the cream in a small bowl until thickened and fluffy, but not firm enough to mound; it should be liquidy. Fold into the mayonnaise. Chill until serving time.

4. Peel off the prawn shells, leaving the tail section intact. Remove the veins; rinse the prawns in the cooled cooking liquid. Serve, or cover and refrigerate until serving time (see Note).

5. Spoon about 2 tablespoons of the sauce onto each of 4 large plates. Cut a slit halfway down the body on the back of each prawn. Open each one and place cut side down so that it stands in the dressing. Distribute the salad greens around the prawns.

Serving: *For less than hearty eaters, serve 3 prawns as an appetizer. For a lunch main course, serve 5–6 prawns per person and arrange on a platter, family-style.*

   For optimum tenderness and flavour, the prawns are at their best if served warm or at room temperature, if your schedule permits.

Options: *Offer cruets of oil and vinegar for those who prefer their salad greens dressed.*

4 SERVINGS AS A FIRST COURSE

MUSSELS WITH FENNEL IN SAFFRON BUTTER

ITALY

Fennel is the dominant note in this first course served at La Pergola restaurant in the Cavalieri Hilton International in Rome. The pale green strips of this quintessentially Italian vegetable are accompanied by a small quantity of mussels which, in their buttery sauce, lend softness and succulence.

2 medium-small fennel bulbs (about 700 g/1½ lb total weight)
80 g (3¼ oz) butter
2 tablespoons finely chopped onion
24 small-medium (or 16 large) cultivated mussels, cleaned (see page 324)

¼ teaspoon saffron threads
175 ml (6 fl oz) dry white wine
Salt and pepper
1 medium tomato, peeled, seeded, and diced
Basil sprigs

1. Cut off and reserve the stalks of fennel for another use. Cut the core out of the base. Slice the fennel bulb into thin layers about 5 cm (2 inches) long.

2. Heat one-third of the butter over moderately high heat in a 25 cm (10-inch) saucepan; stir in the onion and cook until softened. Add the fennel strips and toss over moderate heat for 2 minutes, until shiny and brightly translucent.

3. Add the mussels, saffron, and wine. Cover and boil for a few minutes, just until the mussels open. Remove them with a slotted spoon; set aside and cover four of them for garnish. Shell the remaining mussels.

4. Continue cooking the fennel in the sauce over moderate heat until tender; 3–4 tablespoons of liquid should remain. Place the mussels on the fennel; cover the pan and remove from the heat.

5. In a small frying pan, sauté the tomato in a knob of butter for 2 minutes, or until just softened; set aside. Cut the remaining butter into small pieces. Set the mussels and fennel over lowest heat and stir in the butter. Season with salt and pepper.

6. Divide into 4 small, shallow dishes, placing a mussel in the shell on each. Top with the tomato and basil.

4 SERVINGS AS A FIRST COURSE

FISH FILLETS WITH ASPARAGUS IN HERB SAUCE

AUSTRIA

The dishes offered by Eduard Mitsche at the opulent Rôtisserie Prinz Eugen in the Hilton International Wien are deceptively simple. Arranged in an informal, almost random fashion, the ingredients sparkle with freshness: colourful fish fillets with their iridescent skin are pearly moist; the vivid asparagus are cooked just à point; dressings are room temperature, when appropriate—as here. The success of this dish, less tricky than most of the demanding split-second creations that emerge from the vast kitchen, depends entirely on the quality of fish and asparagus—nothing less than perfect will do. Although the ingredient list looks ominously long, the cause is no more than easy-to-prepare dressings.

2 red mullets or red snappers (each 350–450 g/³⁄₄–1 lb)
50 ml (2 fl oz) dry white wine
½ bay leaf
½ teaspoon lightly crushed peppercorns
1 very small shallot, chopped
12 medium asparagus (about 450 g/ 1 lb), peeled and trimmed closely

Balsamic Vinaigrette
4 teaspoons balsamic vinegar
3 tablespoons olive oil
½ teaspoon finely chopped shallot
Salt and pepper

Creamy Herb Vinaigrette
1 egg yolk
1 tablespoon Dijon mustard

2 teaspoons white wine vinegar
4 teaspoons sherry vinegar
2½ tablespoons dry white wine
150 ml (¼ pint) olive oil
1 teaspoon finely chopped parsley
1 teaspoon finely chopped chervil (or substitute parsley)
1 teaspoon finely chopped chives
½ teaspoon finely chopped fresh tarragon leaves
Salt and pepper

Assembly
Butter, to sauté
1 small head of soft lettuce, such as oakleaf
8 cherry tomatoes, halved
Chervil or parsley sprigs for garnish

1. Remove the gills and innards from the fish but leave the skin intact. Fillet the fish. Alternatively, ask your fishmonger to do this for you, but make sure you ask for the bones and head. Wash the fish bones and heads well; chop into fairly small pieces. Combine in a saucepan with 450 ml (¾ pint) water, the wine, bay leaf, peppercorns, and shallot. Bring to a simmer and skim. Barely simmer for 20 minutes. Strain the fish stock and reserve (you should have about 450 ml/¾ pint).

2. Meanwhile, place the asparagus in a frying pan; cover with boiling water. Simmer until tender, but not soft—5–8 minutes; they should be on the firm side. Refresh in ice water. Drain, dry, and set in a close-fitting dish.

3. Prepare the balsamic vinaigrette: Combine the balsamic vinegar, olive oil, finely chopped shallot, and salt and pepper to taste. Spoon half over the asparagus. Set aside but do not refrigerate.

4. Prepare the creamy vinaigrette: Combine the egg yolk, mustard, vinegars, and wine in a processor or blender; process to mix well. With the motor running, gradually pour in the olive oil. Add the finely chopped herbs and blend. Add salt and pepper to taste.

5. Salt the fish fillets. Butter a frying pan and spread the fillets in it, skin side up. Pour the fish stock over these. Poach just until the fish is no longer translucent in the centre, about 4 minutes. Set on a plate to cool for a moment.

6. Meanwhile, toss the lettuce with the remaining balsamic vinaigrette; arrange on 4 large serving plates. Place a fillet on the lettuce. Halve the asparagus and arrange decoratively over and around this, with the tomatoes. Spoon 2 tablespoons of the creamy vinaigrette alongside each fillet, garnish with chervil or parsley, and serve.

Advance preparation: *You can prepare the fish stock, both sauces, and asparagus many hours in advance, leaving only the few minutes of fish poaching for the last moment.*

4 SERVINGS AS A FIRST COURSE

POACHED SALMON WITH SHERRY CREAM AND TOMATO PARFAIT

GERMANY

Breathtakingly productive, chef Pierre Pfister, of the Hilton International Mainz, is well known in Germany through his gala banquets, television and radio appearances, and books. Experience has given him a sense of just which dishes can be reproduced by the home cook. The following recipe, for example, is easily accomplished in stages, without the last-minute flourishes that distinguish his restaurant food.

Like most of Pfister's dishes, this one contains an element of surprise—in this case, the temperatures: The sherry-touched mayonnaise-like sauce that coats the plate is room-temperature; the slice of salmon is warm, just poached, while the tart and peppery tomato 'parfait' (a slightly fluffy gelatine-bound mixture) is cold. Try this fashionable first course on connoisseurs of contemporary cuisine.

6 g (¼ oz) powdered gelatine
150 ml (¼ pint) tomato juice
2 large tomatoes (about 450 g/1 lb)
½ teaspoon celery salt
Generous amount of white pepper
1 egg yolk
60 ml (2½ fl oz) plus 1 tablespoon
  dry white wine, preferably Riesling (see Note)
1 teaspoon sherry vinegar

1 teaspoon dry sherry
Salt
100 ml (4 fl oz) light olive oil
3 tablespoons walnut oil
60 ml (2½ fl oz) double (or whipping) cream
About 15 g (½ oz) butter
500–600 g (18–20 oz) skinned
  salmon fillet, cut on the bias into
  6 slices
Small celery leaves for garnish

1. Sprinkle the gelatine over the tomato juice in a tiny non-aluminium pan. Peel and halve the tomatoes; squeeze out and discard the seeds. Combine the pulp in a processor or blender with the celery salt and white pepper to taste. Blend just to liquefy (there should be 225–300 ml/8 fl oz-½ pint). Heat the tomato juice mixture until almost simmering, swirling the pan to blend. Add to the purée and blend only until smooth; do not continue to fluff the mixture. Pour into six 60–100 ml (2½-4 fl oz) timbale (dariole, baba) moulds (see Option). Chill for 2 hours or longer.

2. Combine the egg yolk, 1 tablespoon white wine, sherry vinegar, sherry, and salt and pepper in a blender or processor; blend briefly to mix. Combine the olive and walnut oils and cream in a cup. With the machine running, pour in the liquid and blend until light. Scoop into a bowl, cover, and refrigerate (or use within 1 hour).

3. Preheat the oven to 200°C/400°F (gas mark 6). Near serving time, remove the sauce from the refrigerator. Poach the fish: Butter a wide casserole (about 30 x 20 cm/12 × 8-inches) and place the fish in this in a single layer, not touching. Pour over the remaining wine. Set in the centre of the hot oven until barely cooked through, 6–10 minutes depending upon the thickness.

4. Meanwhile, spoon the sherry cream onto 6 plates and tip to distribute evenly. Loosen the tomato parfait by running a knife around the moulds, then dipping the base into warm water for 15 seconds. Unmould onto a fish slice and slip one timbale on each plate.

5. With a fish slice transfer the fish fillets to a towel to dry for a minute. Set on the sherry cream; decorate with the celery leaves.

Note: *It is important to use particularly light, high-quality dry wine for the poaching, as the balance of flavours depends upon the fresh taste of the fish and light seasoning of the sauce.*
Option: *Small timbale moulds or any straight-sided small dishes or moulds do a nice job. However, you may also pour the tomato mixture into a pan or dish to come to a depth of about 2.5 cm (1 inch). This can be scooped into 'quenelles' with teaspoons, rather than unmoulded.*

6 SERVINGS AS A FIRST COURSE

Hilton International Mainz: Expect the Unexpected When You're Entertained by Pierre Pfister

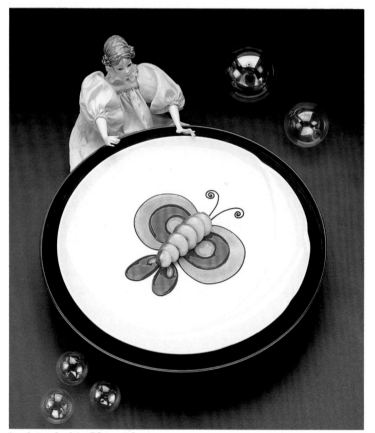

A palate refresher, Pfister-style

D iners seated in the thickly carpeted, richly upholstered Rheingrill can gaze directly into the romantic river through vast windows accented by a brass railing. The ambience is of a sleek cruiser lounge or nautical club. This is Mainz, on the Rhine, and the menu might be fresh trout from the river garnished with baby new potatoes, or a selection of local smoked meats and a profusion of hearty beers.

What arrives at table, however, is a nouvelle cuisine key signature (introduced by Michel Guérard): A white china egg cup bears what at first glance might be a soft-cooked egg, but is, in fact, custard-soft 'scrambled' eggs nestled in a shell, topped generously with caviar. Surprised, but pleased at the execution of the lush appetizer, you smile as the hovering waiter adds more heavy Christofle silver to the already impressive array. As he removes the wide-based egg cup, he uncovers a dainty morsel that had been hiding on the underplate: a petite round of toast, spread with a tartare of beef fillet on which shines the tiniest of yolks—quail.

Apparently enjoying extremes, the chef then sends in a 'serious' plate: A severe arrangement of diamonds of blanched leek and carrot graces the centre of a small, flat soup bowl. Over this the waiter trickles a classically pure consommé of cèpes, deep and woodsy. Creamy layered lasagne follows—but lasagne with a difference: Moist salmon strips are tucked between the filmiest of noodle strata—which are black, tinted with cuttlefish ink—and set in a pool of saffron cream. Although almost austere to behold, it is voluptuous to savour.

A frivolously ornate arrangement arrives (is it dessert?): Fine-drawn wings of chocolate piping, filled in with a mirror of chartreuse and rose confiture, adorn the plate. In the centre is a swirled butterfly of pale orange passion-fruit and wine-dark cassis sorbet. Sweet as it is, it must surely be a palate cleanser, as this meal looks as though it will be banquet-length.

Tradition, miniaturized, ensues in the form of fanned slices of baby lamb fillet, two infant carrots with stems, a tiny potato pancake and peeled cherry tomato.

Solemnly, the waiter announces that two desserts are on their way, as he sets a shining white plate on the crocheted doily on the silver presentation plate beneath. In comes an ice cream cone: a real, ice-cream-man's wafer cone filled with light, smooth nougat ice cream. This is followed by an unmoulded hazelnut soufflé surrounded by vanilla sauce and a toss of raspberries.

If one, two, or three thousand guests are invited, Pierre Pfister revels in the challenge and meets it with similar style. *'Je fais tout,'* exclaims the Alsatian-born chef, *'banquets, cuisine esthétique—hamburgers!'* The annual *Bal des Sports,* a giant Olympic fund-raiser, catches his imagination. Not content with the feat of a *dégustation* meal for 2,500, he may add dancing girls (or elephants), Siberian tigers, or gymnasts between courses of Symphony of Luxury Fish in Turtle Aspic with Two Sauces and Veal Medallions with Creamed Mushrooms and Melted Mozzarella, and has been known to finish off with handmade spun-sugar roses for all. Or, in another mode entirely, a football-pitch-sized bash at the Frankfurt airport featured tables covered in miles of fresh, tender salad greens over which guests sprinkled vinaigrette from watering cans.

But make no mistake. The wild take-offs are somersaults based on firm ground rules. Escoffier is Pfister's hero, he vows, and his cuisine is based on stringent traditional techniques. 'To create as I do, to play, you must have a firm grasp of the reality of food, a serious base to lean on,' he says proudly.

Stashed in the maze of rooms beneath the vast convention hall of the Hilton International Mainz where Pfister reigns over all events (and indeed, some of his dinners could be called happenings), a cache of props attest to the playful side: clown trappings; frying pans large enough to hold a pig or a hundred eggs; Beethoven busts in sugar; balloons, favours, and sprinkling cans for the salad dressing. Numerous plaques, medals, diplomas—tacked to every available scrap of wall—are testament to the mastery of his craft.

One of Pfister's favourite mad creations, an 'homardburger' offers an irresistible and inimitable example of his culinary philosophy: While McDonald's launched a particularly visible advertising campaign in the picture-perfect town of Mainz, Pfister featured an haute cuisine facsimile of the notorious layered burger. Presented on a domed silver platter, the top was removed to reveal the infamous styrofoam container in which rested a sesame-sprinkled 'bun' of the finest puff pastry cradling a 'burger' of the tenderest lobster meat, scrupulously dressed and seasoned.

FENNEL SALAD WITH APPLES AND WALNUTS

SWITZERLAND

Franz Kuhne, executive chef at the Hilton International Basel, describes this as a typical Swiss farmer's salad. The fine strips of crisp red and yellow apple and satiny fennel make a particularly toothsome accompaniment to smoked meats, game, and terrines.

2 medium fennel bulbs (about 700 g/
   1½ lb), chilled
2 medium apples, preferably one red
   and one yellow
About 3 tablespoons lemon juice
About 5 tablespoons dry white wine

Salt
White pepper
50 ml (2 fl oz) walnut oil (see Note)
50 g (2 oz) walnuts, coarsely
   chopped

1. Cut tops from fennel and reserve for another use; save a few sprigs of leaves for garnish. Cut out the core from the base. Remove strings, if necessary, from outer layers (or discard the layers, if less than perfect). Cut the bulbs into thin julienne about 6 cm (2½-inches) long.

2. Core the apples and cut into thin julienne the same length as the fennel. Combine both in a mixing bowl and toss with the lemon juice.

3. Add the wine and salt and pepper to taste, tossing. Add the walnut oil. Toss thoroughly. Taste and adjust seasoning with additional lemon juice, wine, salt, and pepper as desired.

4. Arrange the salad on 4 plates; sprinkle with the nuts; garnish with fennel sprigs.

Note: *Walnut oil, available in most specialist stores, is an extremely assertive and delicious flavour—for those who know and love it. Those unfamiliar with its charms may wish to blend it with an equal amount of light vegetable oil. Those who are familiar may wish to use even more. It spoils rapidly and should be stored in the refrigerator.*
Presentation: *For a more formal presentation, as is done in restaurants, blanch the largest outer layers of fennel bulb to make individual cases for the salad, then garnish with decoratively cut apple slices.*

4 SERVINGS AS A SIDE DISH

PREVIOUS PAGE: Pierre Pfister selecting wines to match his menu

Farmer's Kale Salad

SWITZERLAND

The title tells the tale: a sturdy affair, strong and simple. The rough flavours and textures are independent and contrasting: salty, bitter, oniony, winey, smoky—and good. Served at the coffee shop of the Hilton International Basel, the Café de la Marine Suisse, this warm toss of wilted kale is not a salad in the traditional sense, but more a cooked dish that takes the place of a first-course salad.

700 g (1½ lb) small-stemmed kale
150 g (5 oz) thick-cut rindless bacon, cut crosswise into 5 mm–1 cm (¼–½-inch) strips
1 large onion, cut in half, then sliced thin
1 teaspoon finely chopped garlic

2 tablespoons white wine vinegar
100 ml (4 fl oz) dry white wine
Salt and pepper
1 teaspoon caraway seeds, chopped (see Option)
1 tablespoon finely snipped chives

1. Dunk the kale into a sink filled with cool water. Swish around, then lift out gently so that any debris sinks to the bottom. Repeat, as needed. Pull the stems from the leaves and discard them. Cut the leaves into strips.

2. Heat the bacon over low heat in a wide non-aluminium frying pan until it begins to render some fat, then raise the heat to moderate and toss until lightly browned. With a slotted spoon, transfer the bacon to a plate. Lightly brown the onion in the fat remaining in the pan.

3. Add the garlic and kale; toss for a moment. Add the vinegar and wine. Toss briefly on high heat until most of the liquid has evaporated and the kale has softened sufficiently. Do not cook until tender, but until pleasantly chewy. Season with salt and pepper.

4. Transfer to a serving plate (or 4 individual dishes). Sprinkle with caraway or cumin (see Option), bacon, and chives.

Serving/Presentation: *This dish can be served at room temperature or warm. Accompany with a robust wine— the same that you've used for the preparation of the dish. Follow with veal shanks, or another plain, savoury roasted meat.*
Option: *The word 'cumin', which appeared in the original of this recipe, is used in parts of France, Germany, and Austria to describe what we call caraway. We tested the dish with both (substituting ½ teaspoon ground cumin for the teaspoon of caraway) and found each to be intriguing: the cumin tastes flowery, musky and blooms slowly, while the caraway has a more forthright perfume.*

4 SERVINGS AS A FIRST COURSE OR SIDE DISH

Spinach, Bacon and Egg Salad

BELGIUM

Chunks of bacon, sturdy slices of egg, a heap of baby spinach leaves, and a creamy mustard-garlic dressing make this traditional country-style dish worth reviving. Although similar salads would be equally at home in much of Europe, this version comes from Michel Theurel at the Hilton International Brussels.

---

450 g (1 lb) small-leafed, thin-stemmed spinach
3 slices sandwich bread, crusts trimmed, cut into 1 cm (½-inch) cubes
4 hard-boiled eggs, peeled and halved
1 small garlic clove, crushed

2 tablespoons Dijon mustard
1 tablespoon lemon juice
2 tablespoons sherry vinegar
50 ml (2 fl oz) olive oil
50 ml (2 fl oz) peanut oil
100 g (4 oz) thick-cut rindless bacon, cut crosswise into 1 cm (½-inch) strips

---

1. Preheat the oven to 190°C/375°F (gas mark 5). Dunk the spinach into a sink filled with cool water. Swish around, then lift out carefully so debris falls to bottom. Repeat as needed. Strip the stems from the leaves and discard them. Spin-dry the leaves (or wrap in kitchen paper towels); wrap and chill.

2. Toast the bread dice in a pan in the oven until golden, about 15 minutes.

3. Separate the egg whites and yolks; slice the whites and set aside. Mash the yolks in a salad bowl. Add the garlic, mustard, lemon juice, and 1 tablespoon vinegar; blend well. Gradually whisk in the olive oil, then the peanut oil.

4. Sauté the bacon over moderate heat in a medium frying pan until browned lightly on all sides. Drain off the fat from the pan. Add the remaining 1 tablespoon vinegar; remove from the heat and stir to deglaze the pan.

5. Add the spinach to the bowl with the dressing; toss lightly, using your hands. Divide the mixture between 4 serving plates. Top with the bacon, croûtons, and sliced egg whites.

Serving: *The salad is sufficient as a main course for a light lunch, or serve it as a side dish to grilled meats, or a preamble to a hearty soup meal.*

4 SERVINGS AS A MAIN COURSE

FILLETS OF SOLE WITH SAUTÉED APPLES AND SALAD GREENS

FRANCE

Warm strips of sole, yellowy-green tart apple slivers and feathery leaves of salad are as elegant and beautiful as Oriental porcelain. This surprisingly suited bouquet of tastes and textures comes from executive chef Dominique Michou in Strasbourg, who excels in elegant, understated salads.

700 g (1½ lb) fillet of sole or other firm white fish fillets
Salt and pepper
4½ tablespoons light olive oil
1 tablespoon sherry vinegar
4 medium Granny Smith apples (about 700 g/1½ lb)

40 g (1½ oz) butter
100 g (4 oz) (about 1 medium head) curly endive (*chicorée frisée*) or 2 medium heads chicory, trimmed, rinsed, and dried
1 large bunch (40 g/1½ oz) lamb's lettuce, rinsed and dried

1. Cut the sole fillets crosswise on the diagonal into slices 6–7.5 cm (2½–3-inches) wide with a very sharp knife (you should have about 24 pieces). Set on a sheet of greaseproof paper. Sprinkle with salt and pepper, then paint each slice with olive oil. Turn over the slices, repeat (you'll use about 2 tablespoons of the oil). Place the slices on a baking sheet. Preheat the oven to 240°C/475°F (gas mark 9).

2. Combine the sherry vinegar and the remaining 2½ tablespoons olive oil with salt and pepper to taste.

3. Core and peel the apples; cut them lengthwise into very fine julienne. Heat the butter in a wide frying pan and sauté the apple strips over high heat until just lightly softened and hot, but not cooked through, about 2 minutes. Arrange 3 small heaps around the edge of each of 4 serving plates.

4. Set the fish in the oven for about 3 minutes, to barely cook through. Meanwhile, toss the greens and dressing; set in the centre of the plates. Arrange the fish between the apple heaps.

Serving: *This delicate dish works well for a light summer lunch or supper. Accompany with a chilled Riesling or Sauvignon Blanc. Begin the meal with a consommé madrilène or light puréed vegetable soup, such as asparagus. Although the salad cannot be prepared in advance, it is very easy to assemble and extremely effective.*

4 SERVINGS AS A MAIN COURSE

SALAD OF CHICORY WITH POACHED EGG AND BACON

FRANCE

Lunch at the flowery, wicker-decorated Le Jardin in the Hilton International Strasbourg can be as simple as a hamburger; as sturdily Alsatian as Sauerkraut with Strasbourg sausages, salt pork, black pudding and pork hocks; a spontaneous and luxurious invention of the creative chef, Dominique Michou; or somewhere in-between—such as the following. Fresher and lighter than traditional French bacon-garnished salads, this bistro-style brunch or lunch dish of herb-stippled chicory and poached egg is given a contemporary twist with the nutty dressing, which complements the smoky bacon.

400 g (14 oz) thick-cut rindless
    bacon, sliced across into 2 cm (¾-
    inch) strips
Salt and white pepper
2 tablespoons red wine vinegar
2 tablespoons hazelnut oil

550 g (1¼ lb) medium heads chicory
1½ tablespoons finely chopped
    parsley
1½ tablespoons finely snipped chives
2 tablespoons distilled white vinegar
4 eggs (see Note)

1. Drop the bacon into boiling water; return to a boil. Drain and rinse. Mix together ⅛ teaspoon each salt and white pepper, 1 tablespoon red wine vinegar, and the oil.

2. Halve the chicory and cut out the cores. Soak briefly in water to clean. Drain and spin dry or blot well with towels. Cut the spears across into 5 mm–1 cm (¼–½-inch) slices. Toss with the dressing.

3. Gently cook the bacon in a wide frying pan until slightly crisp, tossing often. With a slotted spoon, transfer to a plate. Discard all but 4 tablespoons of fat. Add the remaining 1 tablespoon red wine vinegar; stir to deglaze the pan. Pour over the chicory and toss. Add the bacon, parsley, 1 tablespoon chives, and salt and pepper. Divide between 4 plates.

4. Poach the eggs in the following manner: In a 25 cm (10-inch) frying pan or saucepan, bring 5 cm (2 inches) of salted water to a boil with the white vinegar. Break each egg into a cup. Slip one at a time into the water and gently scoop up the whites and turn to form neatly covered eggs.

5. When all the eggs have been added, poach below a simmer for 1½ minutes, or until the yolks are not quite set. Lift out with a slotted spoon and drain well.

6. Set an egg on each plate. Sprinkle with the remaining ½ tablespoon chives.

Note: *Poached eggs often have a way of misbehaving, so it makes sense to cook an extra one unless you're very practised.*

4 SERVINGS AS A LIGHT MAIN COURSE

ALSATIAN BEER SOUP

FRANCE

While this version of beer soup hails from Alsace, others warm up wintry evenings in Germany and Switzerland. They can be bound with a pale roux *(such as the following) or a deeply browned one, or with eggs, cream, or bread. Some are spicy and sugary, some savoury and sharp—and this recipe lies in-between: bitter-sweet, with a fruity-yeasty tang, the soup is barely thickened—as if enriched by eggs, although there are none. The zesty, palest beige cream makes a wonderful conversation piece, for few guess the ingredients.*

Be careful about the beer that you choose, for the flavour is intensified—as will be the bitterness. A light, but complex taste will produce the most interesting result.

---

100 g (4 oz) butter
40 g (1½ oz) plain flour
1.25–1.5 litres (2¼–2½ pints) light
   beer, preferably French (Alsatian
   is best)
About ¾ teaspoon coarse kosher salt

About ¼ teaspoon white pepper
About 3 tablespoons icing sugar
½ teaspoon ground cinnamon
225 ml (8 fl oz) double (or whipping)
   cream
6 slices French bread

---

1. Melt half the butter in a saucepan over moderate heat; stir in the flour. Whisk until golden. Gradually stir in the beer. Add salt, pepper, icing sugar and cinnamon.

2. Bring to a boil, stirring. Simmer gently for 20 minutes, uncovered. Add the cream and stir until heated through. Remove from the heat. Check the flavouring, adding further salt, pepper, icing sugar, and cinnamon to taste.

3. Heat the remaining butter in a wide frying pan. Fry the bread over moderate heat until browned on both sides.

4. Place a slice of bread in each serving dish; ladle in the soup.

6 SERVINGS AS A FIRST COURSE

FOREST MUSHROOM BROTH

UNITED KINGDOM

At the Gatwick Hilton International, Graham Cadman put together this deep-brown soup, thick with woodland-wild mushrooms, then topped it with a froth of whipped cream for contrasts of colour, flavour and texture—à la Irish coffee. Easy and unusual.

1.2 litres (2 pints) full-flavoured chicken stock
About 12.5 g (½ oz) dried morels (20 smallish mushrooms)
175 g (6 oz) small wild or 'exotic' fresh mushrooms, preferably a combination—such as *chanterelles* and oyster mushrooms
25 g (1 oz) butter
2 tablespoons finely chopped shallots

About 50 ml (2 fl oz) brandy
About ½ teaspoon fresh thyme leaves, plus sprigs for garnish
About 3 tablespoons finely snipped chives
Salt and pepper
100 ml (4 fl oz) double (or whipping) cream, whipped to form firm peaks

1. Heat 225 ml (8 fl oz) of the stock; combine with the morels. Soak for 2–3 minutes, until tender enough to slice. Trim off the tough tip of the base, then quarter each mushroom lengthwise. Rinse lightly in the broth. Strain the soaking liquid through dampened, fine-meshed muslin, pouring slowly to keep out any sand.

2. Trim the fresh mushrooms, removing any heavy or tough stems. Cut into thin slices. Melt the butter in a wide saucepan. Add the dried and fresh mushrooms. Soften slightly over moderately high heat, about 1½ minutes. Add the shallots; stir for 1 minute. Add brandy and thyme and stir for 1 minute.

3. Add the remaining chicken stock (and the strained stock used to soften the morels). Simmer for 10 minutes. Add 2 tablespoons chives. Season with salt and pepper and additional brandy, thyme, and chives, to taste.

4. Ladle into 4 cups or small bowls, preferably glass, distributing the mushrooms equally. Spoon the cream into the bowls, sprinkle with the remaining chives and garnish with thyme sprigs. Serve at once.

Note: *At Gatwick the soup is ladled into flameproof glass goblets, topped with the cream, then glazed under intense heat.*
Advance preparation: *The soup mellows and develops more body if made a day or two before serving.*

4 SERVINGS AS A FIRST COURSE

Basel: A Melting Pot for
Eclectic Contemporary Cuisine

Trains that run from Geneva in the south to this city in north-west Switzerland, trains that slip punctually alongside groves of espaliered fruit trees, ploughed earth the colour of pumpernickel, diminutive terraced vineyards, and *café au lait* cows, have their signs printed in German, Italian, French, and English (for tourists). Although Basel is only ten minutes from France and two minutes from Germany, its inhabitants speak Swiss-German *(Schwyzerdeutsch),* while those in Geneva are as likely to speak French. In broadest terms there are three regions in the Swiss Confederation: the Deutsch-Schweiz, the French-speaking Suisse-Romande and the Italian Ticino. Composed of 25 self-governing cantons, this tiny country has a wealth (or confusion, depending upon your point of view) of cooking styles to draw from.

Franz Kuhne, executive chef of the Hilton International Basel, was trained at the hotel school in his native town Lucerne, and has cooked his way around the country— and several others. While steeped in the multi-cultural cuisine of Switzerland, he acknowledges that his culinary thinking has been equally affected by a summer spent with chef Jacques le Divellec at La Rochelle, France, where he became enamoured of the 'creative cuisine' that has changed the thinking of so many cooks today. Both influences are clearly visible in the techniques and ingredients of the dishes served in the Wettstein Grill (named after the 17th-century mayor of Basel who, after the Thirty Years War, negotiated the treaty that recognized Switzerland as independent from the German Empire), such as the following graceful dinner assortment:

—A petite slice of rich, deep-flavoured goose liver pâté with *cèpes* affirms that Alsace is just across the border;

—A light vinegar-touched broth with a scattering of brown lentils and bright vegetable dice has roots in local peasant fare;

—An innovative presentation of braided sole fillet in a chive-flecked sauce, accompanied with surprisingly hot-peppery strands of sweet leek and carrot and tender pasta, is a strictly personal expression, inspired by the training with le Divellec;

—Fat, soft white asparagus from a nearby farm are blanketed with thin, moist slices of salmon (one of the favourite fish of Switzerland) and napped with orange-scented butter;

—A quick-cooked crisp and fresh version of ratatouille reminds us of the Mediterranean's proximity, while the generous mint seasoning is Kuhne's own touch;

—The yielding, spicy-winey terrine of prunes with fragile sabayon cream is based on a traditional Swiss dessert (which Kuhne has adapted and lightened)—astonishingly complex in flavour, considering its few ingredients and ease of preparation.

The progression is enhanced by wines and spirits of the country, from a refreshing Fendant to a full-bodied Dézaley, through a berryish, light Pinot Noir, to the unforgettable kirsch and raspberry *eau-de-vie* renowned throughout the world.

OVERLEAF: **Executive chef Franz Kuhne (left) with head cheesemaster Alex Stadelmann, of the Basel Dairy Cooperative selecting a prime Emmentaler**

'Ratatouille' with Mint

SWITZERLAND

Swiss-born chef Franz Kuhne calls this vegetable mélange ratatouille, *although it is not prepared in the same manner as the traditional Provençal dish. (Perhaps this is to remind diners who think Swiss food means cheese and chocolate of the country's connection to Mediterranean cuisines.) The final fillip of mint is Kuhne's own, and delightfully refreshing. Although the dicing takes some time, the quick-cooking method more than compensates.*

5–6 tablespoons full-flavoured olive oil

350 g (¾ lb) firm aubergine, cut into 1 cm (½-inch) dice

350 g (¾ lb) small courgettes, cut into 1 cm (½-inch) dice

350 g (¾ lb) red peppers, cut into 1 cm (½-inch) dice

450 g (1 lb) (about 4 medium) tomatoes, peeled, seeded, and diced

1 large garlic clove, finely chopped

2–4 tablespoons finely chopped fresh mint leaves

Salt and pepper

1. Heat 3 tablespoons of the oil in a wide frying pan over moderate heat. Add the aubergine; toss over high heat until tender, 5–6 minutes.

2. At the same time, heat 2 tablespoons oil in another wide pan; toss the courgettes and peppers over high heat until almost tender, about 4 minutes. Add the tomatoes and toss another minute to heat through. Add the garlic; toss another minute.

3. Add the aubergine to the courgette-pepper mixture. Add the mint and salt and pepper to taste.

4 SERVINGS AS A SIDE DISH

POTATO DUMPLINGS, ALSATIAN-STYLE

FRANCE

While creative contemporary cuisine is the principal focus at the Hilton International Strasbourg, Alsace has a vast repertoire of rich and memorable dishes that have sustained the well-fed inhabitants for centuries. One standard, potato gnocchi or knepfles *(this Alsatian word varies in spelling, ingredients and garnish from one part of the region to another) seems to please diners from the simplest and most sophisticated backgrounds. Soft, chive-dotted, irregular-shaped oval dumplings are strewn with crunchy, butter-drenched croûtons.*

Serve as a hearty side dish with beef or venison stew—with or without the bread garnish. Or set the dumplings and croûtons on tomato sauce and scatter sage leaves over all for a simple main course. Substitute crumbled, butter-fried pumpernickel crumbs for the white bread cubes, in a more German mode. Or omit the chives and serve as a light supper or brunch, accompanied by apples, pears or plums poached in a light syrup.

---

700 g (1½ lb) medium all-purpose potatoes, scrubbed
3 slices white sandwich bread, crusts removed, cut into 1 cm (½-inch) cubes
100 g (4 oz) butter
½ teaspoon salt
¼ teaspoon white pepper

¼ teaspoon nutmeg
1 whole egg
1 egg yolk
3 tablespoons finely snipped chives
125 g (4½ oz) plain flour
100 g (4 oz) grated *Gruyère* cheese

---

1. Bake the potatoes in a 200°C/400°F (gas mark 6) oven until very tender when pressed, 40–60 minutes. During the last 10 minutes of baking, place the bread cubes in a pan in the oven to toast to golden.

2. Holding the hot potatoes with a cloth, halve them and scoop out the pulp. Press through a sieve or the fine disc of a food mill. Stir in 40 g (1½ oz) butter; add the salt, pepper, and nutmeg. Stir in the whole egg, then the yolk, then two-thirds of the chives. Gradually stir in the flour; add the cheese.

3. Using two soup spoons, form oval dumplings (figure on about 20) from the mixture, placing them on strips of lightly oiled waxed paper.

4. Drop the dumplings into a wide pot of boiling, salted water. Keep at a bare simmer for about 15 minutes, or until done to taste. Meanwhile, melt the remaining butter in a medium frying pan until golden-brown; add the croûtons and toss until tawny.

5. With a slotted spoon, transfer the dumplings to a heated dish. Add the croûtons; sprinkle with the reserved 1 tablespoon chives. Serve at once on warmed plates.

4–5 SERVINGS AS A SIDE DISH; 2–3 SERVINGS AS A LIGHT MAIN COURSE

POTATO PANCAKES WITH CHEESE AND CARAWAY

SWITZERLAND

Flat, brown cakes of shredded potato, soft within, are crisped outside, then topped with one of the incomparable cheeses of Switzerland, warmed to barely melting. Caraway seeds, freshly ground over the cheese, lend their pungent scent. (If you don't have an extra mill, grind them in a pestle and mortar or Japanese suribachi.) *At* Le Cygne, *in the Hilton International Genève, Chef Dupont serves the rich concoction alone, as a cheese course, with* vieux vacherin de Fribourg *the cheese of choice; but imported* Gruyère *is an excellent alternative.*

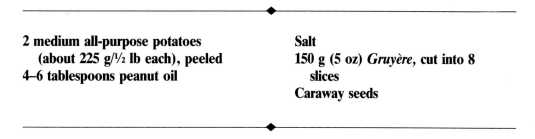

2 medium all-purpose potatoes (about 225 g/½ lb each), peeled
4–6 tablespoons peanut oil

Salt
150 g (5 oz) *Gruyère,* **cut into 8 slices**
Caraway seeds

1. Preheat the oven to 190°C/375°F (gas mark 5). Grate the potatoes on the wide holes of a standing grater.

2. Heat 2 tablespoons of the oil over moderate heat in a wide frying pan, preferably non-stick. Measuring scant 4 tablespoons of the potato (stirring each time you measure), spread and flatten to form 2 or 3 thin neat, rounded cakes, as will fit easily. Sprinkle with salt.

3. Cook over moderately low heat until golden, about 2 minutes per side. Set on paper towels to drain. Continue making pancakes (you should have 8), adding oil generously, as often as needed, to keep the cakes from sticking.

4. Transfer the cakes to a baking sheet; top with the cheese slices. Set in the upper level of the hot oven. Bake until the cheese just melts, 3–4 minutes.

5. Grind a bit of caraway over each and serve hot.

Serving: *Paired with the pleasantly rustic Farmer's Kale Salad (page 133), also a Swiss speciality, the pancakes make a hearty lunch. In a German version, tart apple compote is the accompaniment.*
Advance preparation: *Surprisingly, the pancakes reheat very well. They can remain in a single layer on a baking sheet for hours at room temperature, or longer, refrigerated. At serving time, top with cheese and bake.*

4 SERVINGS AS A SIDE DISH

Risotto with Mint

ITALY

Although the following dish from the Cavalieri Hilton International in Rome adheres to the techniques of traditional risotto-making, the brisk seasoning of fresh mint is in line with the gastronomia creativa *of contemporary Italian chefs. Because mint's intensity varies considerably depending upon the season and variety, you may need more or less. Buy more than you think you'll need, and add gradually, to taste.*

When the dish is served for a first course (which is most common), more broth should be added to the green-flecked grains to achieve a creamy-soupy consistency. As an unconventional side dish to accompany grilled or roasted pork or lamb, less is needed.

About 100 g (4 oz) butter
60 g (2½ oz) finely chopped onion
About 1.75 litres (3 pints) chicken stock (see Note)
450 g (1 lb) arborio rice (see Note)

About 100 g (4 oz) mint leaves stripped from their stems, rinsed
Salt and pepper
Mint sprigs for garnish

1. Heat half the butter in a heavy, wide (25 cm/10-inch) saucepan or sauté pan. Stir in the onion and soften over low heat for a minute or two. Meanwhile, heat the stock to simmering in another pan.

2. Add the rice to the onions and stir for 2 minutes. Ladle in about 175 ml (6 fl oz) hot stock. Adjust the heat so that the rice simmers, but does not boil and stick; stir often until the liquid is almost absorbed. Continue adding hot stock in equal increments and stirring as needed until it is almost absorbed. Meanwhile, finely chop the mint leaves (do not use a food processor).

3. After about 25 minutes the rice should be properly firm-tender in texture; that is, it should be softish on the outside, but remain firm (but not hard) in the centre of the kernel. Remove from the heat; stir in three-quarters of the mint, then additional hot stock, as needed (the mixture will thicken as soon as you remove it from the heat, so add a little more than you gauge necessary).

4. Season with salt and pepper, then add more mint if wished, to taste. Stir in the remaining butter, or more or less to taste. Spoon into heated bowls. Serve at once, garnished with mint sprigs.

Note: *Because a considerable quantity of stock is cooked down to produce the risotto, it should not be salted, or the finished dish will be much too salty.*

Arborio rice, a short-grain Italian rice, is required in order to achieve the special sticky-creamy texture of this dish. It is available in many supermarkets and all Italian grocers.

6 SERVINGS

SPINACH NOODLES WITH MANDARIN CREAM SAUCE

ITALY

At La Pergola in the Cavalieri Hilton International in Rome, lemon, lime and various mandarin seasonings are particularly fashionable, as they are in trendy dining rooms throughout France, Switzerland, Austria, and Germany. The unusual Clementine perfume and colour add a mysterious undertone to the incredibly rich, cream-glossed soft green noodles. Although cheese may seem incongruous, it seems to add saltiness and texture, rather than a defined flavour of its own.

---

3 small Clementines, *or* 2 larger
   mandarins or tangerines
40 g (1½ oz) butter
150 ml (2 fl oz) dry white wine
375 ml (13 fl oz) double (or whipping) cream
Big pinch of cayenne pepper

350 g (¾ lb) fresh (not dried), thin-cut spinach egg pasta (homemade or store-bought)
40 g (1½ oz) grated Parmesan cheese
Salt, if desired
4 basil or mint sprigs

---

1. Finely grate enough Clementine zest to equal 1 teaspoon. With a very sharp knife cut off and discard the rind and pith from 2 fruits; cut neatly between the membranes to free each section. Squeeze and reserve the juice from another ½ fruit—to equal about 2 tablespoons.

2. Heat the butter in a wide, rather deep frying pan—about 25 cm (10 inches) in diameter. Add the grated zest and stir over low heat for 30 seconds. Add the wine and stir over moderately high heat until just a small quantity of liquid remains. Add the cream and a pinch of cayenne pepper. Bring to a boil; cook gently for another minute or so to thicken very slightly. Remove from the heat.

3. Drop the noodles into boiling salted water; cook until not quite tender, only a minute or so (they will continue to cook in the sauce). Drain, rinse lightly. Immediately add to the pan of sauce.

4. Simmer, stirring gently, until the noodles and sauce have reached the desired consistency—only a minute or so (leave extra liquid, as the noodles continue to absorb cream when removed from the heat).

5. Take the pan from the stove. Gradually add the reserved Clementine juice to taste; add the Parmesan, tossing gently. Season to taste with cayenne pepper and salt. Spoon onto 4 heated plates; garnish with the fruit sections and basil sprigs and serve immediately.

Serving: A crisp Alsatian Riesling or Italian Grave del Friuli might accompany the pasta. Plan on a light follow-up to the ultra-creamy opener: a salad of seafood with radicchio and rocket, for example.

4 SERVINGS AS AN APPETIZER

SPINACH AND CARROT TOFU CAKES IN TOMATO SAUCE
'Le Vegetarien'
SWITZERLAND

When executive chef Jean-Claude Bergeret introduced this 'gourmet tofu' at the casual Grignotière restaurant in Geneva, he was responding to a general health and fitness awareness among the hotel guests, but he was sceptical about the dish's survival. In fact the crumb-coated, creamy-textured patties—tinted by the spinach and carrot purées that flavour them—became an immediate best-seller and have remained one. The simple tomato coulis *that moistens them has a fruity bite from the raspberry vinegar, which blends surprisingly well with the touch of soya sauce.*

900 g (2 lb) firm tofu
350 g (¾ lb) carrots, peeled
½ teaspoon nutmeg
1 teaspoon salt
2 heaped tablespoons plain flour
One 275 g (10-oz) package frozen
   spinach, defrosted and drained (or
   900 g/2 lb fresh spinach, trimmed,
   blanched and well-drained)

900 g (2 lb) tinned plum tomatoes
   (see Note)
About 2 tablespoons soya sauce
2–4 tablespoons raspberry vinegar
About 2 teaspoons sugar
Coating
90 g (3¾ oz) plain flour
3 eggs, beaten to blend
225 g (4 oz) fine dry bread crumbs
About 6 tablespoons mild olive oil

1. Place the tofu in a wide shallow dish. Set a pan or lid on the tofu and top with a 2.5–3 kilo (5–6-lb) weight. Let stand for 1–1½ hours. Drain.

2. Meanwhile, simmer the carrots in water to cover until tender, 12–15 minutes. Drain; cut into 2.5 cm (1-inch) chunks. Purée to a rather smooth texture in a blender or processor. Add *half each* of the tofu, nutmeg, salt, and flour. Process to a very fine texture.

3. Press the liquid from the spinach. Purée as fine as possible. Add the remaining tofu, nutmeg, salt, and flour. Purée smooth.

4. Cover a baking sheet with clingfilm. Oil a round 8.5 cm (3½-inch) cookie cutter and set on the sheet. Fill to a depth of 1–1.25 cm (½–¾-inch) with one-sixth of the carrot mixture; smooth with a spoon. Lift off the ring. Repeat, cleaning the ring as necessary, to make 6 cakes of each mixture.

5. Set in the freezer to harden slightly, about 30 minutes. Meanwhile, prepare the sauce. Press the tomatoes through the fine disc of a food mill or purée roughly in a processor or blender and press through a sieve. Add 2 tablespoons soya sauce, 2 tablespoons vinegar, and 2 teaspoons sugar. Boil to reduce to about 450 ml (¾ pint), or until thickened to taste. Adjust the seasonings.

6. Preheat the oven to 200°C/400°F (gas mark 6). Coat each cake thoroughly with the flour, then the eggs; roll in the crumbs to cover entirely. Set each cake on a baking sheet as it is completed.

7. Heat 2 tablespoons olive oil in a wide frying pan over moderately low heat. Lightly brown 4 cakes at a time, about 1 minute per side. Replace on the baking sheet. Add oil as needed to brown 2 more batches.

8. Bake the cakes in the centre of the hot oven for 10 minutes, until sizzling hot. Serve 1 of each cake to each diner, accompanied with the sauce.

Note: *Because this dish is served year-round, and because the quality of tomatoes varies considerably, canned have been used rather than fresh. If sweet, flavourful tomatoes are available, substitute them by all means, and cook down to the desired consistency.*

Advance preparation: *The tofu cakes can be browned, cooled, and refrigerated, then heated in the oven for 15 minutes before serving. Or the uncoated cakes can be wrapped and frozen for months. To finish, defrost slightly, then proceed with Steps 6–8.*

6 SERVINGS AS A MAIN COURSE

VEGETABLE STRUDEL WITH HERBAL CREAM

AUSTRIA

In the sunny Café Am Park that spills out onto a terrace above the rambling city park in Vienna, you can choose from a constantly changing procession of hot desserts and sweet and savoury pastries that flow from the hands of Heinrich Wittman, whose remarkable deftness is on display as he works in view of the customers. The burly, bearded gentleman who presides over the pastry kitchen is well known as a teacher throughout Europe and was named World Strudel-Making Champion. The delicacy of his strudels is due partly to the unusual technique he has evolved for forming the sheets of dough— flinging and spinning pizza-style, rather than in the traditional manner—and partly to the restrained seasoning, which gives fruits and vegetables pride of place. Although it is impossible to teach the strudel-dough technique without Chef Wittman's guidance, the home cook can produce a fine version of his unusual vegetable strudel using packaged strudel or filo sheets.

100 g (4 oz) spinach, stems removed and well washed
100 g (4 oz) French beans, trimmed
3 medium carrots, trimmed and peeled
1 medium kohlrabi, leaves removed, peeled, and cut into 1 cm (½-inch) dice
1 medium-small yellow squash, cut into 1 cm (½-inch) squares
50 ml (2 fl oz) double (or whipping) cream
2 egg yolks
Salt and pepper
400 g (14 oz) packet strudel or filo leaves (see Note)
3 tablespoons melted butter

1 whole egg blended with 1 tablespoon water for egg wash
Sauce
15 g (½ oz) butter
2 tablespoons finely chopped shallots
100 ml (4 fl oz) dry white wine
100 ml (4 fl oz) veal or chicken stock
225 ml (8 fl oz) double (or whipping) cream
1 tablespoon finely chopped chives
2 tablespoons finely chopped parsley
8 large sorrel leaves, stems removed, leaves finely sliced
15 g (½ oz) cup finely chopped watercress leaves
Salt, pepper, and lemon juice

1. Preheat the oven to 180°C/350°F (gas mark 4). Drop the spinach leaves into a large pan of boiling salted water; return to a boil. Scoop out the leaves with a strainer; drop into iced water. Drain, then spread flat on a tea towel.

2. Drop the beans into the boiling water; boil until tender, about 4 minutes; with a slotted spoon transfer to iced water. Quarter one carrot lengthwise, cut the others into 1 cm (½-inch) dice. Drop into the water; boil 1 minute. Add the kohlrabi; boil another minute. Add the squash; boil 30 seconds longer. Pour into a colander to drain, then spread on a tea towel. Drain and dry the beans; cut in 1 cm (½-inch) lengths.

3. Purée the cooked, quartered carrot in a processor or blender, scraping down the sides. Add the cream and egg yolks; purée fine. Combine with the diced vegetables and toss to coat. Season with salt and pepper.

4. Spread one leaf of strudel on a dish towel, a long side towards you. Brush with melted butter to coat completely. Continue layering and buttering until you have used 7 sheets.

5. Lay the spinach leaves in the centre of the filo to form a rectangle about 30 x 15 cm (12 × 6 inches), a long side towards you. Spread the vegetable mixture over this. Fold in the short edges of filo where they meet the filling, then the long sides. Butter these folded margins. Begin rolling from the long side close to you, using the towel to shape a neat cylinder.

6. Place seam side down on a buttered baking sheet. Brush with the egg wash. Bake in the centre of the moderate oven for 25–30 minutes, until nicely browned.

7. Meanwhile, make the sauce: Melt the butter in a medium saucepan. Add the shallots; cook over moderately low heat until soft. Add the wine; reduce almost to a syrup. Add the stock and cream; boil to reduce to 225 ml (8 fl oz). Add the chives, parsley, sorrel, and watercress. Process until frothy in a blender or processor (see Option). Reheat. Season to taste with additional salt, pepper, and lemon juice.

8. Cut the strudel into 12 slices. Distribute the sauce onto 6 warmed plates, then place 2 slices on this. (For an appetizer, cut up to 16 pieces—one per person—and serve a tablespoon of sauce with each slice.)

Note: *Strudel and filo doughs vary in size, and may have to be trimmed to size. Some are more brittle than others, so it is prudent to have on hand more than the 7 sheets required in case of breakage. If the dough looks fragile, cover with a sheet of greaseproof paper, then a damp towel.*

Because packaged doughs are more brittle than Mr Wittman's, we have cubed the vegetables instead of cutting them in narrow sticks, which makes the slicing of the strudel somewhat easier. If you use homemade dough, you may prefer to cut 5 mm (¼-inch) bâtonnets, as the chef does; you may also find the egg wash unnecessary, as homemade pastry will colour more deeply and evenly.

Option: *If you have an electric hand-blender, place it directly in the saucepan and whisk to create a lovely froth, as the chef does.*

Advance preparation: *The strudel can be made up to a day ahead and refrigerated. Brush with the egg wash just before baking. Although the sauce can be prepared ahead, it loses its fluffy texture and becomes somewhat heavier and more prominently sorrel-flavoured.*

6 SERVINGS AS A MAIN COURSE, UP TO 16 AS AN APPETIZER

Vienna's Rôtisserie Prinz Eugen: A Trend-Setting Restaurant in a City That Resists Change

A contemporary presentation of traditional Austrian desserts in miniature, at the Rôtisserie Prinz Eugen

In a grand-scale trio of authentically and opulently decorated Baroque rooms (named after Prinz Eugen, the military strategist who delivered Austria from Turkish domination), the meals served are as apparently simple as Vienna is ornate. In a city where customs and tastes change slowly and food standards are unusually high, the local elite has singled out (as have *Michelin, Gault et Millau,* and a score of other guides) this deluxe, spacious restaurant as one of the most favoured in the city—and the country.

In fact, it was the opening of the Rôtisserie Prinz Eugen in Hilton International's largest European hotel and the influence of its first chef, Werner Matt, that transformed the cuisine of Vienna, beginning a trend now called *Neue Wiener Kuche,* or Nouvelle Cuisine Viennoise. As in most contemporary French cooking, the ingredients of the day's market dictate the dishes that appear on the menu. Lighter than the usual Viennese fare, the larder is adventurous (containing such newcomers as tropical fruits, wild rice, and a wide range of seafood, previously little used in the region), but still stocked with traditional Austrian delicacies, such as plump white asparagus, wild mushrooms, and an abundance of game and offal. Gradually, Viennese residents came to trust (and look forward to) the unusual intrusions in their classical *plats;* guests began to expect the imaginative smaller courses and less formal presentations. The dining room became the testing ground for subtle creations that are now a matter of fact.

Eduard Mitsche, sous-chef in the kitchen of 70 that provides for the hotel's five eating places, moved to the position of executive chef and added his own graceful touch. Lean and energetic, sunny and communicative, Mitsche pulls out books to illustrate his points as he speaks. Interested, absorbed, his long fingers understand the qualities of the fruits and vegetables he is showing and describing, automatically sensing the potential of the raw material. An Austrian ('a kitchen in Vienna will not tolerate anything else,' he laughs), he has a love for the traditional foods of the country which he interprets in sturdier and more conventional ways for the four other hotel restaurants. Widely travelled, he was the first non-British employee on the *Queen Elizabeth 2,* as its VIP chef, then went on to the London Hilton on Park Lane, before returning to Cunard to sail around the world on the same vessel. His experience has led him to prefer a kitchen staff in which cooks of different nationalities meld and clash—a challenge to co-ordinate and a source of stimulation and information. It seems to be working beautifully as a philosophy in this hotel. And as testament to the kitchen's successful approach, it is interesting to note that at the time of writing, almost every other fine dining room in Vienna is headed by a chef who worked in the kitchen of the Hilton International Wien somewhere along the line.

While the performance of the dining room staff is as polished and old-world as the array of glittering glasses and formal flower arrangements, when the silver domes are removed from diners' plates (with the simultaneous precision of the violin section of the Vienna State Orchestra), the arrangements within are deceptively simple. An *amuse-gueule,* cute and simple, begins the meal: A miniature money-bag unadorned, perched next to a slim cylinder of tissue-thin strudel dough, tied with a chive, scroll-like. The little pouch is stuffed with wild rice, the cigarette with salmon, each cuts with the slight pressure of a fork to make two delicate bites. Long slices of soft breast of guinea-hen touched with a hazelnut vinaigrette follow, strewn casually over warm, crisp *haricots verts,* barely but quintessentially dressed. A pure, fresh broth with ribbons of courgette, carrot, and onion hold a scallop, a shelled lobster claw, a rectangle of turbot and another of red mullet with its silvery crimson-etched skin—each poached to individual perfection, *à point*. A shallow bowl coated with a bare slick of marbled purées of unsweetened kiwi, mango, strawberry, and blackcurrant with a spiral of thin sour cream ('a dialogue of fruit purées') is briskly tart and perfumed, truly a palate refresher. A medallion of pink, pale veal barded with a thin Savoy cabbage leaf is inset with sweetbread and a fine herbed veal *farce,* then daubed with its own juice. A tiny fried potato cornucopia spills baby potato balls, mangetout peas, slivers of turnip and carrot *bâtonnets*. For dessert, slices of rosy papaya surround a light honey and ginger ice cream.

Each statement in the meal is clear and subtle. As gifted gardeners instinctively pluck a fruit from a tree just at its peak, so some cooks have a feeling for cooking and seasoning food until it reaches the stage that most naturally underscores the finest qualities of the fish or fowl, fruit or vegetable in question. Such are the dishes that come from the kitchen of the Prinz Eugen.

LOBSTER, RED SNAPPER, SCALLOPS AND SOLE WITH VEGETABLE STRANDS IN LIGHT STOCK

AUSTRIA

The essence of understated luxury: arranged with Japanese simplicity, the finest seafood is presented with no frills, but much care, each ingredient given equal billing in the pale stock. You must be an admirer of this type of pure, light food to make the expense and effort worthwhile. Perfect ingredients and split-second timing are crucial, or you wind up with casual—albeit pleasant—fish soup.

To accompany this dish, its creator, chef Eduard Mitsche of the Hilton International Wien, suggests a soft leafy salad for the first course and a side dish of wild rice or steamed potatoes for the seafood.

---

1 red snapper, red mullet, or sea bream (about 1.1 kilos/2½ lb)
100 ml (4 fl oz) dry white wine or dry vermouth
½ teaspoon bruised peppercorns
½ bay leaf
1 small shallot, chopped
Salt
1 lobster (about 1.5 kilos/3 lb)
15 g (½ oz) butter
2 rather large carrots, peeled and cut into fine julienne about 7.5 cm (3-inches) long

4 tender inner celery stalks, cut in fine julienne about 7.5 cm (3-inches) long
1 small leek, dark green tops removed, well washed, and cut into very thin rounds
White pepper
4 large or 8 medium sea scallops
175–225 g (6–8 oz) sole fillets, cut into 4 pieces
Basil sprigs for garnish

---

1. Halve each fish, keeping the skin intact. Remove the gills and innards and discard; rinse the bones well and cut them small. Combine in a saucepan with 1.2 litres (2 pints) water, the wine, peppercorns, bay leaf, and shallot. Bring to a boil, skimming. Gently simmer for 20 minutes. Strain the fish stock through dampened cheesecloth; you should have about 750 ml (1¼ pints). Season with salt, as desired.

2. Drop the lobster into boiling salted water. Simmer gently for 10 minutes. Remove and cool slightly. Halve the body lengthwise and remove the carapace. Jiggle open the small pincers, then crack and gently remove the shells from the claws. Remove the tail meat. Halve the meat from each in neat diagonals. Remove the meat from the large front legs. Combine all the meat in a saucepan with 100 ml (4 fl oz) of the fish stock.

3. Heat the butter in a wide frying pan; add the carrots, celery, and leek and toss until coated. Add 100 ml (4 fl oz) fish stock and toss on moderately low heat until just cooked through, 7–8 minutes. Add salt and pepper, as desired.

4. Meanwhile, butter a deep frying pan. Spread the snapper fillets in this, skin sides up. Heat the remaining fish stock; add it and the scallops and bring to a simmer; add the sole and cook until barely translucent inside. At the same time, warm the lobster.

5. Divide the seafood evenly between warmed, wide soup plates. Strain the stock into the vegetable mixture and bring to a boil. Divide evenly into the soup plates. Serve immediately, garnished with basil.

4 SERVINGS

FISH TERRINE WITH BASIL

BELGIUM

Remarkably clean and uncomplicated, this terrine is also freshly pretty: a mosaic of red snapper fillets speckled with basil is enclosed between layers of smooth fish purée, the whole wrapped in spinach leaves. The festive, summery slices are sparked by a bright plum-tomato garnish.

The terrine, like most at the Hilton International Brussels, is the creation of Christian Albrecht, the transplanted German sous-chef who, with the French executive chef Michel Theurel, has worked there since the hotel's opening. The unusually long-lived team has been variously described as 'the visionary Frenchman and the pragmatic German', 'the artist and the technician', 'the flexible doer and the perfectionist brainchild' by their colleagues. Both are dedicated teachers and recognized as Master Chefs of Belgium.

350 g (¾ lb) skinned red snapper
  fillets
2 tablespoons lemon juice
1 medium-large bunch basil (100 g/4
  oz), trimmed and chopped
350 g (¾ lb) smooth spinach leaves,
  cleaned, stems removed
450 g (1 lb) skinned sea bass fillets,
  well chilled and cut into 2.5 cm
  (1-inch) pieces
1 egg
1¼ teaspoons salt
½ teaspoon white pepper

375 ml (13 fl oz) double (or whipping) cream
Tomato garnish
8 medium plum tomatoes, peeled,
  seeded, and diced
Salt and pepper
1 tablespoon lemon juice
2 tablespoons olive oil
2 tablespoons peanut oil
About ¼ teaspoon each dried basil,
  thyme, tarragon, and fennel seeds
Basil sprigs for garnish

1. Cut the snapper fillets into strips of more or less equal thickness about 3.5 cm (1½-inches) wide and 10–12.5 cm (4–5 inches) long. Arrange in a non-aluminium dish; sprinkle with the lemon juice and chopped basil; toss to coat. Cover and let stand at room temperature while you prepare the rest of the dish.

2. Drop the spinach into boiling salted water; return to a boil, then drain and drop into ice water. Drain, then spread flat between towels to dry.

3. Preheat the oven to 180°C/350°F (gas mark 4). Line a 22.5 × 12.5 cm (9 × 5-inch) loaf tin with greaseproof paper to overhang somewhat. Line completely with the spinach, placing the leaves so that they hang over the edge a few inches.

4. Chop the sea bass to a fairly fine texture in a food processor. Add the egg, salt, and white pepper; blend to barely mix. Add the cream and purée fine.

5. Spread one-third of the fish purée in the mould, smoothing some up the side to lightly coat the spinach. Place half the fillets on this, arranging in a single layer. Spread half the remaining purée on this; top with the rest of the fillets. Cover neatly with the remaining purée, smoothing with the back of a spoon. Overlap the spinach to cover the dish, adding a few more leaves if necessary. Fold over the greaseproof paper to seal tightly.

6. Set in a pan and pour in boiling water to reach halfway up the mould. Set in the centre of the oven and bake for 1 hour. Remove from the water and cool on a rack. Chill well (do not remove the greaseproof paper)—at least 6 hours or for up to 1½ days.

7. Combine the tomatoes, salt and pepper to taste, the lemon juice, olive and peanut oils; crumble the herbs and add; chop the fennel seeds and add. Let stand for at least 1 hour at room temperature; adjust the seasoning to taste.

8. Unmould the terrine, remove the greaseproof paper, then slice with a serrated knife. Place the slices (2 for a main course, 1 as an appetizer) on each of the serving plates. Spoon the sauce alongside. Garnish with basil sprigs.

Serving: *Simple and attractive, this works beautifully for a buffet, with the slices arranged on a platter and the sauce alongside to spoon over. A cucumber salad makes a nice accompaniment.*

8 SERVINGS AS A MAIN COURSE, 16 AS AN APPETIZER

FISH FILLETS IN RED WINE BUTTER SAUCE

GERMANY

Executive chef Gerhard Heusing of the Hilton International Düsseldorf (the first German hotel-restaurant to receive a Michelin *star) has an ability to balance flavours unerringly, to contrast textures, temperatures, and tastes in a way that might be considered the culinary equivalent of perfect pitch: a terrine of smooth, cool, goose liver is dabbed with crème fraîche and escorted by apple julienne; a rosette of raw petals of turbot inlaid with salmon and transparently dressed with vinaigrette is caviar-touched; sliced fillet, kidney, and liver of rabbit are accompanied by a velvety black olive purée and fresh herbed noodles; frozen Grand Marnier parfait is set on clouds of unsweetened cream around a pool of bitter-sweet kumquat sauce.*

Unfortunately, although the presentation of each dish is unaffected, preparation is most often extremely labour-intensive and ingredients are very difficult to obtain, making home-cooking nearly impossible. Thus, we have but one easily realized example of Heusing's provocative work. The sauce is fruity, slightly sweet, thin-bodied, with great depth—and is a most unlikely blueberry-violet-grey. The fish fillets that nearly float in it are coated with a moist layer of taupe-brown mushrooms and crumbs. And somehow, the flavours and colours magnify the beauty of the fish; they do not mask or overwhelm it.

Two 700–900 g (1½–2-lb) sea bass (or other firm, small white-fleshed fish)
1 medium carrot, cut into chunks
1 small onion, cut into chunks
1 medium stick celery, cut into chunks
¼ teaspoon peppercorns
175 ml (6 fl oz) dry red wine
75 ml (3 fl oz) white port
75 g (3 oz) butter

100 g (¼ lb) mushrooms, very finely chopped
50 g (2 oz) soft fresh white bread crumbs
1 tablespoon finely chopped chervil (or parsley with a touch of tarragon)
Salt and pepper
2 tablespoons double (or whipping) cream

---

1. Remove and discard the innards and gills; fillet the fish, keeping the skin intact; rinse the bones and heads. Combine in a saucepan with the carrot, onion, celery, peppercorns, and about 750 ml (1¼ pints) water to just barely cover. Simmer gently for 20 minutes, skimming occasionally. Strain out the solids. Skim the fish stock and simmer to reduce to 350 ml (12 fl oz).

2. Preheat the oven to 200°C/400°F (gas mark 6). Combine 225 ml (8 fl oz) of the fish stock with the red wine and port in a non-aluminium saucepan. Boil to reduce the sauce to a scant 225 ml (8 fl oz).

3. Melt one-third of the butter. Toss with the mushrooms, crumbs, and chervil. Season the fillets and place in a buttered ovenproof dish or Swiss-roll tin. Distribute the crumb mixture over the fillets, patting firmly to form a neat covering. Spoon the remaining fish stock around the fillets.

4. Set in the upper level of the hot oven. Bake for about 8 minutes, until just cooked through. Meanwhile, heat the sauce. Take it off the heat and whisk in the remaining butter, a small piece at a time (see Note). Whisk in the cream. Set over lowest heat.

5. When the fish has cooked through, pour about 60 ml (2 fl oz) of sauce into each of 4 warmed serving plates. Set the fillets on this.

Note: *If you have an electric hand-blender, place it directly in the sauce pot and whisk to create a lovely froth, as the chef does.*
Serving: *Plates must be heated for this tender, sauced fish. This is spoon food, not designed for forks.*
Advance preparation: *The sauce can be prepared through Step 2 up to two days ahead and the bread-mushroom topping completed a few hours in advance.*

4 SERVINGS

BROCHETTES OF MONKFISH AND SALMON WITH LIME
SWITZERLAND

(continued)

This pastel-pretty, citrusy brochette is a best-seller at the lively Grignotière restaurant of the Hilton International Genève. Monkfish (also called lotte, bellyfish, goosefish, angler) is particularly favoured for its firm flesh, but executive chef Jean-Claude Bergeret suggests halibut as an alternative; fettuccine or rice soaks up the thin wine cream sauce.

2 small limes
225 g (½ lb) boneless, skinned
    salmon fillet
350 g (¾ lb) boneless monkfish steak
    or thick fillet, membranes
    trimmed
400 ml (14 fl oz) dry white wine

3 tablespoons chopped shallots
4 teaspoons tarragon vinegar
50 ml (2 fl oz) double (or whipping)
    cream
100 g (4 oz) butter
Salt and white pepper

1. Thinly pare the zest from 1 lime using a vegetable peeler; cut into fine julienne. Remove and discard the white pith. Bring the julienned zest to a boil with water to cover. Drain and cool.

2. Cut all the rind and pith from the other lime; cut the lime in half lengthwise, then across into very thin half-rounds. Cut both types of fish into 3 cm (1¼-inch) squares. Alternate salmon and monkfish on 4 thin wooden skewers about 20 cm (8 inches) long, placing a lime slice between each and beginning and ending with monkfish.

3. Combine the white wine, shallots, and vinegar in a wide non-aluminium saucepan or frying pan. Boil to reduce to 50 ml (4 fl oz). Strain into a small non-aluminium pan. Add the cream; boil to reduce to 50 ml (4 fl oz). Stir in 60 g (2½ oz) butter; remove from the heat. Add salt and pepper to taste, and half of the lime julienne.

4. Melt the remaining butter in a wide frying pan. Salt and pepper the brochettes. Place them in the pan and cook for about 1½ minutes on each of the two wide sides, or until barely cooked through. Serve with the sauce; sprinkle with the remaining lime julienne.

Note: *Although the colours are pale, the lime flavour is sharp and dominant—so cut down on the quantity of slices on the skewers if you're not a citrus devotee.*

4 SERVINGS

The Hilton International Genève team of Gilles Dupont (left) and Jean-Claude Bergeret in Lake Geneva, heading towards the hotel and the spectacular Jet d'Eau.

SEA BASS FILLETS WITH ARTICHOKES AND CORIANDER

SWITZERLAND

Gilles Dupont, the young French chef at Le Cygne in the Hilton International Genève, trained in his native country in Annecy, Juan-les-Pins and Cologny, then went on to Sweden, England, and Canada before joining the Hilton staff in 1980 in Geneva. His inventive combinations, particularly seafood dishes with intensified essential sauces—such as the following harmonious mélange—have drawn numerous accolades from food critics throughout Europe, and two Michelin stars.

Although artichoke hearts and fish are uncommon plate-mates, they have a rare affinity, particularly when underscored by coriander. The effect is multifaceted, with hints of tastes that are bitter-sweet, earthy, briny, mushroomy, and acid without being disparate.

Two 800 g (1¾-lb) sea bass or red snappers, filleted with skin intact, heads and bones reserved
A few peppercorns, bruised
1 bay leaf
1 medium bunch coriander (about 75 g/3 oz), rinsed
225 ml (3 fl oz) dry white wine
2 tablespoons chopped shallots

2–3 tablespoons lemon juice
4 large artichokes
350 ml (12 fl oz) double (or whipping) cream
Salt and pepper
Peanut oil
4 firm medium plum tomatoes, seeded, peeled, and diced

1. Remove and discard the gills and innards from the skeletons. Rinse the heads and bones well; combine in a saucepan with 1.5 litres (2½ pints) water, the peppercorns, and bay leaf. Simmer for 20 minutes; skim. Strain the fish stock into the pan. Chop and add the coriander stems, white wine, shallots, and 2 tablespoons of lemon juice.

2. Break the stems from the artichokes. Break off the outer leaves until you reach the tender, pale centre. Slice across the tops of these leaves to remove about half. Trim off any additional dark leaf parts. Pare away the dark base of the underneath part.

3. Bring the fish stock to a boil. Add the artichoke bottoms; set a dish on top to keep them submerged. Simmer until tender (timing can vary considerably; begin checking at about 25 minutes). Cool slightly in the liquid. Scrape away the hairy chokes and cut each into 8 wedges.

4. Strain the stock. Return to the pan and boil until reduced to 65 ml (2½ fl oz). Add the cream and boil the sauce to reduce to about 300 ml (½ pint) and slightly thickened. Add lemon juice to taste. Chop fine enough coriander leaves to equal 2½ tablespoons (reserve a few sprigs for garnish); add to the sauce. Add salt and pepper to taste.

5. Set a foil-covered grill rack as close to the heat as possible and preheat the grill. Paint the fish fillets on both sides with peanut oil. Grill until just barely cooked, about 5 minutes.

(continued)

6. At the same time, combine the artichoke hearts and sauce and warm over low heat. Add the tomatoes.

7. Arrange the artichokes and tomatoes on 4 warmed plates with the fish fillets. Garnish with the reserved coriander sprigs.

Serving: *This lush sauce is lovely with a light grain, particularly a scented rice such as Basmati, if available, or couscous.*
Advance preparation: *Although this dish is rather labour intensive, it can be almost completely made a few hours in advance—through Step 4.*

4 SERVINGS

MONKFISH FILLET WITH FENNEL AND RED ONION

UNITED KINGDOM

When chef Graham Cadman put together this dish at the Gatwick Hilton International, the ingredients were considered altogether unusual. In fact, when French and English fishermen met in the Channel, monkfish was commonly exchanged for fish more to British taste. Also called goosefish, bellyfish, and angler, only the tail end of this firm-fleshed fish is marketed. Well known in France and Italy (where you will find it as lotte, baudroie, rape*), the fish has just recently become part of the repertoire of other nations' chefs.*

The marinating (begun a day before cooking) tenderizes the flesh and adds a gingery Oriental edge to the traditional French white wine sauce, which is brightly verdant from its generous helping of parsley and chives. The garnish of crisp-tender sweet onion and aromatic fennel is particularly pleasant alongside baby new potatoes in their pink jackets.

550 g (1¼ lb) monkfish fillet, cut
    into 16 slices (medallions)
Salt and white pepper
1 tablespoon grated fresh ginger
120 ml (4 fl oz) olive oil
25 g (1 oz) butter
2 teaspoons finely chopped shallot
1 tablespoon plain flour, plus flour
    for dusting the fish
225 ml (8 fl oz) fish stock (see
    page 326)

100 ml (4 fl oz) dry vermouth
450 g (1 lb) fennel bulb, weighed
    without large stalks
1 large red onion, halved, then
    thin-sliced
15 g (½ oz) chives cut into 3.5 cm
    (1½-inch) lengths
1 tablespoon finely chopped parsley

1. Sprinkle the fish slices on both sides with salt and pepper to taste. Mix the ginger and 60 ml (2 fl oz) olive oil; spread evenly on both sides of the fish. Cover with clingfilm; refrigerate for about 24 hours.

2. Preheat the oven to its lowest heat. Heat half the butter in a small saucepan. Stir in the shallot and cook until softened over moderately low heat. Add 1 tablespoon flour and cook until slightly coloured. Add the fish stock and half the vermouth; bring to a boil, whisking. Cook over lowest heat for 15 minutes, stirring often. You should have slightly more than 175 ml (6 fl oz) of sauce.

3. Meanwhile, trim off the fennel stalks completely, if necessary, saving the small inner leafy parts for garnish. Halve or quarter the bulb(s), as size dictates, then cut across in thin slices. Heat 30 ml (1 fl oz) olive oil in a medium-large frying pan over moderate heat. Add the fennel and cook, tossing often, for 3 minutes, until partly tender. Add the onion and continue cooking until just tender, about 2 minutes. Season to taste. Divide the portions on serving plates and set in the low oven.

4. Heat half of the remaining oil in a 23 cm (9-inch) non-stick frying pan (or use a very good stainless or copper one; the fish sticks) over moderate heat. Dust half the fish slices with flour. Cook until lightly browned on both sides, about 2 minutes. Arrange on the plates with the vegetables. Repeat with the remaining oil and fish (or use 2 pans and cook all at once).

5. Add the remaining vermouth to the pan in which the fish cooked; stir over moderate heat until the brown bits have been loosened. Add to the vermouth sauce. Pass through a strainer. Add the chives and parsley; bring to a simmer. Off the heat, stir in the remaining butter.

6. Remove the plates from the oven, spoon the sauce around the fish and vegetables. Serve at once.

Advance preparation: *The recipe can be completed through Step 2 a day ahead.*

4 SERVINGS

A Quiet Coup: Graham Cadman at the Gatwick Hilton International

Graham Cadman and his son, Ben, at home

'I can't help it. I was born with an English handicap,' says lean, affable Graham Cadman, a native of Sheffield. 'My teachers told me that I should change my name if I wanted to get on in the field, that I could never make it.' But he has, and so have the restaurants with which he has been affiliated in his 21 years in the business—13 of them with Hilton International. 'It's a fluke my being a chef, anyway. My mother, a fine farm cook, made nice jams and bread, but never touched a piece of garlic or other "strange things". The closest I ever came to cooking or caring much about it was picking berries.' At sixteen, an average student and avid soccer player, he was persuaded by a school career's officer to try his hand at cooking. Christmas season being near and hotel kitchen help never sufficient, he found himself peeling mountains of turnips and potatoes—and happy as a lark. 'There was steam everywhere, turkeys were tossed through the air, grown men were swearing at each other and running around with pots and platters; it was as much fun as a soccer match.'

Cadman apprenticed for four years in England, then went on to Switzerland—where he realized he knew just about nothing, and virtually began again. As a foreigner in a Swiss kitchen, he managed to achieve the almost unheard-of high rank of sous-chef, then decided to glean some international experience. But the giant beach-barbecues and rum-and-Coke atmosphere of the Caribbean where he was transferred were too much of a shock to his system after the chilly precision of Zurich. And, more important, there was *beurre rouge* ('not *beurre blanc,* but a new sauce, a new world to discover')! A friend had sent an innovative menu from Europe—subtle dishes with classic under-pinnings and daring new ingredients and techniques—the burgeoning of Nouvelle Cuisine. 'If I stay away from Europe too long, I may never know *beurre rouge,*' proclaimed the brave young sous-chef, and had himself moved to Europe, even though the change meant a lesser position. He learned to make a red wine butter and much more, and became executive chef of the Amsterdam Hilton. A three-year stint in Holland found him a bit homesick, and when an appropriate place became available in England, he relocated to the Gatwick Hilton International.

Just imagine driving out of the way to an airport hotel to have dinner prepared by an English chef—on purpose! Of course, that's just what happened. Cadman's calm, sensitive style, his unflagging enthusiasm, his ability to sense guests' preferences, his seasonal menus based on the fine national products—simple vegetables, Welsh lamb, Angus beef, perfect turbot and Dover sole, Dublin Bay prawns, remarkable cheeses—and his ability to meld traditional English ingredients with continental ones, resulted in an award-winning restaurant 'worth the detour' and loved by locals. 'The restaurant started out serving giant portions of English food kept in *bain maries* large enough to swim in, and wound up—with Hilton's blessing, and the help of a remarkable team—with a European kitchen built to produce European food.' Candid and direct, he says, 'I cannot tell you how I love the commitment it takes to be a chef. The involvement of so many people along the line, the fact that you see a product from the beginning to the end. I couldn't dream of doing anything else.' From the following 'sampler' meal, we should all be grateful for this last statement.

—Smooth, thin slices of burgundy-red, salt-marinated raw duck slicked with olive oil, truffle-topped, served on warm potato slices;

—Miniature medallions of golden-sautéed sweetbreads and pine nuts tossed with crunchy stir-fried *bâtonnets* of asparagus and carrots, touched with a mere gloss of balsamic vinegar and lightest walnut oil;

—A cool terrine of mixed poultry and wild mushrooms, cut in large morsels, Madeira-touched, served with warm slivers of herb-flecked tawny forest mushrooms;

—Tenderest prawns and baby papaya balls in a thin, fresh chilli-spiked sauce of the puréed fruit, shellfish stock, and finished with butter and cream to barely bind;

—A small salmon fillet, pan-seared, deglazed with currant-vinegar purée, served on a bed of tart-sweet, diced peppers (yellow, red, and green), aubergine, courgette, and capers;

—Two diminutive lamb chops from the rack, mahogany-toned from a light smoking, served with a scant spoon of reduced juices, tiny turned turnips, a miniature carrot flan, and *haricots verts;*

—A tulip biscuit cup containing strawberry, pear, and mango sorbet surrounded by a marbled fantasy design of cream and sour raspberry purée, escorted by slices of lightly liqueur-macerated strawberries, mango, and pear.

OVERLEAF, TOP: Monkfish Fillet with Fennel and Red Onion (see page 166 for recipe) BOTTOM: Lamb with Minted Red Wine Sauce and Mustard Seeds (see page 171 for recipe)

Lamb with Minted Red Wine Sauce and Mustard Seeds

UNITED KINGDOM

The origin of some dishes is less poetic than others. In this case Graham Cadman was confronted upon his arrival at the Gatwick Hilton International by a huge supply of mustard seeds, left by his predecessor—who was passionately fond of the spice. A number of weekly specials were thus inspired by inherited mustard seeds.

Try this new approach to lamb with mint sauce: a wine reduction accented with fresh mint leaves moistens long, rosy slivers of loin.

Rack of lamb (8 ribs; 1.1 kilos/2½ lb), meat removed in one long cylinder, bones and trimmings hacked into small pieces
1 tablespoon vegetable oil
2 small onions, cut into chunks
1 carrot, sliced
½ teaspoon peppercorns, crushed slightly with the blade of a knife
½ bay leaf

1 garlic clove
8 g (⅓ oz) cleaned mint leaves
450 ml (¾ pint) dry red wine
1 large shallot, finely chopped
65 g (2½ oz) butter
Salt and pepper
About 1 teaspoon mustard seeds, crushed slightly with a knife blade
Mint sprigs for garnish

---

1. Discard the fat from the lamb trimmings and bones. Heat the oil in a very wide frying pan over high heat; add the bones and trimmings, onions, and carrot and toss until well browned, about 15 minutes, pouring off the fat as it accumulates. Add the peppercorns, bay leaf, and garlic; toss for 5 minutes longer. Add 450 ml (¾ pint) water and bring to a boil slowly. Boil, stirring occasionally, to reduce the liquid to 300 ml (½ pint), 10–15 minutes. Pour the lamb stock into a container. Spoon off the fat.

2. Preheat the oven to 200°C/400°F (gas mark 6). Combine the lamb stock, mint, wine, and shallots in a saucepan. Boil until the sauce is reduced to 175 ml (6 fl oz).

3. Meanwhile, heat 15 g (½ oz) butter in a flameproof casserole. Sprinkle the meat with salt and pepper; brown it lightly on both sides. Set in the hot oven for 6–10 minutes for rare. Set on a cutting board to rest for 5 minutes or so, lightly covered with foil to keep warm.

4. Add the reduced sauce to the pan with any juices that have accumulated from the meat. Boil to reduce to 100 ml (4 fl oz). Strain into a small saucepan. Bring to a boil. Remove from the heat and stir in the remaining butter and 1 teaspoon mustard seeds. Season to taste, adding more mustard seeds, if desired.

5. Cut the meat into about 24 slices. Spoon 3 tablespoons of the sauce onto each of 4 heated plates. Arrange the meat over, garnish with mint sprigs, and serve at once.

Note: *If you like meat very rare, there is no need to roast it in the oven. Simply cook over direct heat.*
Advance preparation: *The lamb stock and wine reduction can be made 2–3 days ahead.*

4 SERVINGS

SWEETBREADS WITH HONEY SAUCE AND MELON

BELGIUM

This finely tuned and understated dish comes from Michel Theurel of La Maison de Boeuf in Brussels, where it is served with Chinese rice noodles, glazed pearl onions, a snippet of lime zest, and mint sprigs. It is one of those inventions in which the sum equals far more than the parts. The melons are no mere fanciful garnish, but lend their sweetness and acid to the gingery-meaty sauce which burnishes the pale sweetbreads.

---

1 pair veal sweetbreads (about 700 g/ 1½ lb)

½ small ripe honeydew, *or* a whole Galia melon

½ ripe cantaloupe, orange melon, or an equivalent amount of another orange-fleshed melon

Salt and white pepper

40 g (1½ oz) butter

2 tablespoons light fragrant honey

3 tablespoons sherry vinegar

150 ml (¼ pint) chicken or veal stock

½ teaspoon very finely grated fresh ginger

---

1. Soak the sweetbreads in a bowl of water in the refrigerator for about 24 hours, changing the water 4–8 times, as convenient; all blood spots should be soaked clean.

2. Slip the sweetbreads into a pan of simmering salted water to cover. Simmer for 10 minutes. Drain and cool slightly. Set the sweetbreads in a pan; place a dish and a 5–6-lb weight on top. Let stand for ½–1 hour. Trim and discard the heavy membranes.

3. Preheat the oven to its lowest heat. Scoop out and reserve the melon seeds and attached fibres. With a 2.5 cm/1-inch melon ball cutter, scoop about 20 balls of each melon; cut each of these in half. Scrape both seeds and enough remaining ripe flesh from each melon to make about 150 g (5 oz).

4. Sprinkle the sweetbreads with salt and pepper. Heat half the butter in a medium frying pan over moderately low heat. Cook the sweetbreads until golden on both sides, about 5 minutes. Spoon the honey over the sweetbreads; lower the heat and cook for about 10 minutes, basting and turning often, until the sweetbreads are richly browned and glazed. Set on a dish in the warm oven.

5. Pour the vinegar into the pan in which you glazed the sweetbreads; stir over high heat for a moment until the steam dies down. Add the reserved melon seeds and pulp and the stock. Bring to a boil, stirring; boil for 1 minute. Strain into a small pan.

6. Boil the sauce to reduce it until it becomes slightly shiny and sticky—about 50 ml (2 fl oz). Add the ginger and the remaining butter; pour in the juice that has accumulated from the sweetbreads.

7. Cut the sweetbreads into diagonal slices. Spoon the sauce onto 4 warmed plates. Arrange the sweetbreads on it. Shake the melon balls in a frying pan over high heat for a moment to heat through. Distribute over and around the sweetbreads.

Advance preparation: *The sweetbreads can be soaked, poached, and flattened in advance.*

4 SERVINGS

VEAL MEDALLIONS WITH APPLES AND WALNUTS

SWITZERLAND

Franz Kuhne, executive chef at the Hilton International Basel, and Marcel Roth, food and beverage manager, have been at the hotel since its opening in 1975. Both native Swiss, they work together with Rolex precision. Meticulous craftsmen, they stress a traditional education and are dedicated to the training of young chefs. They are not of the wild individual school of cooking, but rather advocate more subdued personal expression, rooted in the classics.

This dish then, of tender veal morsels in a generous gilding of glossy sauce is (reluctantly spoken by chef Kuhne) 'a creation', but based on beloved Swiss ingredients—palest meat, walnuts, and apples—in a classic veal reduction.

2.3 kilos (5-lb) veal rib roast (6 chops), meat removed in one long cylinder, bones and trimming hacked into small pieces

2 medium carrots, peeled and cut into thick slices

3 medium onions, peeled and cut into chunks

1 stick celery, cut into thick slices

½ teaspoon crushed white peppercorns

Salt and white pepper

35 g (1¼ oz) plain flour

50 g (2 oz) butter

225 ml (8 fl oz) dry white wine, preferably Swiss (Dézalay or Fendant) or a dry Riesling

225 ml (8 fl oz) double (or whipping) cream

2 tablespoons Calvados or apple brandy

3 Golden Delicious apples, peeled and cored

1 tablespoon lemon juice

100 g (4 oz) walnuts

Basil sprigs for garnish

1. Preheat the oven to 200°C/400°F (gas mark 6). Cut the meat into 12 equal medallions. Spread the bones and trimmings in a wide roasting pan. Set in the preheated oven and roast for 30 minutes, until well browned. Add the carrots, onions, celery, and peppercorns. Roast for 30–40 minutes longer, until well browned. Pour off the fat. Transfer the contents of the pan to a stockpot. Add 1 litre (1 ¾ pints) water to the roasting pan and bring to a boil over high heat, stirring. Pour into the stockpot. Bring to a boil with an additional 1 litre (1¾ pints) of water. Simmer, uncovered, for about 1½ hours. Strain out the solids, then boil the stock to reduce it to 225 ml (8 fl oz).

2. Lower the oven heat to a minimum. Sprinkle the veal with salt and pepper; dust evenly with the flour. Heat a quarter of the butter in a very wide frying pan over moderate heat; add half the veal; cook until lightly browned on both sides, about 2 minutes. Transfer to a platter in the warm oven. Repeat with the remaining veal, using another quarter of the butter. Pour out the fat.

3. Add the wine to the pan; stir over high heat until reduced to a syrupy consistency. Add the cream and reduced veal stock; boil, stirring, until reduced to about 300 ml (½ pint). Add the Calvados and salt and pepper to taste. Remove from the heat; add half the remaining butter.

4. Cut each apple into 12 wedges; toss with the lemon juice. Heat the remaining butter in a wide frying pan. Add the apples; sauté until nicely coloured on both sides, about 3 minutes. Add the walnuts; toss for 2 minutes. Arrange with the veal on the platter. Spoon some sauce over the meat. Garnish with basil sprigs.

Serving: *Accompany with noodles, or the snipped Swiss noodles,* spätzli, *or rounded* knöpfli *(little buttons). Serve the remaining sauce alongside.*

6 SERVINGS

Pigeon and Chicory with Salad Greens

FRANCE

The Maison du Boeuf in the Hilton International Strasbourg began as a showcase for the finest American meat. It seemed foolhardy for an American hotel chain to compete with the many celebrated restaurants in this much-starred Alsatian food town. However, when Dominique Michou began to make his imprint, he not only managed to attract the tourists, but the critical locals—and a Michelin *star. Grilled and roasted meats were gradually replaced with trendy versions of local specialities, such as this dish.*

The gamey flavour and deep-rose colour of pigeon are well suited to the bitter-sweet chicory, barely butter-braised, and jewel-bright mâche and radicchio combination.

4 pigeons (each about 350g/¾ lb)
Salt and pepper
2 tablespoons sherry vinegar
50 ml (2 fl oz) hazelnut oil
450 g (1 lb) chicory
75 g (3 oz) butter

1 small head of radicchio (about 6 oz), rinsed and dried and torn into bite-size pieces
1 large bunch of lamb's lettuce *or* 1 small head of imported curly endive *(chicorée frisée)*, rinsed and dried

1. Cut the leg-thigh pieces from the pigeons. Cut off the wings (leave the first joint of the wings intact), then remove the breast meat from the birds. (Save the wings, carcasses, giblets, etc. for future stock-making.) Sprinkle with salt and pepper.

2. Mix together the vinegar and salt and pepper to taste; blend in the oil.

3. Halve the chicory and trim out the cores. Rinse and pat dry. Cut crosswise on a slant into 3 sections, if large, 2 if small.

4. Heat half the butter in a very wide frying pan (see Note) over moderately high heat. Cook the pigeon pieces until deep pink within, about 2 minutes on each side. Set on a cutting surface and cover lightly to keep warm.

5. Heat the remaining butter in a wide, rather deep frying or sauté pan over moderately high heat. Add the chicory pieces; toss until they lose their raw crunch, about 3 minutes. Season with salt and pepper.

6. Toss the salad greens with the dressing; divide onto one side of 4 large serving plates. Arrange the chicory next to this. Quickly slice the breasts lengthwise; cut apart the leg-thigh sections. Arrange the pigeon over the chicory. Serve at once.

Note: *If you cook the pigeon in a black cast-iron pan it will brown more thoroughly and the skin will be crisper.*
Serving/Presentation: *This composed salad will be most attractive served on very large plates, especially dark-coloured ones.*

4 SERVINGS

DUCK IN TWO ACTS:
CRACKLING SALAD AND SLICED DUCK WITH SPRING VEGETABLES IN BROTH
UNITED KINGDOM

British chef Graham Cadman is reluctant to call a dish his invention or confess to personal preferences, but he does allow that this creation is his ('although based on the classic boeuf à la ficelle*'), a response to the overload of richness in most haute cuisine preparations.*

A new way of looking at duck, this recipe supplies both salad and main course for four with one bird. Satiny chicory and radicchio are tumbled with crunchy strips of duck skin for an appetizer salad, then the meat is served with a bouquet of springtime vegetables in a modicum of full-flavoured broth. Not a soup, not a stew, the combination is clean, light, Japanese in feeling; a natural, pure ensemble of rewarding simplicity.

2.3–2.7 kilo (5–6-lb) duck
1 large onion, cut in chunks
1 large carrot, cut in chunks
1.5 litres (2½ pints) cold unsalted chicken (or duck) stock
4 small red potatoes, scrubbed and sliced 5 mm (¼ inch) thick
175 g (6 oz) *haricots verts* (or tiny string beans), trimmed
4 medium carrots, quartered lengthwise, cut into 3.5 cm (1½-inch) lengths
225 g (½ lb) (3 small) turnips, cut the same size as the carrots

100 g (4 oz) mangetout peas, strings removed
Salt and pepper
1½ tablespoons red wine vinegar
3 tablespoons olive oil
1 medium head radicchio (about 150 g/5 oz), cored, rinsed, and torn into bite-sized pieces
2 medium heads chicory, halved, cored, and sliced across
2 tablespoons finely chopped parsley
1 tablespoon finely snipped chives
2 teaspoons soya sauce

---

1. Prepare the duck stock: Cut the leg-thigh pieces from the duck; trim neatly. Cut off the wings (leave the first joint of the wing attached). Halve the breast down the centre and remove the 2 pieces from the carcass with the wing joints. Trim these, saving the trimmings. Cut up enough fat to yield about 225 g (8 oz) (discard the remainder). Heat in a very wide frying pan over moderate heat. Chop the carcass, wings and neck into small chunks and add to the pan. Cook over moderate heat until browned, about 15 minutes, turning occasionally; pour off fat as it accumulates. Add the onion and large carrot; stir now and then until well browned, about 10 minutes. Remove from the heat; tip the pan so the fat runs to one side; let stand for a few minutes. Pour off the fat. Add the chicken stock; bring to a boil. Simmer until reduced to 825 ml (28 fl oz), 25–30 minutes.

2. Preheat the oven to 220°C/425°F (gas mark 7). Prepare the vegetables: Drop the potatoes into a large pot of boiling, salted water. Boil for 30 seconds. Add the beans and carrots; boil for 1½ minutes, until half-cooked. Add the turnips and mangetout peas; boil for 1½ minutes longer, until all the vegetables are just cooked through. Drain; drop into iced water. Drain again.

3. Cook the duck: Heat 1 tablespoon of duck fat or oil in a clean flameproof casserole. Salt and pepper the breast and thigh pieces and place skin-side down in the pan. Brown lightly, then turn and sear the meat. Pour off the fat. Set the breast pieces on a plate. Place the pan with the thighs in the hot oven for 15 minutes. Add the breast; roast about 10 minutes longer, until the meat is pink within. Transfer to a cutting board. Pour the fat from the pan.

4. Prepare the salad: Add the vinegar to the pan; stir over low heat for 30 seconds to deglaze. Strain into a small bowl. Whisk in salt, pepper, then olive oil to make a dressing. Remove the duck skin/fat from the roasted pieces; cut this into thin, even strips. Toss in a medium frying pan over moderate heat until golden and crisp. Toss the radicchio and chicory with the dressing, then top with the duck skin and serve as a first course.

5. To prepare the main course: Combine the duck stock, parsley, chives, and soya sauce in a wide saucepan. Bring to a simmer, covered. Add the blanched vegetables; return to a simmer. Taste; adjust seasoning and herbs. Meanwhile, cut the duck meat into thin strips. Spoon the vegetables into 4 wide, heated serving bowls. Top with the duck meat, dividing breast and leg-thigh meat equally. Pour the hot stock over all.

Serving: *You can also serve the two dishes together, as is done at the Gatwick Hilton International.*
Advance preparation: *The duck stock and blanched vegetables can be prepared in advance. If you don't want to make the dish ahead of time, the vegetables can be blanched, drained and added to the hot stock at serving time.*

4 SERVINGS, AS BOTH SALAD COURSE AND MAIN COURSE

OVERLEAF: **An innovative meal for four from one duck: Sliced Duck with Spring Vegetables in Broth (left); Crackling Salad (right—with a few crisp bits in the foreground)**

POUSSINS WITH GREEN BEANS IN HAZELNUT DRESSING
AUSTRIA

Executive chef Eduard Mitsche, in Vienna, is partial to salads of lightly cooked warm fish or poultry nestled against a toss of tender greens touched with nut-oil dressings (as is Dominique Michou, in Strasbourg). He serves the following as an appetizer course, but for home cooks this is more likely to be a featured main course. As with all of Mitsche's dishes, there is no hiding place: the simple flavours are the focus, so ingredients must be perfect.

2 poussins
225–285 g (8–10 oz) *haricots verts*
    (or tiny string beans)
2 tablespoons balsamic vinegar
1 teaspoon sherry vinegar
Salt and pepper
50 ml (2 fl oz) hazelnut oil

50 ml (2 fl oz) plus 2 tablespoons
    olive oil
1 tablespoon finely chopped shallots
4 quail eggs (optional, but desirable)
1 medium head of soft lettuce, such
    as oakleaf, rinsed and dried
12 cherry tomatoes, halved

1. Preheat the oven to 180°C/350°F (gas mark 4). Cut the leg-thigh sections from the poussins, then the breasts. Remove the wings from the breasts and the bones from both breast and leg-thigh pieces (freeze and reserve these for stock).

2. Trim the beans and drop into boiling salted water; boil until barely tender, about 3 minutes. Drain, cool in iced water; drain and dry. Blend the 2 vinegars and salt and pepper; whisk in the hazelnut oil and 50 ml (2 fl oz) of the olive oil; add the shallots. Toss the beans with half the dressing.

3. Sprinkle the poussins with salt and pepper. Heat the remaining olive oil in a wide ovenproof frying pan over moderate heat. Place the leg-thigh pieces in the pan and brown lightly on both sides. Leave these in the pan and add the breasts, skin side down. Cook until golden; tip the pan and spoon the fat over the meat. Set the pan in the oven for 10 minutes, or until just barely cooked.

4. Drop the quail eggs into boiling water; boil for just under 2 minutes. Drop into cold water to cool slightly; gently crack shells and remove them. The eggs should be warm.

5. Arrange the lettuce and beans on 4 large plates. Cut the thigh pieces into fairly thick slices on a diagonal. Place these on the lettuce. Cut the breasts into thin, long slices and arrange these on the plate. Stir the dressing and spoon over poussins and lettuce.

6. Garnish with the cherry tomatoes. Halve the eggs and set on the plates. Serve at once.

4 SERVINGS AS A MAIN COURSE

CHICKEN BREASTS WITH RED PEPPER SAUCE

SWITZERLAND

La Grignotière, a casual restaurant at the stunning Hilton International Genève, spills out onto a broad terrace once the weather warms. This is not surprising, as the view may be one of the most beautiful any restaurant can claim. Right on the shore of the glittering lake, one can see as far as Mont Blanc and as near as the graceful swans that sail along the shore below.

Although a 'fast-food' restaurant in comparison to Le Cygne (the luxury dining room of the hotel) La Grignotière, supervised by executive chef Jean-Claude Bergeret, a Hilton International veteran of 23 years standing, is by no means standard—as is clear from the following recipe for a best-seller of juicy chicken served with a tart-sweet, vividly orange pepper sauce and egg noodles.

4 chicken breasts with wings (175–
   200 g/6–7 oz each)
Salt and pepper
40 g (1½ oz) butter
350 ml (12 fl oz) chicken stock
2 large, meaty red peppers, halved,
   seeded and coarsely diced

2–3 tablespoons raspberry vinegar
2–3 teaspoons sugar
1 large green pepper, halved and
   seeded
50 ml (2 fl oz) dry white wine

1. Preheat the oven to 190°C/375°F (gas mark 5). Trim the wing tip and attached joint from each piece (reserve for stock-making); sprinkle breasts with salt and pepper. Heat the butter in a wide ovenproof frying pan until foaming; add the chicken breasts, skin side down. Cook over moderate heat until browned, about 5 minutes. Turn to barely colour, about 1 minute. Cover; transfer to the hot oven. Roast until cooked through, about 15 minutes.

2. Meanwhile, combine the stock and red peppers in a saucepan. Simmer until tender, about 10 minutes. Purée in a blender or processor. Add 2 tablespoons of the vinegar and 2 teaspoons sugar; purée fine. Add sugar, salt, pepper, and vinegar to taste. Bring to a boil and cook for a minute or two.

3. Drop the green pepper into boiling, salted water. Return to a boil. Refresh in iced water. Dry and cut into very fine strips.

4. Transfer the chicken to a platter (remove breast bones, if desired); cover with foil.

5. Boil the liquid in the roasting pan until the fat rises to the top and the particles beneath are browned. Pour off the fat. Add the wine to the pan and bring to a boil, scraping the pan bottom. Simmer for 2 minutes on low heat. Strain into the pepper purée. Bring to a simmer.

6. Serve the chicken and sauce garnished with the green pepper.

Note: *For a velvety sauce, grill and peel the peppers before simmering.*

4 SERVINGS

Chicken Breasts Stuffed with Liver in Light Basil Cream Sauce

UNITED KINGDOM

This recipe is slightly adapted from the version developed by chef Graham Cadman and served at the Gatwick Hilton International, where chicken is stored and cooked in vacuum-sealed pouches that maintain freshness and yield a flavourful, moist finished product. The presentation resembles a miniature ballottine: *pale chicken breasts wrapped in spinach leaves are centred with rosy livers. The warm slices are arranged on an ivory* sauce suprême *sparked with a generous amount of basil.*

---

40 g (1½ oz) butter
2 tablespoons plain flour
450 ml (¾ pint) chicken stock
100 ml (4 fl oz) double (or whipping)
    cream
8 g (⅓ oz) finely chopped basil
    leaves

4 medium chicken livers, cleaned
    and halved (about 175 g/6 oz)
Salt and pepper
About 225 g (½ lb) spinach leaves,
    as smooth and flat as possible;
    cleaned, with stems removed
4 boned and skinned chicken breast
    halves (100 g/4 oz each)

---

1. Heat 25 g (1 oz) butter over low heat in a small saucepan. Add the flour and stir for 2 minutes; do not brown. Add the stock, whisking. Bring to a boil, stirring, then simmer gently for 15 minutes, or until reduced to 300 ml (½ pint). Add the cream; simmer gently until reduced to a little less than 300 ml (½ pint). Add the basil. Cool.

2. Heat the remaining butter in a small frying pan over moderate heat. Season the livers with salt and pepper, then sear on both sides. Set aside to cool.

3. Drop the spinach into boiling salted water; return to a boil. Drain; refresh in iced water. Spread about 6 overlapping leaves on paper towels to form a rectangle the size of each breast piece. Form 4 of these. Dry the remaining leaves on tea towels.

4. Enclose each liver piece in a leaf of spinach. Cut a pocket running the length of each chicken breast piece; insert 2 spinach-wrapped liver packets. Place each chicken piece on a spinach rectangle; sprinkle with salt and pepper. Enclose each breast in the spinach (adding additional leaves as needed), to cover completely.

5. Wrap each chicken packet in buttered foil to make a neat cylinder, leaving the ends open. Place the packets on a steamer rack set over boiling water. Steam for 10 minutes, until just cooked through; the liver will still be slightly pink. Let cool for 5 minutes.

6. Slice the chicken into rounds and arrange on a warm platter. Gently rewarm the sauce, then spoon a little over the slices; serve the rest separately.

Option: The chicken can also be chilled, sliced, and served with basil mayonnaise as a cold hors d'oeuvre.

4 SERVINGS

Rabbit and Chicory in Cream with Walnut Dressing
FRANCE

Most of the diners who spend the evening at La Maison de Boeuf in the Hilton International Strasbourg are locals. They have come to expect meals that depend on the day's market, and on the creative whims of chef Dominique Michou—rather than a traditional fixed menu. Michou is particularly fond of warm, lightly cooked fish or meat, arranged around salad greens tossed with nut oil and sherry vinegar. Here, creamy chicory shreds accompany port-scented rabbit slices brushed with walnut-sherry dressing. While the presentation of this dish is simpler than most of Michou's, the flavours are characteristically subtle. You'll need to plan on marinating the rabbit for about a day.

Two 1.1 kilo (2½-lb) rabbits
300 ml (½ pint) double (or whipping) cream
60 ml (2½ fl oz) port
2 tablespoons light vegetable oil
5 large heads chicory (about 700 g/1½ lb)

25 g (1 oz) butter
2 tablespoons walnut oil
1 teaspoon sherry vinegar
Salt and pepper
1 very small head of oakleaf or other soft lettuce, rinsed and well dried

---

1. Remove the hindquarters, then the forelegs from the rabbits. Bone the loin/breast section carefully, so that it remains in one piece. (If you are less than practised, you might ask the butcher to take over.) Roll and tie this large piece to form a cylinder. Bone the hind quarters (keep the forelegs, bones, and trimmings for future stock-making). Combine 175 ml (6 fl oz) cream and the port in a non-aluminium dish. Turn the rabbit pieces around in the cream; cover, and refrigerate for 12–24 hours.

2. Preheat the oven to 180°C/350°F (gas mark 4). Remove the meat from the dish, scraping off some of the marinade. Heat the oil in a wide gratin pan or pan with ovenproof handle. Lightly brown the rabbit on both sides. Set in the moderate oven for 30 minutes, or until tender. Let stand for 5 minutes before slicing.

3. Meanwhile, halve the chicory and trim out the cores. Cut across into thin slices. Heat the butter in a 30 cm (12-inch) frying pan. Add the chicory and toss over high heat until most of the juice has exuded, about 2 minutes. Add the remaining cream. Toss frequently over high heat until the cream has thickened to a slick.

4. Blend together the walnut oil and sherry vinegar with salt and pepper to taste. Arrange the lettuce on 4 plates.

5. Divide the chicory over the lettuce. Slice the rabbit and arrange around the two salad leaves. Brush the meat with the walnut dressing and sprinkle a little on the lettuce. Serve at once.

Serving: *The aromatic, bone-dry white wines of Alsace are the natural accompaniment to this creamy dish. A Riesling or Tokay, if available, will serve beautifully.*

4 SERVINGS

Hilton International Brussels:
From Vegetarian Club Sandwiches
to Foie Gras on Rose Petal Gelée,
a Kitchen That Stays in Tune

Residents of Brussels are knowledgeable—and passionate—about fine food, and so are most of their cosmopolitan visitors. In the city that is home for NATO and the European Parliament, heads of state wind up meetings on time to keep their reservations in the many prestigious eating establishments. In fact, for anyone attempting to choose a dining spot, whether casual or formal, the abundance of restaurants is almost daunting. It is therefore quite remarkable that the three large restaurants of a de luxe, modern American hotel, which handles 1,200 meals on an average day (banquet service included), should all be highly rated in numerous European restaurant guides and that 85 per cent of the clientele is local.

In the glassed-in terrace of the Cafe d'Egmont (overlooking the château of the Count of Egmont, inspiration to Goethe and Beethoven) you can order a quick snack or meal anytime. Enjoy crunchy rolls and fine croissants for a continental breakfast, or try the Belgian-style sweet *pain perdu* with a glass of buttermilk, into which large brown sugar crystals are stirred. After noon, listen to the pleasant hum of Swiss-German, French, Dutch, and English as businessmen, tourists, and sleek ladies-who-lunch fill the tables. Gloved and veiled dowagers take over with their dachshunds and poodles at teatime, downing copious quantities of tartes and tortes, coupes and creams, coffee and chocolate. Evening finds a menu of seasonal specials that changes weekly—such as the silky white May asparagus, in a mousse of eel and basil, or in a gamut of salads and soups, or in puff pastry with watercress mousseline alongside, or with rabbit in mustard.

Lunch or dine any day of the year in the easy atmosphere of La Maison du Boeuf (like the restaurant of the same name in Strasbourg and the San Francisco Grill in Düsseldorf, beef was once the raison d'être of these restaurants, which have now come to feature light, creative cuisine as well). A floor above the café, over the same cool, wooded park, the comfortable room is frequented by regulars. Genial Willy Raye-makers, one of the three long-term maîtres d's, greets many guests by name. Luxuriate in the imaginative, constantly changing menu: wild mushrooms in cream, steamed goujons of sole and ribbons of chicory in pale butter with chives, sweetbreads in a slick of ginger-tinged honey essence with tiny melon rounds, traditional but lightened veal kidneys *liégeoise* with juniper sauce, a full-flavoured orange and bitter chocolate parfait with a thin, fresh *coulis* of pears, or crunchy *tulipes* filled with wild strawberries and almond ice cream.

The place to go for special occasions is En Plein Ciel (In Mid-Sky), from where you can look out onto the twinkling city from the 27th floor. There the accomplished captain, Jacques Ingerhoets, takes charge amid the candles, flowers, and couples in formal dress dancing to live music sung in a dozen tongues. While the atmosphere is festive, the

Chef Michel Theurel (left) with Marc Roger, his produce supplier, at the spotless wholesale market in Brussels

food is altogether serious—in the best gastronomical sense. A menu will speak for itself:

—Tuna and salmon tartare with lime (barely marinated slivers, sea-breeze fresh, with a few pale salmon eggs, fine radish julienne, and snippets of chive);

—A slice of the freshest goose liver set on a mirror of cool gelée made of an infusion of rosebuds in which are suspended mere threads of pink and yellow petals;

—Langoustines, halved, cooked with only a little butter and pink peppercorns, served with slivers of deep-fried chicory and a julienne of courgettes;

—Red mullet fillets, their gaudy skin intact, lightly crumbed and browned, accompanied with a deep-dark purée of purple onions set against a pale fennel foam;

—Fanned slices of duck breast around a shallow flan of pears in a peppery, minted custard, alongside a paper-thin basket of deep-fried celery root cradling baby broad beans and mushrooms;

—Ovals of iced nougat cream and kiwi sorbet set in a pool of vividly bright, sour raspberry *coulis*.

To create such variety you need a devoted group, with a wide range of talents. The 190 in the food staff at this hotel have shown unusual constancy and devotion: Christian Albrecht, head sous-chef (and himself a *maître cuisinier de Belgique*) has spent 20 years in the same kitchen, the technical strength that supports many of the creative efforts. Other sous-chefs, the butcher, and pastry chef, have been part of the team for 10 years; the maîtres d'hotel have been there longer, as have many of the 46 on the kitchen team. Most agree that it is the captain of the team who sets the pace and the standards.

Michel Theurel—*chef des cuisines, maître cuisinier de Belgique,* a strong-minded, vigorous, humorous man—has been at the helm since the hotel's opening in 1967. From the Vegetarian Club Sandwich in the cafe (three layers of fine-grained warm toast, grated carrot and paper-thin apple slices, tomato, cucumber, and slivered chicory, all lightly coated in mayonnaise) to the *soufflé du soir,* from birthday party to embassy banquet, he is the man in charge. He thanks and blames his maternal grandmother for his energy and gregarious nature: 'She kindled the spark that became my career and my pleasure. Although widowed early and living alone, she loved the garden and kitchen dearly. She would cook all day to feed 50 even if there were never that many.' The favourite grandchild of four, he spent days with her watching the progress in the garden, rabbit hutches, and chicken yard. They put up the winter produce together, neatly layering conserves and pickles, *confits* and terrines ('I still wish I knew how she made that incredible rabbit terrine!'). A confident, organized Lyonnais who bounces into the kitchen in sweatpants in a city where it seems appropriate to wear a tie and jacket to bed, this chef champions the camaraderie of the job, loves the challenge of working with other stimulating chefs and the process of choosing and developing new talent. In fact, all the fine hotel kitchens in Brussels are headed by his disciples.

Layered Orange and Chocolate Parfait with Pear Sauce (recipe on next page)

LAYERED ORANGE AND CHOCOLATE PARFAIT WITH PEAR SAUCE

BELGIUM

At the Hilton International Brussels, this dessert is frozen in small timbales, then un-moulded onto the pear sauce, which is scattered with white and milk chocolate shavings and bright, sour airelles (like tiny cranberries). The creamy dessert, which fluffs as it softens, is the result of the combined efforts of Michel Theurel, executive chef, and Jacky Chartier, the sous-chef who runs En Plein Ciel, the more formal of the hotel's restaurants. Although a labour-intensive dish, the result is elegant, unusual, and serves a goodly number of guests.

Orange parfait mixture
2 medium juicy oranges
175 g (6 oz) sugar
2 eggs, at room temperature and separated
A drop of lemon juice
Pinch of salt
225 ml (8 fl oz) double (or whipping) cream

Chocolate parfait mixture
75 g (3 oz) bittersweet chocolate, broken into small bits
3 eggs, at room temperature and separated thoroughly (no white should remain in the yolks)

60 g (2⅓ oz) sugar
Pinch of salt
225 ml (8 fl oz) double (or whipping) cream

Sauce
3 tablespoons honey
1–2 tablespoons lemon juice
3 medium-large very ripe pears (about 700 g/1½ lb)
¼ vanilla bean pod, halved length-wise
Orange zest for garnish

1. Prepare the orange parfait mixture: Remove the orange zest with a peeler, avoiding all the bitter white pith beneath. Combine the zest in a food processor with 90 g (3½ oz) of the sugar; process the rind into small particles. Scrape into a very small, heavy pan. Squeeze the juice from the oranges to make 100 ml (4 fl oz). Add to the orange sugar; bring to a boil, stirring. Lower the heat; simmer until the syrup reduces to a syrupy texture—slightly less than 100 ml (4 fl oz)—about 10 minutes. Strain.

2. Beat the egg yolks in a small bowl with an electric mixer; gradually add the hot syrup, beating until the eggs form a thick, slowly dissolving ribbon when the beater is lifted—about 5 minutes.

3. Combine the egg whites, lemon juice, salt, and the remaining sugar. Beat until soft peaks form; when you dip a finger in the meringue and hold it up, the mixture should form a soft hook, not a firm peak. Beat the cream until softly mounded, not stiff. Transfer the egg yolk mixture to a larger bowl; stir in one-third of the meringue mixture to blend well. Delicately fold in the remainder. Gently fold in the cream. Cover and refrigerate.

4. Prepare the chocolate mixture: Melt the chocolate over hot, but not simmering, water; it should be about blood heat. Remove from the heat; stir in the yolks, one at a time. Beat the egg whites, sugar, and salt to form firm but not stiff peaks. Whip the cream to form soft peaks; blend into the whites. Scrape the chocolate into a mixing bowl. Scoop a quarter of the cream-egg white mixture into the chocolate; blend well. Add the remainder and fold in gently.

5. Line a pan (see Options) with clingfilm. Spoon in half the chocolate mixture, smoothing lightly. Top with half the orange; gently distribute the remaining chocolate over this, then the rest of the orange. Fold over the clingfilm; freeze for at least 6 hours.

6. Meanwhile, make the pear sauce: Combine the honey, 150 ml (¼ pint) water, and 1 tablespoon lemon juice in a non-aluminium saucepan. Bring to a boil. Meanwhile, peel, quarter, and core the pears, placing them directly in the syrup. Cover and simmer for 10–15 minutes, until soft. Purée in a blender or processor. Scrape in the vanilla seeds to taste. Cover and chill.

7. To serve: Slip the loaf from the pan and unwrap the plastic. Gently cut slices, rinsing the knife with warm water between each cut. Place on chilled dessert plates. Spoon 2–3 tablespoons sauce alongside each serving (if the sauce has thickened, add a little water or pear liqueur). Sprinkle with the orange zest.

Options: *You can mould the dessert in any fairly smooth form of about 1.5 litre (2½ pint) capacity: a long narrow terrine, a* rehrücken *mould, triangular ice cream mould, or simple loaf tin.*

ABOUT 12 SERVINGS

FROZEN POPPY SEED AND CINNAMON PARFAIT WITH RUM DATES
AUSTRIA

*A traditional European ingredient—poppy seeds—distinguishes this creamily soft con-
fection, from the Hilton International Wien. The tiny, black, oily seeds are most commonly
used as a topping for loaves and rolls. Here, they present a visual and textural contrast*

to the cinnamon-scented parfait mixture. Oozingly rich, the sweetness intensified by the dates in rum, this is a dessert to be savoured in small portions.

25 g (1 oz) poppy seeds (see Note)	4 egg yolks
100 ml (4 fl oz) milk	2 whole eggs
3 cinnamon sticks, broken into small splinters	115 g (4½ oz) sugar
100 ml (4 fl oz) double (or whipping) cream	12 pitted dates (about 350 g/¾ lb; see Note)
	175 ml (6 fl oz) dark rum

1. Gently simmer the poppy seeds and milk in a small pan until almost all of the milk has evaporated. Stir often as the mixture thickens.

2. Meanwhile, combine the cinnamon in a tiny pan with cream. Cook over *lowest* heat (or all the liquid will cook off), tightly covered, for 5 minutes. Let steep, covered, off the heat.

3. Combine the egg yolks, whole eggs and sugar in a heatproof bowl. Whisk to blend. Set over a pan of simmering water and whisk constantly until meringue-like, thick and shiny; when the whisk is lifted, the egg mixture should leave slowly dissolving ribbons on the surface. Remove from the heat, set in a pan of iced water, and whisk until cooled.

4. Whip the remaining cream to form firm peaks; add it gently to the eggs, folding with a spatula. Scoop the poppy seeds into a mixing bowl; stir in a few spoons of the egg-cream to lighten the texture, then fold in a little less than half of the remaining mixture. Strain the cinnamon cream into the unflavoured egg-cream mixture, scraping off as much as you can from the shards of cinnamon; fold to mix well.

5. Scoop about 100 ml (4 fl oz) of the poppy seed mixture into each of six 225–350 ml (8–12 fl oz) ramekins, bowls, or other fairly straight-sided, smooth moulds. Top with the cinnamon mixture, dividing evenly. Cover with clingfilm and freeze for at least 6 hours.

6. Meanwhile, halve the dates lengthwise. Combine with the rum in a saucepan. Bring to a simmer over low heat. Scoop into a bowl, cover, and let stand until serving time (there is no need to refrigerate).

7. To serve, dip the base of each mould into hot water for 15 seconds; run a knife around the edge, then turn out onto icy-cold plates. Garnish each with 4 of the date halves. Serve immediately.

Note: *Poppy seeds have a very high oil content and become rancid quickly. Taste before you use them, to be sure they are not musty.*

Although dates were the chef's choice, we found prunes to be an effective, somewhat less sugary complement.

6 SERVINGS

HONEY-GINGER ICE CREAM WITH PAPAYA AND MANGO

AUSTRIA

Eduard Mitsche, executive chef at the Hilton International Wien, serves this honeyed dessert with sunset-pink papaya slices. If papayas are less than fragrant, substitute mangos, nectarines, or peaches. But do find a special fruit, for the smooth, intense frozen cream needs the contrast, both for taste and visual effect.

100 ml (4 fl oz) dry white wine	450 ml (¾ pint) milk
250 g (9 oz) light fragrant honey	4 egg yolks, whisked to just blend
40 g (1½ oz) grated fresh root ginger	1 ripe papaya (about 350 g/¾ lb)
	1 medium mango

1. Combine the white wine, two-thirds of the honey, and the ginger in a small non-aluminium saucepan. Boil to reduce to 150 ml (¼ pint). Strain and reserve.

2. In the top of a double boiler, heat the milk. Measure out 225 ml (8 fl oz) and whisk slowly into the egg yolks; add this mixture to the remaining milk.

3. Set the pan over simmering water. Stir for about 5 minutes, until the mixture coats the back of a metal spoon, leaving a path when you draw your finger down it. Remove from the heat at once, strain into a bowl set in iced water.

4. Cool the custard, stirring often. Add the strained honey-ginger mixture and the remaining honey.

5. Pour into the container of an ice cream maker. Freeze according to the manufacturer's instructions. Pack into a freezerproof container; place in the freezer for at least 12 hours.

6. Halve, seed, and peel the papaya. Cut into thin diagonal slices. Do the same to the mango. Arrange on 6 plates. Place a ball of the ice cream on each.

Note: *As the ice cream is particularly concentrated and sweet, this small quantity is sufficient to serve 6 in combination with the fruit. However, if you prefer to make a large amount, the recipe can be doubled, then stored for a week.*

6 SERVINGS (SEE NOTE)

ICE CREAM WITH MELON AND JASMINE TEA SABAYON

GERMANY

Another unusual concept from flamboyant Pierre Pfister of the Hilton International Mainz: a strong infusion of jasmine tea tints and flavours the warm, barely sweet sabayon sauce that clings to the ice cream and floats over the summery melon balls.

450 ml (¾ pint) vanilla ice cream	3 tablespoons jasmine tea leaves
1 very small ripe honeydew or large Galia melon (about 1 kilo/2 lb)	1 whole egg
	1 egg yolk
60 ml (2½ fl oz) boiling water	2 tablespoons sugar

1. Using a large scoop, form the ice cream into 4 neat balls; place on 4 dessert plates. Set in the freezer.

2. Halve and seed the melon. With a 3.5 cm (1½ inch) melon ball cutter, scoop out about forty rounds. Set these in the refrigerator.

3. Pour the boiling water over the tea leaves and infuse for 4 minutes; strain, pressing lightly.

4. Just before you are ready to serve the dessert, distribute the melon balls equally around the ice cream. Return to the freezer.

5. Combine the whole egg, egg yolk and sugar in the top of a double boiler or in a bowl set over a pot of simmering water. With an electric mixer, beat in the tea gradually. Continue beating until very pale, fluffy and creamy, and quite warm—3–4 minutes.

6. Remove from the heat, beating. Spoon the sauce over the ice cream, and serve at once.

Advance preparation: *Steps 1–3 can be done ahead.*

4 SERVINGS

CHAMPAGNE SORBET WITH CAMPARI

SWITZERLAND

The popular French Kir royale *(a rosy quaff of Champagne and blackcurrant* Cassis *liqueur) has an Italian cousin of sparkling wine flavoured and coloured with the vividly red, bitter* aperitivo, *Campari. Chef Franz Kuhne of the Hilton International Basel adapted it to sorbet form, lightening the Campari to a mere hint that barely modifies the flavour of the bubbly base and transforms the colour to an innocent blush.*

200 g (7 oz) sugar
6 g (¼ oz) powdered gelatine
400 ml (14 fl oz) boiling water
600 ml (1 pint) Champagne or other
   sparkling dry white wine

3 tablespoons Campari
2–3 tablespoons lemon juice

1. Combine the sugar and gelatine in a bowl; add the boiling water and stir to dissolve. Set in a container of iced water.

2. Add the Champagne, Campari, and lemon juice to taste. Cool the mixture, stirring now and then. Pour into a metal pan.

3. Set in the coldest part of the freezer until frozen almost solid, but still mushy in the centre.

4. Scoop into a bowl and whisk with an electric mixer until rather fluffy, but not liquefied. Immediately return to the metal pan and freeze almost solid, about 2 hours (although timing varies).

5. Beat the sorbet until soft and homogenized in texture. Scoop into a storage container, cover tightly, and freeze until firm, for at least 4 hours or up to 3 days.

Note: *If you have an ice cream maker that contains its own freezing unit, this ice can be made quickly and will have a finer, silkier texture, closer to the snowy sorbet served by Chef Kuhne.*

ABOUT 1½ QUARTS

ENGADINE NUT CAKE

SWITZERLAND

The tuorta de nusch Engiadinaisa, *made of shortbread dough packed with caramelized nuts, is a confection for serious sweet lovers. Each slice is more like a toffee bar wrapped in biscuit crust than a cake.*

Crust
250 g (9 oz) butter (room temperature)
150 g (5 oz) sugar
¼ teaspoon salt
1 egg
350 g (12 oz) plain flour
Filling
250 g (9 oz) sugar

400 ml (14 fl oz) double (or whipping) cream
85 g (3½ oz) honey
400 g (14 oz) walnuts, coarsely chopped
1 egg, beaten lightly with 1 tablespoon water for egg wash

1. Prepare the crust: Combine the butter, sugar and salt in the small bowl of an electric beater. Beat until very light and creamy. Add the egg. On lowest speed, add the flour, mixing until barely incorporated. Divide the dough into 2 balls, making one slightly larger than the other. Wrap and chill for at least 1 hour.

2. For the filling: Combine the sugar and 60 ml (2½ fl oz) hot water in a heavy-based medium saucepan and let stand for a few minutes to moisten evenly. Cook over medium-low heat until the sugar dissolves completely; cover and cook over low heat for 1 minute to be sure all the crystals have washed down the sides. Raise the heat and swirl the uncovered pan until the syrup turns medium-deep amber.

3. Remove from the heat and stir in the cream, keeping clear of the considerable splatters (don't worry when the caramel lumps: it will smooth out). Return to the heat and bring the mixture to a boil, stirring. Add the honey and walnuts. Let cool.

4. Soften the pastry for about 15 minutes at room temperature. Preheat the oven to 190°C/375°F (gas mark 5). Roll out the larger round on a lightly floured board to form a 33 cm (13-inch) circle. Ease into a 23 cm (9-inch) springform pan. If the pastry breaks, patch as necessary. Press it up the sides to make a wall about 5 cm (2-inches) high; even it by pressing downward to form a slight lip.

5. Pour in the filling. Roll out the remaining dough to form a 25 cm (10-inch) circle. From this cut a 23 cm (9-inch) circle. Paint the rim of the lower pastry with the egg wash; lay the top crust on this (it will be easy if you have another 23 cm (9-inch) tart or cake pan bottom to use as a spatula). Press lightly. Paint the crust generously with egg wash. Seal the edge with a fork, then mark a pattern on the surface.

6. Bake in the centre of the oven for 30 minutes, until nicely browned. Set on a rack to cool for at least 30 minutes. Slowly slip a knife around the edge of the pan, then remove the side. Without covering the pie, let stand overnight before serving.

10 SERVINGS

FLAMBÉED BLACKBERRIES WITH PERNOD AND ICE CREAM

SWITZERLAND

Deft tableside preparation of spectacular desserts is one of the pleasures of the Hilton International in Geneva, from where this recipe comes. If you have a chafing dish, the effect and efficiency are well worth the effort of assembling the ingredients and performing for your guests, for the luscious dessert truly takes minutes to prepare. It is important to shake the pan throughout the brief cooking, but do not be tempted to stir the mixture, which will become runny.

The warm berries swell and create a dramatically garnet sauce that is lightly syrupy and coats the ice cream (here set in a tulipe cup). The fruit flavour dominates, while the tart-sweet sauce adds its liquorish punch.

---

450 g (1 lb) blackberries	**1 teaspoon lemon juice**
450 ml (¾ pint) vanilla ice cream	**5 tablespoons Pernod**
45 g (1¾ oz) sugar	**3 tablespoons dry red wine**
15 g (½ oz) butter	**3 tablespoons Cointreau**
1 tablespoon orange juice	

---

1. Pour the berries into a bowl of water; gently scoop out and spread on a clean, absorbent tea towel; pick up the corners of the towel to roll the berries gently until dry. Scoop 4 large balls of vanilla ice cream and place on a sheet of greaseproof paper in the freezer.

2. Measure and set out all the remaining ingredients.

3. Sprinkle the sugar evenly in a 25 cm (10 inch) frying pan. Over moderate heat tip the pan as the sugar melts to dissolve it fairly evenly. When the sugar has melted, lower the heat and tip for a minute or two until the syrup turns amber. Add the butter and stir to blend.

4. Add the blackberries and gently shake the pan (do not stir the berries) until some juice seeps out, about 30 seconds. Add the orange and lemon juices and shake the pan.

5. Pour in the Pernod, then ignite. Shake the pan gently until the flame is extinguished. Add the red wine and Cointreau and return to a simmer. Remove from the heat.

6. Immediately divide the berries and juices onto 4 large dessert plates. Place a scoop of ice cream on top of each. Serve at once.

4 SERVINGS

GÂTEAU DEVIDAL
(Chocolate Mousse Cake)
SWITZERLAND

Looking over beautiful Lake Geneva from a dining room panelled in mirror-finish Brazilian rosewood, there is little question about being in one of the most comfortable laps that luxury can provide. When the dessert course arrives at Le Cygne restaurant in the Hilton International Genève, six trolleys (silver-serviced, flower-bedecked) bear the burden of sweets offered as an end to a memorable meal. The sleek chocolate confection that is a favourite of the pastry chef, Régis Devidal, seems almost austere among the cascade of choices. No buttery embellishments, no triumvirate of sauces: just fine chocolate lightened with cream and egg to a mousse consistency, melded to rum-moistened chocolate génoise. Simple and very special.

Génoise

3 whole eggs
85 g (3½ oz) sugar
60 g (2½ oz) plain flour
15 g (½ oz) unsweetened cocoa
  powder
1 tablespoon melted butter, lukewarm

Rum Syrup

2 tablespoons sugar
50 ml (2 fl oz) dark rum

Chocolate Cream

250 g (9 oz) bittersweet chocolate
  (with cocoa butter content of 50
  per cent or more; check the label)
450 ml (¾ pint) double (or whipping) cream
2 egg yolks

Final Assembly

40 g (1½ oz) bittersweet chocolate
About 2 tablespoons unsweetened
  cocoa powder

---

1. Prepare the génoise: Preheat the oven to 180°C/350°F (gas mark 4). Grease a 23 cm (9-inch) springform cake pan. Line the bottom with parchment or greaseproof paper. Grease this, then flour the pan well.

2. Place the whole eggs and sugar in a mixing bowl; set over simmering water, whisking until the sugar dissolves and the mixture is barely lukewarm. Remove from the heat and, using an electric whisk, beat on high speed until tripled in volume, about 4 minutes.

3. Sift together the flour and cocoa powder. Gradually add to the eggs, beating on lowest speed until not quite incorporated. Add the melted butter and beat for another moment, until barely mixed in.

4. Pour at once into the prepared pan; smooth the top with a rubber spatula. Tap the pan gently on the worktop to release air bubbles.

5. Bake in the lower third of the oven until the cake begins to pull away from the sides and the centre feels moistly spongy, not liquid, when pressed (do not open the oven before almost baked), 25–30 minutes.

6. Place on a rack to cool for 5–10 minutes. Run a thin knife around the pan to release

(continued)

One of the dessert trolleys at Le Cygne in Geneva, with the signature Gateau Devidal in the foreground the cake, then remove the side of the pan. Invert on the rack, remove the base of the tin, then the paper. Cool completely.

7. Prepare the rum syrup: Combine the sugar and 2 tablespoons water in a tiny pan; bring to a boil, swirling. Off heat, stir in the rum. Cut the cake into 2 equal layers with a long serrated knife (wrap and freeze one layer for future cake-making). Set one layer, cut side up, back in the springform pan on a round of greaseproof paper. Brush evenly with the rum syrup.

8. Make the chocolate cream: Break up the chocolate in small pieces and set in a bowl over hot, but not simmering, water. When barely melted (the chocolate should be only about blood heat) remove from the heat. Whip 400 ml (14 fl oz) cream until thickened and fluffy, but not firm enough to mound; it should be slightly liquid. Blend together the remaining cream and the egg yolks; pour this into the chocolate all at once, then stir lightly but rapidly with a rubber spatula to blend. Pour the whipped cream over this and blend in gently. Scoop the chocolate cream onto the cake; smooth with a spatula. Chill for at least 4 hours (see Advance Preparation).

9. Final assembly: Run a knife around the rim of the pan, then carefully remove the side. Grate the chocolate on the medium holes of a standing grater. Press this gently onto the side of the cake to coat evenly. Sift the cocoa over the top.

Advance preparation: *The génoise base can be made a day ahead of assembling and refrigerated (or weeks ahead and frozen). The cake can be finished through Step 8 up to 48 hours in advance.*

8 SERVINGS

Thurgau Apple Cake

SWITZERLAND

The canton of Thurgau, in north-east Switzerland, is notable for its apples, which appear in cider and a wide range of cakes and tarts. Among the more casual and simple of the baked goods, this light, lemony, slightly sweet cake is easy to make and pretty: a snowfall of sugar dusts overlapping crescents of apple inlaid in a puffed golden batter that rises between the slices.

85 g (3½ oz) butter,
  at room temperature
163 g (5½ oz) granulated sugar
4 eggs, separated
Pinch of salt
1 teaspoon grated lemon zest
2 tablespoons lemon juice

150 g (5 oz) plain flour
1 teaspoon baking powder
3 medium-large apples, preferably
  Golden Delicious
Icing sugar
Whipped cream (optional)

Thurgau Apple Cake (sugar-dusted) and caramel-rich Engadine Nut Pie (see page 199 for recipe)

1. Preheat the oven to 190°C/375°F (gas mark 5). Butter a 25 cm (10-inch) springform pan. In the small bowl of an electric mixer, beat the butter with 45 g (1½ oz) granulated sugar until light. Beat in the egg yolks, one at a time; add the salt, lemon zest, and lemon juice (do not worry if the mixture curdles).

2. Beat the egg whites until soft peaks form; gradually beat in 100 g (3½ oz) granulated sugar, whipping until firm. Blend one-third of the whites thoroughly with the butter-yolk mixture; gradually incorporate the remainder with a rubber spatula.

3. Sift the flour and baking powder into the mixture, folding gently. Scoop into the prepared springform pan.

4. Peel, halve, and core the apples. Cut into thin crosswise slices. Arrange them overlapping closely to cover the cake, pressing lightly into the batter. Sprinkle with the remaining granulated sugar.

5. Bake in the centre of the oven for about 45 minutes, or until a cocktail stick or skewer poked into the centre comes out clean. Cool briefly on a rack, then unmould.

6. Serve the cake warm, lightly sprinkled with icing sugar. Offer whipped cream alongside, if you like.

Serving: *Do not reheat the cake or prepare far in advance, as it will dry out, as do most baking powder cakes. Enjoy it warm and soft as breakfast, brunch, or teacake, with or without cream, or with a glass of apple brandy or sherry alongside.*
Option: *This simple cake can withstand plenty of variation: Play with the design of apple slices so that the batter squeezes up between them. Experiment with other fruit—such as peeled peaches, apricots, cherries, or tender pears.*

8 SERVINGS

BAKED APPLE CUSTARD WITH CARAMEL PEPPER SAUCE
GERMANY

Every autumn the Hilton International München holds a game festival to celebrate the bounty of its forests—with hare, chamois, red deer, elk, and more. Among the desserts suggested as finales for these specials are rose cream, chestnut mousse, blueberry pancakes, and this tender egg custard topped with a fan of hot apples and doused with a chilled, peppery caramel sauce—a unique complement to the creamy-fruity flan.

Sauce

60 g (2½ oz) sugar
100 ml (4 fl oz) double (or whipping) cream
1 teaspoon freshly ground black pepper
2 tablespoons Calvados or other apple brandy

Apple Custard

4 large Golden Delicious apples
3 eggs
225 ml (8 fl oz) milk
100 ml (4 fl oz) double (or whipping) cream
1 teaspoon vanilla extract
2 tablespoons plus 2 teaspoons sugar
½ teaspoon ground cinnamon

1. Prepare the sauce: Combine the sugar and 3 tablespoons hot water in a small heavy-based pan: let stand a few minutes to moisten evenly. Cook over low heat until the sugar dissolves completely; cover and cook over low heat for 1 minute to be sure all crystals have washed down the sides. Raise the heat and swirl the pan until the syrup turns medium amber. Remove from the heat and drizzle in 3 tablespoons hot water, keeping clear of considerable splatters. Return to the heat and stir a moment until the caramel has completely dissolved. Add the cream and pepper and simmer for 2 minutes. Cool to lukewarm. Strain through a sieve; add the Calvados. Chill (see Note).

2. Make the custard: Preheat the oven to 150°C/300°F (gas mark 2). With a corer, remove the core and seeds from the apples; then peel and halve them lengthwise. Cut crosswise into thin slices. Arrange 1 apple in an overlapping flower pattern in a shallow gratin or baking dish about 15 cm (6-inches) in diameter. Repeat to fill 3 more dishes.

3. Blend together the eggs, milk, cream, vanilla, and 2 tablespoons sugar. Spoon gently over the apples, distributing evenly. Mix the remaining 2 teaspoons sugar with the cinnamon. Sprinkle evenly over the apples, coating lightly.

4. Arrange the dishes in a roasting pan. Set in the centre of the oven and pour in boiling water to reach halfway up the sides of the moulds. Bake until the custard has just set in the centre, 30–35 minutes.

5. Serve warm with the sauce alongside.

Note: *If the sauce is chilled, the pepper flavour becomes pleasantly pronounced; however, if served at room temperature, it helps retain the appealing warmth of the custard.*

4 SERVINGS

DIALOGUE OF FRUIT PURÉES

AUSTRIA

A lengthy, elegant meal at the Rôtisserie Prinz Eugen in Vienna is served with the kind of exquisite attention one would expect from a host of footmen at a royal home—which is what this spacious, darkly handsome trio of rooms is modelled on.

Surprisingly, the free-form 'painting' of this stunning, unusually tart palate-freshener seems altogether appropriate in the regal library setting. At a more modest meal than Chef Mitsche's you would probably wish to enjoy the mélange as a dessert. However it is offered, it is imperative that the fruit be in peak condition, as it forms the majority of the sweetness and flavour. Consider ripe apricots or mangos as alternatives to the peaches, if they are in finer form.

4 ripe kiwi fruits (about 450 g/1 lb)
4 medium peaches (about 450 g/1 lb)
225 g (8 oz) blackcurrants
About 1 tablespoon blackcurrant or
**   raspberry jam**

450 g (1 lb) strawberries
350 ml (12 fl oz) sour cream
1 tablespoon lemon juice

1. Remove the kiwi skins with a swivel peeler. Slice the fruit and press through the fine disc of a stainless-steel food mill into a bowl.

2. Drop the peaches into boiling water; return to a boil. Drop into cold water, drain, and dry. Remove the skins and pits. Press through the fine disc of the food mill.

3. Press the blackcurrants through the disc with 1 tablespoon jam; taste and add more jam if desired. Press the strawberries through the mill into another bowl.

4. Stir together the sour cream and lemon juice. Thin with about 1 tablespoon water to the texture of double cream.

5. Spoon about one-quarter of each of the purées and the cream gently into wide plates to make 5 wedge-shaped pools that almost touch. Shake the plate slightly so that they run together. With a chopstick or wooden skewer, swirl the purées slightly to give them a somewhat marbled appearance; do not mix.

Note: *This is the kind of dish that will be different every time you make it, depending upon the quality of the fruit. Try for a balance of sweet and sour and contrasting colours. Enjoy the palette of colours and play with the food, dipping, dotting and marbling at whim.*
Advance preparation: *All of the purées can be prepared in advance and refrigerated, covered, in separate bowls.*

4 SERVINGS

PRUNE TERRINE WITH SABAYON CREAM

SWITZERLAND

Although this lacquer-brown loaf of winey prunes and chewy nuts is based on a traditional recipe from an old cookbook ('it has been a Swiss grandmother's dish forever,' says Franz Kuhne, executive chef of the Hilton International Basel), this elegant version, graced by a billowy sauce, is suited to the most contemporary dining room. As fragrant as fruitcake, the dessert seems spicy and very rich, even though it is neither. (In the Wettstein Grill where this is featured, a small scoop of cinnamon ice cream completes the picture.) A unique, satisfying sweet that is easy to prepare.

---

350 ml (12 fl oz) dry red wine
6 g (¼ oz) powdered gelatine
45 g (1¾ oz) sugar
800 g (1¾ lb) pitted presoaked
   prunes
25 g (1 oz) shelled unsalted
   pistachio nuts
50 ml (2 fl oz) Armagnac or brandy
25 g (1 oz) walnuts, chopped

25 g (1 oz) pine nuts (pignolia)
1 navel orange
Sauce
58 g (2¼ oz) sugar
4 egg yolks
50 ml (2 fl oz) dry white wine
50 ml (2 fl oz) Armagnac or brandy
225 ml (8 fl oz) double (or whipping)
   cream

---

1. Combine 50 ml (2 fl oz) water and 50 ml (2 fl oz) of the red wine in a cup; sprinkle the gelatine over this and let stand to soften. Combine the remaining wine with the sugar and prunes in a non-aluminium saucepan; bring to a simmer, stirring. Cover and simmer until tender, about 5 minutes. Add the gelatine mixture and bring to a simmer, stirring gently so as not to break up the fruit. Remove from the heat.

2. Drop the pistachios into a small pan of boiling water; return to a boil. Drain, then rub in a towel to remove the husks. Add to the prunes with the Armagnac, walnuts, and pine nuts. Cut the rind and membrane from the orange. Cut between the interior membranes to section out the pulp; cut into 1 cm (½-inch) pieces. Add to the prunes.

3. Rinse a 23 × 12.5 cm (9 × 5-inch) glass or ceramic loaf dish with cold water. Pour in the prune mixture. Press down firmly so that the solids are covered by the liquid. Cool completely, then cover and refrigerate for at least 4 hours, preferably overnight.

4. Make the sauce: Combine the sugar and 2 tablespoons water in a small pan and bring to a boil, swirling. Whisk the egg yolks in a bowl to blend well. Whisk in the hot syrup gradually. Set the bowl in barely simmering water and whisk (or use a small electric whisk) until hot and thickened to the consistency of soft whipped cream. Remove from the heat and continue whisking until cooled and pale. Whisk in the white wine and Armagnac. Whip the cream to form soft peaks. Pour the egg sauce over it. Fold together gently with a rubber spatula. Serve at once, or chill, covered, for up to 5 hours before serving.

5. To serve, dip the loaf dish into warm water for 15 seconds; slip a knife gently around the side of the loaf to release it. Invert onto a cutting board. Ladle 50 ml (2 fl oz) of sauce onto each dessert plate; tip to distribute neatly. Using a very sharp or serrated knife carefully cut the terrine, placing a slice on each pool of sauce. Serve at once.

Advance preparation: *The terrine can be prepared a day in advance, the sauce up to 5 hours ahead.*

12 SERVINGS

BERRIES PERFUMED WITH KÜMMEL

FRANCE

Here is one example from the hundreds of problems that arise when converting chefs' recipes for home use: The Food Research Center received a recipe from chef Dominique Michou—'Soup of Berries Perfumed with Kümmel'—that called for four kinds of berries, honey, and Kümmel (caraway liqueur). The directions read: 'Heat the Kümmel. Add the honey. Place the fruits in a bowl. Pour the Kümmel onto the berries.' We tried to test it by feel, guessing how many it was meant to serve, whether it should be hot or chilled, whether the Kümmel was sweet or dry, what we should substitute for bilberries, whether the strawberries were small wild ones or large cultivated ones, how to arrange the berries, why it was called 'soup' with only 4 tablespoons liquid specified. In short: Dieter Hannig came up with his own version, given below.

Later, there was the opportunity to taste the 'original' in Strasbourg: Thin slices of fresh figs were pressed against the sides of an enormous balloon glass overflowing with whole strawberries, raspberries, an abundance of passion fruit, and topped with fresh strawberry sorbet, mint leaves, and a julienne of candied orange peel. A soupçon of Kümmel perfumed the accumulated juices. When asked about the recipe we had 'tested', Michou explained that it had been inspired by a dessert from the Crémaillère d'Orléans where he had worked previously, and that of course *dishes were different every time you made them, no? Pinning down specifics with a fine chef may be compared to trapping lightning. It is worth the trip to Strasbourg to sample Michou's 'Soup' of the day.*

225 g (8 oz) raspberries
450 g (1 lb) strawberries, rinsed and hulled
225 g (8 oz) blackberries or blueberries, gently rinsed and tenderly patted dry
350 ml (12 fl oz) Kümmel (see Note)
75 g (3 oz) clear honey

1. In each of 4 shallow soup dishes or deep plates arrange the raspberries in a ring around the outer edge. Quarter or halve the strawberries and place them inside the circle; arrange the blackberries or blueberries in the centre. (Or place the berries in a single layer in any design that suits your taste.)

2. Combine Kümmel and honey in a small pan; bring to a boil. Spoon 50 ml (2 fl oz) of hot liquid over each of the plates of fruit. Cover with clingfilm; chill for 2 hours or more.

Note: *Of the several varieties of dry-to-sweet Kümmel (the word means caraway in German and Dutch), those most frequently available are quite sweet.*
Serving/presentation: *Try this clean, light 'soup' as an appetizer for a multi-course meal.*
Advance preparation *is a must, as some mellowing time must be allowed for the full flavour to develop. An hour is sufficient, about 12 maximum. The longer it stands, the pinker the pale syrup becomes.*

4 SERVINGS

PREVIOUS PAGE: **Executive chef Dominique Michou with a typical** *menu dégustation* **in La Maison du Boeuf in the Hilton International Strasbourg**

ASIA AND AUSTRALIA

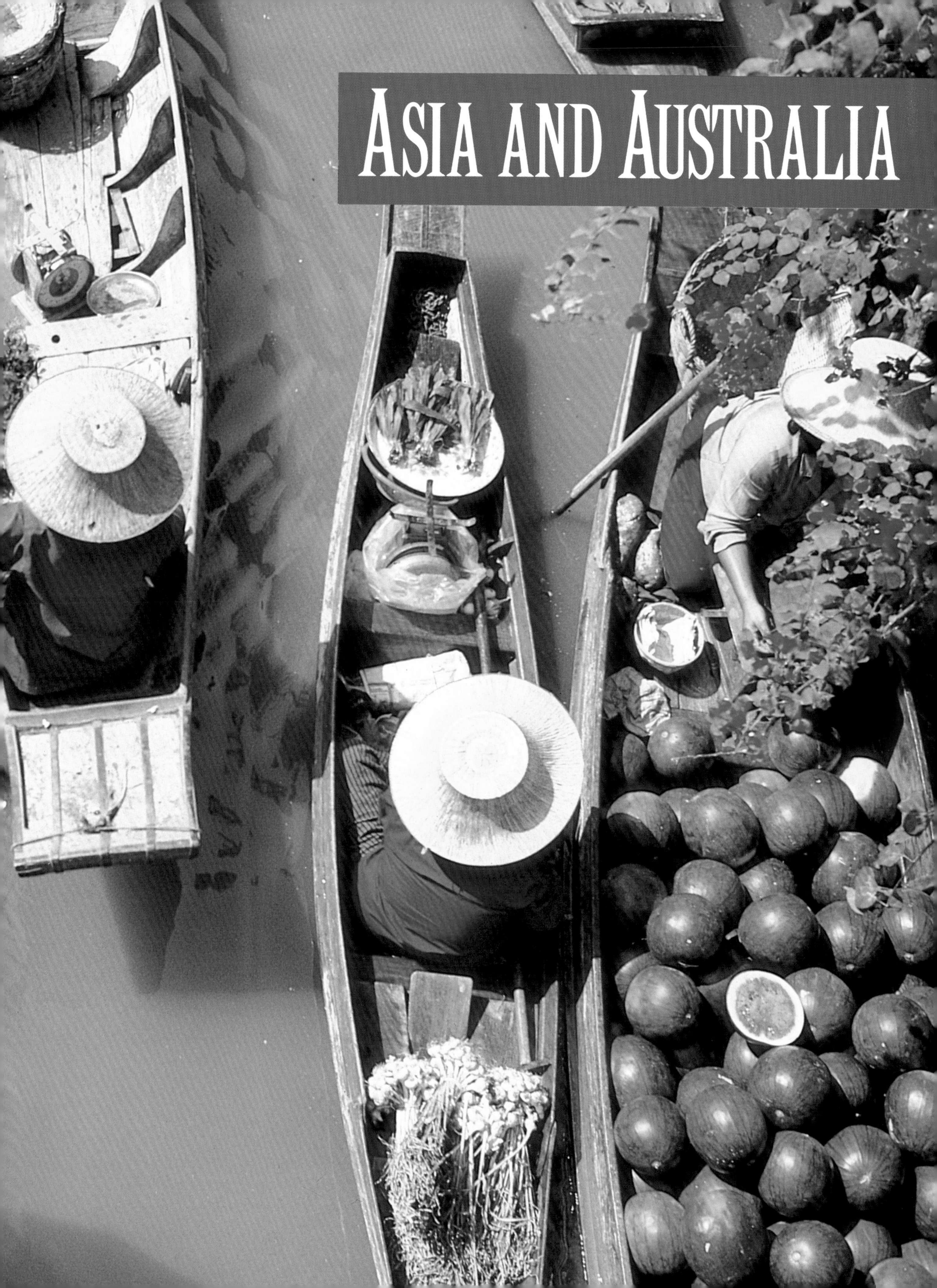

RECIPES

APPETIZERS

Herbed Prawn Terrine in Aspic *(Australia)* 219
Marinated Raw Salmon with Coriander-Green Peppercorn Sauce *(Australia)* 220
Oysters Wrapped in Raw Beef with Horseradish Vinaigrette *(Australia)* 223
Pork, Prawn and Vegetable-Filled Rolled Crêpes *(Philippines)* 224
Terrine of Mixed Fresh Mushrooms *(Japan)* 226
Lobster Dumplings with Sea Urchin Sauce *(Japan)* 229
Spiced Red Snapper with Herbs *en Papillote (United Arab Emirates)* 231

SALADS

Prawn Salad with Cucumbers, Chilli, Garlic, Mint and Lemon Grass *(Thailand)* 232
Hot and Spicy Glass Noodle, Shrimp and Pork Salad *(Thailand)* 236
Salad of Pepper-Seared Beef Fillet *(Japan)* 241

SOUPS

Pigeon Consommé with Quail Eggs *(Singapore)* 246
Oyster Consommé with Seaweed Twists *(Australia)* 250
Chicken Broth with Coriander Dumplings *(Thailand)* 252
Thai Soup of Mixed Oriental Vegetables and Shrimp *(Thailand)* 254
Red Bean Soup with Ginger *(Indonesia)* 256
Clear Prawn Soup with Lemon Grass *(Indonesia)* 258

VEGETABLES, GRAINS AND PASTA

Asparagus with Thai Sauce *(Thailand)* 263
Stuffed Tofu with Prawns *(Taiwan)* 264
Roasted Root Vegetable Strips with Caraway *(Australia)* 265
Aromatic Rice with Nuts, Raisins and Shallots *(Indonesia and Malaysia)* 266
Fried Egg Noodles with Mixed Vegetables *(Indonesia)* 268
Spaghetti Sakura *(Japan)* 270
Spiced Chick-peas with Fresh White Cheese *(India)* 271

PREVIOUS PAGE: **The floating market at Damnoen Saduak, outside of Bangkok**

SEAFOOD

Prawns in Coconut-Chilli Sauce *(Indonesia)* 277
Prawns in Papaya Sauce *(Singapore)* 278
Fillet of Sole with Sour Turmeric Sauce *(Indonesia)* 280
Pomfret with Ginger Fragrance *(Singapore)* 283
Fancy-Cut Squid Stir-Fried with Asparagus *(Taiwan)* 284
Salmon Fillets with Vinegar Sauce on Diced Vegetables *(Singapore)* 286

MEAT AND POULTRY

Beef Steaks with Mustard Cream *(Japan)* 292
Buffalo Fillets with Pumpkin Sauce and Goat Cheese *(Australia)* 295
Smoked Duck Breast Salad, Javanese-Style *(Indonesia)* 297
Pork Loin with Quince *(Australia)* 298
Stir-Fried Pork and Cashew Nuts *(Thailand)* 300
Hainanese Chicken-Rice Dinner *(Singapore, China and Taiwan)* 302
Chicken Terrine with Coconut-Chilli Sauce *(Indonesia)* 304
Chicken Stir-Fried with Tree Ears and Ginger Julienne *(Thailand)* 307
Chicken and Cashews with Chinese Mustard Greens *(Taiwan)* 310
Braised and Grilled Chicken in Coconut and Javanese Spices *(Indonesia)* 312

DESSERTS

Cucumber-Ginger Granita *(Indonesia)* 314
Strawberry and Yogurt Mousse with Grand Marnier Sauce *(Singapore)* 315
Guava Fritters and Mango with Blueberry Tofu Cream *(Taiwan)* 316
Dried Fruit Bread *(Australia)* 321
Dampers *(Australia)* 323

HERBED PRAWN TERRINE IN ASPIC
(Adaptation of Potted Moreton Bay Bugs)
AUSTRALIA

Of the many colourfully-named crustaceans that inhabit the waters in and around Australia, Moreton Bay bugs, a species of small, flat marine lobster, are among the sweetest and meatiest. They are served in an appetizer terrine at the darkly handsome Victoria's, a sleek restaurant done up in silken dusky plum, the luxury dining room of the shining new Hilton International Brisbane. The terrine is thickly studded with the tender lobster meat, dotted with yellow and white chopped egg, coriander leaves, red pepper, chive snippets, and sharpened with green peppercorns. The dressing, similar in colour and texture to the terrine, is mellowed with creamed Caboolture cheese, a cottage cheese made in an area north of Brisbane that is renowned for its dairy products. Serve one of the many fine Australian Chardonnays to complement the fresh-flavoured dish.

1.35 litres (2¼ pints) fish stock (see recipe, page 326)
3 eggs
2 small red peppers (about 200 g/7 oz)
Salt
550 g (1¼ lb) raw medium prawns in the shell (see Note)
5 teaspoons powdered gelatine
60 ml (2½ fl oz) dry vermouth
20 g (¾ oz) coriander leaves (no stems)

1 tablespoon drained green peppercorns, coarse-chopped
3 tablespoons finely snipped chives
Dressing
450 g (1 lb) firm, sweet-ripe tomatoes, peeled, seeded, and cut into tiny dice
15 g (½ oz) finely snipped chives
50 ml (2 fl oz) cider vinegar
Salt and pepper
150 ml (6 fl oz) olive oil
40–50 g (1½–2 oz) small-curd creamed cottage cheese

---

1. Gently pour the stock through a sieve lined with several layers of dampened fine muslin, being careful to avoid any sediment that may have accumulated. Simmer the stock, skimming as necessary, until reduced to 750 ml (22 fl oz).

2. Meanwhile, place the eggs in a pan of boiling water. Simmer for 12 minutes. Place under cold running water, tap the shells to crack them all over; leave to cool completely.

3. Boil the red peppers for 2 minutes, turning occasionally. Halve, seed, and cut into tiny dice; spread on paper towels. Peel and halve the eggs; chill briefly.

4. Bring 1 litre (1¾ pints) water and 1 tablespoon salt to a boil; add the prawns. Cover and bring to a simmer over highest heat. Remove from the stove; drain. Remove the shells, halve each prawn lengthwise, then remove the veins as needed. Cut each half into 2–3 pieces. Chill.

(continued)

5. Sprinkle the gelatine over 100 ml (4 fl oz) water; let stand 2–3 minutes. Combine with the hot stock over moderate heat. Stir to dissolve completely, scraping the bottom. Stir in the vermouth. Add salt, as desired. Pour 100 ml (4 fl oz) of the aspic into a narrow terrine mould about 28 × 9 × 9 cm (11 x 3½ x 3½ inches). Chill briefly until set, but not hard. Chill the remaining aspic until cold, but not set.

6. Meanwhile, cut the coriander leaves into coarse slivers. Mince the egg and yolks separately, then combine in a bowl with the red peppers, coriander, green peppercorns, and chives. Gently toss to mix.

7. Spread half the egg mixture on the aspic layer, then press down firmly with a spatula. Arrange half the prawns on this, then the remaining egg mixture, then prawns, leaving a small margin of uncovered aspic all around. Slowly pour the remaining liquid aspic into the terrine. Chill for at least 12 hours.

8. Make the sauce: Combine the tomatoes, chives, and cider vinegar. Add salt and pepper to taste. Stir in the olive oil; chill.

9. To unmould, dip the base of the mould in hot water, then run a knife gently around the edge to release the loaf. Invert onto a cutting board, rapping sharply. Immediately return to the refrigerator for a few minutes to firm any melting exterior aspic.

10. Add the cottage cheese to the tomato dressing, adjusting the quantity to taste. With a serrated knife, gently cut the prawn loaf into 1-inch slices. Serve the sauce alongside.

Note: *If you have access to cooked, picked crayfish, it is a superior substitute for Moreton Bay bugs. Fourteen to fifteen ounces of cleaned meat should be used. Or you can substitute, rock lobster tails, or a combination of shellfish, all cut in smallish pieces.*

8–10 SERVINGS

MARINATED RAW SALMON WITH CORIANDER-GREEN PEPPERCORN SAUCE

AUSTRALIA

Adapted from the silky appetizer developed by Gerard Taye, executive chef of the Hilton International Adelaide, this sumptuous course requires waiting time for its preparation, but little labour. The tangy, pleasantly biting sauce is laced with coriander leaves and green peppercorns, and bound with tomato, mustard, and grapeseed oil. If this pale, delicate oil is not easily found, substitute another mild, light oil, such as sunflower seed.

1 kilo (2-lb) salmon fillet (with skin)
75 g (3 oz) coarse sea salt
1 teaspoon coarse-ground black
  pepper
75 g (3 oz) thin-sliced shallots
Leaves from 1 medium bunch fresh
  coriander
100 ml (4 fl oz) dry, light white wine

Sauce
1 tomato (150–175 g/5–6 oz),
  peeled, seeded, and chunked

1 tablespoon drained green peppercorns
15 g (½ oz) coriander leaves (no
  stems)
1 tablespoon Dijon mustard
150 ml (6 fl oz) grapeseed oil
Lemon juice
Coriander sprigs

1. With tweezers or fine pliers, pull out any small bones that may remain in the salmon fillet. Trim off any fatty or membranous areas. Place the fish skin side down in a heavy plastic bag. Rub with the salt to coat evenly. Close the bag; refrigerate for 12–24 hours, turning once.

2. Rinse the fish well. Pat dry. Coat with the pepper. Spread half the shallots and half the coriander in a dish just large enough to hold the fish. Place the salmon on top, skin side up. Cover with the remaining shallots and coriander. Pour over the wine; cover closely with clingfilm.

3. Refrigerate for 2 days, turning occasionally.

4. Remove from the marinade and scrape clean. Wrap tightly in clingfilm and refrigerate until serving time.

5. Prepare the sauce: Combine the tomato, green peppercorns, coriander leaves, and mustard in the container of a blender or processor. Whirl to form a smooth purée, scraping down the sides. With the motor running, gradually add the oil; process until as smooth as possible. Add lemon juice to taste. Chill until serving time.

6. Cut the salmon on the bias into thin slices. Either lay flat, or coil to form rose shapes, as they do at the restaurant. Ladle a pool of sauce alongside. Garnish with coriander sprigs.

8–10 SERVINGS

OYSTERS WRAPPED IN RAW BEEF WITH HORSERADISH VINAIGRETTE

AUSTRALIA

This trendy recipe comes from chef Herbert Franceschini of the Hilton International Brisbane, who devised the hors d'oeuvre with one of the local specialities, rock oysters. These are so small that one can be wrapped in beef, set on a lettuce nest, crowned with marinated pear slivers—and still fit into a teaspoon, which is the way the appetizer is presented in Australia, five per serving. Where oysters are larger, we suggest placing the rosy beef packages on pale leaves of soft lettuce set into oyster shells.

The lush oysters and soft meat topped with the crisp pear and crunchy sesame create an effect that is mainly textural, with a flavour far less complicated than the list of ingredients indicates.

150–175 g (5–6 oz) fillet of beef
3–4 tablespoons fresh-grated horse-radish (or prepared horseradish in vinegar, squeezed dry, to equal that amount)
1 tablespoon finely chopped shallot
2 teaspoons Dijon mustard
2 tablespoons raspberry red wine vinegar (or simple red wine vinegar)
1 tablespoon dry white wine or vermouth
½ teaspoon pepper

¼ teaspoon finely chopped garlic
150 ml (¼ pint) light olive oil
Salt
20 medium oysters on the half-shell
1 or 2 heads soft lettuce (20 leaves)
2 medium firm-ripe pears; cored, peeled, and cut into finest julienne about 4 cm (1½-inches) long
2 tablespoons hulled white sesame seeds
20 coriander sprigs

---

1. Set the beef fillet in the freezer until not quite frozen solid (timing will depend on your freezer). Meanwhile, prepare the dressing: Combine 2 tablespoons of the horse-radish, the shallot, mustard, vinegar, wine, pepper and garlic in a small bowl; whisk to blend. Gradually whisk in the oil. Add salt to taste. Set aside.

2. Remove the oysters from their shells and set them aside in a strainer. Rinse the shells; set 4 on each of 5 serving plates and place a lettuce leaf, trimmed to fit if necessary, in each shell. Toss the pears with a scant 50 ml (2 fl oz) dressing and set aside. Stir the sesame for a few minutes in a frying pan over low heat, until golden.

(continued)

3. Let the frozen beef stand for a few minutes, then cut into 20 thin slices (see Note). Place between layers of clingfilm and flatten with the side of a cleaver or meat pounder. Distribute the remaining horseradish (1–2 tablespoons, to taste) over the meat. Place an oyster in the centre of each slice; roll up neatly. Set in a shell.

4. Top each roll with a little of the pear julienne; drizzle the remaining dressing over each. Top with the sesame, then a coriander sprig.

Note: *For paper-thin slices, cut the fillet on a meat slicer or have the butcher do this, then pack between sheets of clingfilm.*
Serving/presentation: *Although finger food, these appetizers are a bit unwieldy for stand-up service. Instead, offer them as a first course to be enjoyed while seated. Try them for brunch, with sparkling wine. In Australia the packets are tied with chives.*
Advance preparation: *The dressing can be prepared and the meat cut, pounded, layered between sheets of clingfilm, and refrigerated.*

5 SERVINGS AS AN APPETIZER

PORK, PRAWN AND VEGETABLE-FILLED ROLLED CRÊPES
(Lumpia Ubod)
PHILIPPINES

The Filipino wrappers (lumpia) *that here enclose crisp shreds of iceberg lettuce, prawn, and pork bits (although sweet fillings are as common as savoury) are soft as chamois and pale as ivory. The size and shape of smallish egg rolls, these traditional delicacies are dipped into a lightly thickened, sweetened soya sauce and topped with paper-thin fried garlic chips.*

150 g (5 oz) plain flour
75 g (3 oz) cornflour plus 1½ tablespoons for sauce
3 eggs, beaten to blend
About 3 tablespoons peanut oil
350 g (¾ lb) raw prawns in the shell
150 g (5 oz) whole, drained bamboo shoots (see Note)
350 g (¾ lb) pork loin, cut into 5 mm (¼-inch) dice
60 ml (2½ fl oz) fish stock (see page 326)

½ teaspoon granulated sugar
3 tablespoons lightly packed brown sugar
2 tablespoons soya sauce
400 ml (14 fl oz) chicken stock
½ head of garlic, peeled and thin-sliced
About 250 g (9 oz) thinly shredded iceberg lettuce

1. With a whisk, blend together the flour and 75 g (3 oz) of the cornflour. Gradually whisk in 650 ml (26 fl oz) water, then add the eggs.

2. Heat a 15 cm (6-inch) crêpe pan (or non-stick frying pan) over moderately low heat. Brush with a little oil. Remove from the heat. Taking a scant 3 tablespoon portion at a time, ladle the batter into the centre of the pan; immediately tip and shake to distribute the thin batter evenly. Cook only until the sides of the *lumpia* separate from the pan, about 30 seconds (do not brown or turn). Gently transfer to a work surface, cooked side down. Continue making pancakes, stirring the batter often, and placing each crêpe separately on the work surface (see Advance Preparation).

3. Shell and devein the prawns as needed; cut into 1 cm (½-inch) pieces. Cut the bamboo shoots into fine dice. Heat a wok over high heat; pour 1 tablespoon oil around the rim and tip to distribute. Add the pork and toss for 2 minutes. Add the bamboo and toss for 2 minutes longer. Add the fish stock; toss for 1 minute. Add the granulated sugar; toss for another minute or so, until the liquid has evaporated. Add the prawns; toss just until pink. Set aside to cool.

4. Prepare the sauce: Blend together the remaining cornflour and the brown sugar. Add the soya and mix; add the chicken stock. Heat 2 tablespoons oil in a small saucepan. Add the garlic and cook over moderately low heat until golden-brown. Remove with a slotted spoon and reserve. Pour the stock mixture into the oil and stir over moderate heat until thick. Pour into a small bowl and cool to room temperature.

5. Spread a heaped tablespoon of lettuce shreds in the centre of each pancake; spread a heaped tablespoon of the filling over this. Turn in the sides slightly over the filling, then roll each gently but firmly. Place seam side down on a serving dish. Accompany with the garlic and sauce.

Note: *Canned, whole bamboo shoots are available in all Oriental groceries and some supermarkets. If raw prawns are unavailable, cooked prawns may be used, but add them to the wok when the stir-frying is completed.*
Serving/presentation: *Either pick up the rolls with your fingers and dip in the sauce, or place a few on each diner's plate and pour the sauce alongside, then eat with fork and knife. Sprinkle over garlic slivers to taste. If you have time to spare, tie each roll with a length of narrow spring onion. The* lumpia *work beautifully as a summer buffet or hors d'oeuvre. Or for a light lunch, serve 4 rolls per person along with a clear soup and fresh fruit mélange.*
Advance preparation: *You can prepare the pancakes 3–4 hours ahead, stack them, and cover with kitchen paper. Stuffing and sauce can be made far ahead and brought to room temperature. The rolls can be assembled about 2 hours in advance.*

36–40 ROLLS

TERRINE OF MIXED FRESH MUSHROOMS
(Terrine Forestière)

JAPAN

Light but sumptuous, this creamy beige terrine is thickly studded with woodland mushrooms in different shapes and sizes and punctuated by confetti of chives, parsley, and tomato dice. The work of Siegfried Jaeger, executive chef of the vast Tokyo Hilton International, this is the type of dish favoured by Japanese diners in the primarily Western restaurant of the hotel, the Imari: top quality ingredients presented in more-or-less traditional guise, no fussy garnishes, direct but subtle flavours.

8 fresh medium *shiitake* (100–150 g/
  4–5 oz), stems removed and
  reserved for another use, caps
  cut into 1 cm (½-inch) slices
175 ml (6 fl oz) dry white wine
350 g (¾ lb) medium button mushrooms, cleaned and quartered
12 fresh small morels (about 25 g/
  1 oz), halved and rinsed
  (see Note)
100 g (¼ lb) small oyster mushrooms, trimmed of heavy stems
15 g (½ oz) powdered gelatine
350 ml (12 fl oz) double (or whipping) cream

1 teaspoon salt
¼ teaspoon white pepper
1½ teaspoons thin-sliced chives
1½ teaspoons finely chopped parsley
2 tablespoons Cognac, Armagnac,
  or brandy
2 medium plum tomatoes, peeled,
  seeded, and diced
⅛ teaspoon nutmeg

Relish

5 medium plum tomatoes, peeled,
  seeded, and diced
Finely chopped chervil or parsley
Salt and pepper
Lemon juice

1. Combine the *shiitake* and two-thirds of the wine in a non-aluminium pan; bring to a boil, covered. Simmer gently until soft, about 10 minutes. Add the button mushrooms, morels, and oyster mushrooms. Cover and simmer until tender, about 8 minutes. With a slotted spoon transfer the fungi to a mixing bowl. Boil the liquid to reduce to 2 tablespoons. Add to the mushrooms.

2. Combine 50 ml (2 fl oz) water with the remaining 50 ml (2 fl oz) wine in a small pan; sprinkle the gelatine over this; let soften for a few minutes. Add one-third cream and the salt and pepper and bring to a simmer, stirring, over low heat. Pour this over the mushrooms. Add the remaining cream, the chives, parsley, Cognac, tomatoes and nutmeg. Set in a larger bowl of iced water. Stir often until jelled.

3. Line a mould of about 1.2 litres (2 pints) capacity, preferably about 9 × 28 cm (3½ × 11-inches) (or use a 23 × 12.5 cm/9 × 5-inch loaf pan—although the slices will be less trim), with clingfilm. Pour in the mushroom mixture. Cover and chill for at least 4 hours or up to 24.

4. Meanwhile, prepare the relish: Combine the plum tomatoes, chervil and salt, pepper and lemon juice to taste. Refrigerate until serving time.

5. Let the terrine stand at room temperature for about 30 minutes before slicing. Serve with the tomato relish spooned alongside.

Note: *If you cannot find fresh morels, use dried ones. Select 12 tiny ones, soak in warm water until barely cuttable, a matter of a few minutes. Trim off any coarse base parts. Halve the mushrooms lengthwise and rinse lightly. Add to the cooking liquid at the same time you would the fresh morels—and expect a stronger, smokier flavour.*

8–10 SERVINGS

LOBSTER DUMPLINGS WITH SEA URCHIN SAUCE

JAPAN

Thin rounds of pasta (wonton wrappers) filled with herbed lobster sail in a golden, buttery sea urchin cream sauce. The Japanese who dine at the polished, low-key Imari restaurant in the Tokyo Hilton International are partial to lobster, pasta, and sea urchin—which is why chef Siegfried Jaeger assembled this dish. It exemplifies the style of luxurious Western haute cuisine, Japanese-tinged, that comes from his kitchen. Interestingly, although eating habits in that country are based on awareness of the lightest, healthiest foods, this extraordinarily rich dish is a best-seller. Perhaps it represents the quintessential indulgence?

Lobster Dumplings
2 lobsters (each about 550 g/1¼ lb; see Note)
23 g (¾ oz) butter
1 tablespoon finely chopped shallots
3 tablespoons dry white wine
100 ml (4 fl oz) double (or whipping) cream
1 tablespoon finely chopped parsley
1 tablespoon finely chopped basil
Salt and pepper
36 wonton wrappers (see Note)
1 egg beaten with 1 teaspoon water

Sauce
6–10 sea urchins (see Note)
25 g (1 oz) softened butter
1 teaspoon finely chopped shallot
50 ml (2 fl oz) dry white wine
75 ml (3 fl oz) dry vermouth
300 ml (½ pint) double (or whipping) cream
Salt and white pepper
About 2 teaspoons lemon juice
Basil sprigs for garnish

1. Prepare the lobster dumplings: Place the lobsters on a rack over boiling water; cover and steam for 8 minutes (or drop into boiling water for 5). Cool until you can handle them, then cut off the claws where they attach to the body. Twist off the tail; snip the cartilage with scissors; remove the meat and chop coarsely. Cut the claws from the attached joints; halve these joints lengthwise, pull out the meat and chop coarsely. Jiggle the small pincers on the claws to pull out the cartilage; then crack the heavy shell with the dull side of a knife or a lobster cracker. Gently withdraw the lobster meat; cut in neat lengthwise slices. Set aside in a saucepan with liquid from the steamer to partly cover (refrigerate if you won't be using within the hour).

2. Heat the butter in a frying pan over moderate heat. Add the shallots and toss for a minute. Add the wine and cream and boil until thick, or reduced to about 60 ml (2½ fl oz). Add the chopped lobster meat and toss to coat. Off the heat, add the finely chopped herbs. Season with salt and pepper. Cool and chill. *(continued)*

3. Place 18 wonton rounds on a work surface. Place a heaped tablespoon of the lobster filling in the centre of each. Paint the surrounding area with the beaten egg. Place a round of the remaining dough on top of each, press to flatten the filling a bit, then press down the edges to seal tightly.

4. Prepare the sauce: Combine the sea urchins in a sieve with half of the softened butter. Press through, scraping every bit into a bowl. Heat the remaining butter in a small frying pan. Add the shallot; stir over low heat to soften slightly, but not to colour. Add the wine and vermouth; boil to reduce to 60 ml (2½ fl oz). Add the cream; boil, stirring, to reduce to 225 ml (8 fl oz). Season with salt and white pepper. Remove from the heat.

5. Slip the dumplings into a large, wide pan of boiling water. Simmer until soft, about 2 minutes. Meanwhile, heat the lobster claw meat. Drain the dumplings carefully. At once warm the cream reduction; remove from the heat and stir in the sea urchin butter and the lemon juice to taste.

6. Place 3 dumplings on each of 6 plates, spoon over the sauce, garnish with the drained lobster meat and basil sprigs.

Note: *If you do not wish to cook and clean lobsters, you can buy 175–200g (6–7 oz) fresh lobster meat and forgo the garnish of claws.*

Round skins for boiled dumplings, about 9 cm (3½-inches) in diameter, are available in Oriental shops. Square wonton skins the same dimension are easily found in many supermarkets and all Oriental groceries. To use these, cut circles by trimming and rounding off the corners or impress a circle on each skin and cut off the excess.

Cleaned fresh sea urchin roe can be purchased in Japanese and other Oriental supermarkets, neatly packed in little boxes. If you buy the sea urchin in the shell from a fishmonger, be sure that there is no off odour and that the spines stick straight out, porcupine-fashion, with no flattened or tired looking stickers. Holding a sea urchin with a pan holder or in a thick glove, insert the point of a pair of scissors into the soft depression in one side, cutting out a round lid of about one-third of the shell. Gently rinse the interior, then carefully spoon out the ochre roe, avoiding the dark membranes. The roe should be rather strong smelling, but sea-like, not unpleasant.

Advance preparation: *The dumplings (or just the filling, if you like) can be made up to a day ahead, then tightly wrapped in a single layer, and refrigerated.*

6 SERVINGS AS A FIRST COURSE

SPICED RED SNAPPER WITH HERBS EN PAPILLOTE

UNITED ARAB EMIRATES

At the Hilton International Dubai, a rainbow of fishes from the Persian Gulf takes pride of place at the Al Fahidi Grill, under the guidance of executive chef John Dolan. Among the various best-sellers on the menu are Poached Paupiette of Baby Hammour, *Fried Fillet of* Gaian, *Baked Fillet of* Khen, Moussa *with Apricot Essence,* Beiah *with Fine Vegetables, and* Nagrour *with Pistachio. Fortunately, there is also a fish we can recognize: red snapper.*

Unlike most red snapper recipes, this one is hot and spicy, with a big, brash bouquet. The intensity makes it a more likely candidate for a first course than a main one, but if you double the quantity of fish (two fillets in each pouch), keeping spicing the same, it will be fine in the latter role. Do not be put off by the long list of ingredients, which are simply seasonings, called collectively, 'Arabic Spice' in recipes from the area.

½ teaspoon pepper
½ teaspoon ground cumin
½ teaspoon ground paprika
¼ teaspoon ground cloves
¼ teaspoon ground cinnamon
¼ teaspoon ground coriander
¼ teaspoon salt
Large pinch of ground cardamom (optional)

1 lime
1 tablespoon finely chopped coriander leaves
1½ teaspoons finely chopped parsley
1 tablespoon olive oil
4 red snapper fillets with skin (each about 75 g/3 oz; or substitute another firm, white-fleshed fish)
25 g (1 oz) butter, cut into small pieces

1. Preheat the oven to 200°C/400°F (gas mark 6). Combine the pepper, cumin, paprika, cloves, cinnamon, coriander, salt and cardamom. Peel the zest from the lime and cut into very fine julienne; add ½ teaspoon to the spices. Squeeze the juice from the lime and add to the spices with the fresh coriander and parsley. Rub the fish with the mixture, dividing evenly.

2. Cut four 28 cm (11-inch) circles of aluminium foil. Brush with the oil. Place a fillet, skin side down, on one-half of each circle, dot with the butter; fold the other half of the foil as you would a turnover. Crimp together the edges.

3. Set the packets on a baking sheet in the lower third of the oven. Bake for 8 minutes, until just cooked through. Serve the remaining lime zest in a tiny dish, so each diner can sprinkle some on his or her fish when the aromatic package is cut open.

Serving: A cucumber-yogurt sauce alongside is a refreshing complement. You might follow this with a room-temperature vegetable main course, then a cooling fruit dessert.

4 SERVINGS AS A FIRST COURSE

PRAWN SALAD WITH CUCUMBERS, CHILLI, GARLIC, MINT AND LEMON GRASS
(Goong Plar)
THAILAND

A traditional hot/aromatic Thai dish interpreted by Viboon Roongrojpanawan, sous-chef of the Hilton International Bangkok. This easy assembly embraces the primary flavours of the sultry country: garlic, chilli, lemon grass, nam plah, *and seafood—which should be just barely cooked through in this recipe. Fiery and garlicky is the Thai rule of thumb and the strength on which the balance depends, so you might wish to experiment to the hilt for the full impact. But if you are timid-tongued, cut down on chilli and garlic.*

32 raw medium prawns in the shell (about 900 g/2 lb)
3 medium stalks lemon grass (see Note)
50 ml (2 fl oz) *nam plah* (see Note)
50 ml (2 fl oz) lemon juice
1 tablespoon finely chopped garlic
About 1 tablespoon fine-sliced hot green chilli-pepper, seeds and veins removed

25 g (1 oz) small shallots, sliced
50–100 g (2–4 oz) small mint leaves (removed from stems), plus a few sprigs
2 small cucumbers
4 ripe plum tomatoes, quartered lengthwise

1. Pour boiling salted water over the prawns in a wide frying pan. Bring to a simmer. Remove from the liquid and let cool just until they can be handled. Remove the shells; devein prawns, as necessary. Cool completely. (But do not chill.)

2. Meanwhile, remove the upper leaves, heavy outer leaves, and thick base tip from the lemon grass. Halve the stalks lengthwise, cut out any tough core, then cut across into the finest slices possible. Mix together half of the lemon grass, the *nam plah,* lemon juice, garlic, 2 teaspoons of the sliced chilli-pepper, the shallots, and 50 g (2 oz) mint leaves, crushing lightly with a spoon. Add the prawns and taste for seasoning, adding mint and lemon grass if not sufficiently assertive.

3. Rinse the cucumbers and remove alternating strips of peel lengthwise. Cut into very thin slices. Arrange these around 4 serving plates. Divide the salad in the centres. Top with tomato wedges and mint sprigs.

Note: *If raw prawns are unavailable, substitute cooked and omit step 1. Simply peel and devein. Long stalks of greyish-green fresh lemon grass can be found in Oriental shops and some supermarkets. It adds a subtle, inimitable lemon pungency.*

Nam plah *(Thai) or* nuoc mam *(Vietnamese) is a thin, fermented sauce somewhat like light soya sauce with a fishy taste. It is easily obtained in all Oriental supermarkets.*

Serving and presentation: *With half the quantity of prawn and dressing, this becomes a versatile appetizer. Or prepare a large platter and serve the dish buffet-style for a party.*

Do not be tempted to serve the dish chilled, as the prawns become too firm and the strong flavours of the sauce quickly overpower the delicate seafood if left to marinate.

In Bangkok unpeeled cucumbers are cut in thinnest lengthwise strips, to make wide ribbons. These are folded in half to form a flower-like design around the central prawns. If you have a mandoline or other slicing device to cut the full length of the cucumber in thin slices, present the salad this way.

4 SERVINGS AS A MAIN COURSE; 6–8 AS AN APPETIZER

The water lily pond at the Hilton International Bangkok

Floating atop the world's largest water lily species, in the pond of the Hilton International Bangkok, is a selection of the flavours that characterize Thai cuisine: mint, kaffir lime leaves, chilli-peppers, shallots, and stalks of lemon grass. In the centre, presented as it is made at the hotel's garden restaurant Suan Saranrom, is the pungent Prawn Salad with Cucumbers, Chilli, Garlic, Mint and Lemon Grass.

SALAD OF PEPPER-SEARED BEEF FILLET

JAPAN

Gentle murmurs are the loudest sound in the Imari of the Tokyo Hilton International, where the Japanese take dining seriously—and often silently. Raw dishes, particularly the bright-rose beef of Kobe and Matsuzaka (astronomically-priced and much in demand in fine restaurants) are among the favoured first courses and luncheon dishes. This unusual treatment from executive chef Siegfried Jaeger produces meltingly soft slices that are black-seared without, raw within, somewhere between carpaccio and pepper steak in appearance. (It is imperative that you buy beautifully marbled prime beef for this dish, or the point is lost.) Ever-so-slightly dressed with a soya-sesame sauce and combined with a trio of leaves of various chicories, the flavours are Oriental-Italian.

2 tablespoons black peppercorns
1½ teaspoons coarse sea salt
500 g (1¼ lb) trimmed prime beef
    fillet
1 tablespoon vegetable oil
2 tablespoons lemon juice
3 tablespoons olive oil
Additional salt and pepper
1½ tablespoons chicken or beef
    broth
1½ tablespoons soya sauce

1 tablespoon rice or white wine
    vinegar
¾ teaspoon sugar
2 teaspoons dark sesame oil
2 medium heads chicory, trimmed,
    rinsed, and dried
1 small head of radicchio, trimmed,
    rinsed, and dried
1 very small head of imported curly
    endive (*chicorée frisée*) *or* ½
    bunch watercress, trimmed,
    rinsed, and dried

1. Crush the peppercorns with a heavy knife blade or meat pounder. Combine with the salt. Coat the fillet with the mixture. Let stand at room temperature for 1–2 hours.

2. Heat a frying pan until very hot over moderate heat. Add the vegetable oil, then the beef. Sear over highest heat until just browned all over (do not cook through). Cool, then chill, lightly covered, for several hours or longer.

3. Mix together the lemon juice and olive oil with salt and pepper to taste. In a separate bowl blend the chicken broth, soya sauce, vinegar, and sugar. Add the sesame oil.

4. Toss the cleaned salad leaves with the olive oil dressing; divide onto 4 serving plates. Cut the meat into about 24 slices and arrange alongside the greens, very slightly over-lapping. Stir the sesame dressing and spoon evenly and sparingly over the meat.

Serving and presentation: *Several alternative presentations are part of the repertoire of the Imari: The beef may be accompanied by a few thin onion rings and watercress alone, or by several asparagus and* kaiware *(daikon or Oriental radish sprouts). Or paper-thin slices of completely raw fillet (no pepper, no searing) are served as an appetizer with 4 chicory spears, a small bunch of cress in the centre, and long chive stalks atop each beef slice.*

4 SERVINGS AS A MAIN COURSE; 8 AS A FIRST COURSE

A World Tour, Luxury Class, at the Tokyo Hilton International

In the world's most populous city, living space is minuscule, home kitchens often nonexistent, and dining out simply a way of life. In fact, eating in Tokyo is both a recreational and business pastime, with as many secretaries and salesmen likely to spend a large chunk of their salaries on dinners and afternoon cakes and tea as bank presidents. After a time of post-war isolationism and relative conservatism, the last 15 years or so have seen a meteoric rise in the variety of cuisines and number of restaurants in the city.

At the Tokyo Hilton International, three to four thousand meals are served daily, about 85 per cent of these to Japanese. Among the world's most demanding and knowledgeable diners and, contrary to the ideas of most Westerners, the Japanese also happen to be among the most open-minded and adventurous eaters on the globe. With the city itself and the hotel in particular as indications, the desire for new tastes seems boundless. Provided that service is absolutely exquisite (and the Tokyo Hilton International is frequently cited as having the finest in Asia), presentation superb and never fussy, and ingredients beyond compare—money is no object.

Because no single approach could begin to satisfy the Japanese appetite for the unknown, the food outlets at the Tokyo Hilton International, already diverse in styles, offer ever-changing menus based on a score of national cuisines and on strictly seasonal products. The Imari, for example, the hotel's showcase of creative haute cuisine, adds a spate of weekly specials—such as meals by foreign chefs, desserts of American cherries, oyster dishes, fresh caviar—to its already extensive Continental menu. With caviar prices ranging from 7,800 yen (about £35, at the time of writing) for a tasting portion to 12,000 (£60) for a regular one, you can imagine the willingness to eat well. The immaculate service and individual attention in this hushed and spacious room are the kind allotted to royalty. The display cases of museum-quality porcelain ware and the picture-perfect seafood still-life wheeled to each table as a visual 'menu' of the day's specials set the tone for a dining room that is serious about food: rounds of raw beef without equal are barely touched with sesame and soya; a custard of vibrant orange peppers set on velvet avocado cream has no distracting interference from outside seasonings; tissue-thin packets of lobster meat float in a pale ochre pool of sea urchin butter; crisp-sautéed red snapper is decked with fresh *shiitake* slivers; fanned slices of lean duck breast with a blackcurrant reduction are escorted by stuffed baby turnip halves; a symphony of fresh fruits and fruit sorbets follows; then, bonbons set on wildly misting dry ice that engulfs the diners in the theatrical finale—for restaurant is theatre in Japan.

Meanwhile, round the corner, the Dynasty room is in full swing. This classical Chinese restaurant with 200-plus dishes that represent the regions of China has a kitchen staff

A quartet of culinary gems from an elegant *kaiseki ryori* dinner presented at the Musashino restaurant in the Tokyo Hilton International

that does the same. As if such a range were not sufficient, constantly shifting menu schemes for specialities—such as cold noodle dishes, seasonal shellfish, new liqueurs—keep the insatiable diners on their toes.

The casual coffee shop Sakura offers a mixed menu of hamburgers, spaghetti Bolognese, Indian chicken samosas, Indonesian *nasi goreng*—then takes a monthly detour to Switzerland, Thailand, Hungary, a world of Hollywood soda fountain extravaganzas or an American Thanksgiving.

The clubby, British Saint George Bar in the lobby, handsomely turned out in green marble, brass, leather and plushy dark chairs, is the regular home of roast beef, other carvery items and salads, but at a moment's notice can become the backdrop for an Oktoberfest or Swiss food buffet.

In the morning, the sleek, modern Marble Lounge in the lobby, its colossal, dappled cream columns creating intimate conversational oases, is the scene of the power breakfast. By noon the popular Continental lunch buffet, its platters refreshed at such a rate that each guest is virtually the first to serve himself, takes over the same comfortable area. At 2:30 the place is peacefully packed with women—from teenagers to dowagers, who in a two-hour period may pack in (without adding a centimetre to their delicate frames) a pastel profusion of 80 cakes, 20 monumental platters of French pastry, and 50 litres of ice cream from the Austrian-style dessert buffet. Come early evening, snacks and drinks take over (in that order, for Japanese request first food, then alcohol), and the lively lobby keeps hopping into the night.

Behind the scenes, spread out in numerous private rooms, are the banquets, meals usually containing six or more courses—fresh goose liver from France, lobster from North America and Japan's fillet of beef are *de rigueur*—whether for a fashionable society ball or wedding (both the hotel's Shinto and Christian chapels are booked for an average of eight marriages every day).

Who better to oversee the execution of this multinational carnival than Siegfried Jaeger, an Austrian chef who grew up speaking French, German, and English, moved from Switzerland and England to a position on round-the-world cruisers, landed in Bombay, then took on Singapore, Manila, Seoul, and, finally, opened the mammoth food operations of the award-winning new Tokyo Hilton International? While familiar with a wide range of cuisines, he is particularly at ease with Japanese aesthetics, sensibilities, and work ethics. 'I don't like messy or fussy food, and neither do the cooks I work with,' he explained. 'Nor do I like wasting time. Once you show a Japanese cook how to do a recipe—that's it. It will never vary. You don't need to check; you can relax, knowing it will always be produced as agreed.' The lanky chef lopes around the kitchen, towering over most of the staff and grazing all the door frames, even as he stoops to accommodate. 'Nowhere have I encountered such an appreciation of quality as here in Japan. Every fruit and vegetable is examined and evaluated,' he marvels. Bespectacled and trimly mustachioed, with his imperial fingers calmly designating various tasks throughout the kitchen, he looks more the part of a chief surgeon or scientist in a secret laboratory than the man in charge of a food staff of 550.

Perfection is the password at this smoothly-run operation, and no detail is too small to warrant attention. Each food outlet has a training manual that specifies virtually every move to be made by each employee—and the reasons why. Eight steps are required to explain the proper way to change a tablecloth in The Imari; four pages describe the correct serving of various desserts—a page each for cakes, pastries with sauces, ice creams and coupes, and fruits. The service of tea requires two pages, and French bread must be sliced on a 45° angle, and of a specific thickness, while German rye needs a vertical cut at a thickness a quarter of that for a baguette.

Imagine the scrutiny to which a sumptuous Japanese restaurant in the only American-run hotel in the city is subjected, how flawless it must be! The Tokyo Hilton's Musashino—in effect a collection of restaurants housed in a single, gleaming space, the areas divided by brass-edged screens of bevelled glass—provides the lover of true Japanese dishes with happy choices: The sushi room, where ingredients and execution are religiously pristine, vies with the finest in the country; famed Matsuzaka beef and peak-quality vegetables are cooked to order with balletic precision on the grills of the *teppan-yaki* room; the tempura area opposite, graced with an arrangement of the day's most stunning produce, offers a seasonal cast of characters that may include minute aubergines and okra pods, plumpest shrimps and gingko nuts, tiny shining fish, and the mushrooms of the moment. For a menu composed from the gamut of raw, deep-fried, simmered, grilled, vinegared foods, and soup and pickles that make up the more formal *kaiseki-ryori* dinners, move to the small dining rooms and tatami rooms for memorable feasts, each course displayed in unique dishes by kimono-clad beauties as graceful as the porcelain, glass, and ceramic accoutrements. Among the parade of unique presentations are a free-form, ice-filled carved crystal bowl (too heavy to lift with one hand) that bears a chrysanthemum on which rest furled petals of raw tuna and red snapper; squares of silver flying-fish enclosing slices of fragrant *matsutake* (pine mushrooms) are sandwiched between scented cedar shingles (the packet is untied at the table, its aromas unleashed for the guest) and served with shoots of pale-pink fresh ginger; an iced Champagne coupe holds a purée of sweet-sharp Asian pear crowned with emerald cubes of *suizen-ji nori* (lake algae), baby bay scallops, carved cucumber ovals and red-tipped white radish shreds—and on and on as long as you enjoy the flow of perfectly executed art that streams from the kitchen of chef Matsuda.

Pigeon Consommé with Quail Eggs

SINGAPORE

A hallmark of quality in many fine dining rooms, this deep-flavoured amber essence (developed by chef Peter Knipp of Shanghai when he was a sous-chef in Singapore) is a luxury to be savoured as one would fine wine. The tender pigeon breast and poached quail egg must be prepared at the last minute, to the exact degree of doneness, or they will cloud and cool the sparkling liquid. For connoisseurs and comfortable cooks.

3 pigeons (about 1 kilo/2¼ lb total
   weight)
1 stick celery, sliced
1 medium carrot, sliced
½ small onion, sliced
Top green part of 1 small leek,
   sliced
10 peppercorns, roughly crushed

1 small bay leaf
1 teaspoon fresh thyme
2 egg whites
2.2 litres (4 pints) cold, *very* strong
   homemade chicken stock (see
   Note)
Salt and pepper
25 g (1 oz) butter
12 quail eggs

1. With a boning knife, cut the breast meat from the pigeons; remove and discard the skin. Trim any fat or membranes from the meat; cover tightly and refrigerate. Chop the rest of the birds into small pieces.

2. Combine the pigeon pieces in a stockpot with the celery, carrot, onion, leek, peppercorns, bay leaf and thyme. Whisk together the egg whites with a few cups of cold chicken stock. Add to the stockpot with the remaining stock. Whisk to blend very thoroughly.

3. Bring to a simmer over moderately low heat. As soon as the stock begins to simmer, turn the heat so low that only an occasional bubble floats to the surface. Do not stir or in any way disturb the foamy crust that floats atop the stock or the essence will not be clear. Keep at this level, uncovered, for about 3½ hours. The flavour should be pronounced and full.

4. Carefully remove the crust. Ladle the soup gently through a muslin-lined sieve. (You should have about 1.5 litres/2¼ pints of consommé.) Cool; cover, and refrigerate.

5. At serving time, skim off all fat particles; place the consommé over low heat. Set 6 shallow, wide soup plates in a warm oven to heat. Season the breast pieces with salt and pepper. Melt the butter in a medium frying pan over moderate heat. Sear the pigeon for 1 minute on each side, to medium-rare. Place between kitchen paper towels for about 5 minutes.

6. Meanwhile, tap a quail egg sharply with a knife to break it in half. Drop into a small cup or dish, then slip into a frying pan of not-quite-simmering water (or preferably, light stock). Continue until all the eggs are in the water. They will be poached in a matter of minutes, as you finish the slicing of the breasts.

7. Cut each piece of breast meat in long, narrow slices. Arrange in a fan in a heated soup plate. Place 2 quail eggs in the dish. When all the pigeon and eggs have been arranged, bring to the table. Immediately divide the hot consommé over each, about 225 ml (8 fl oz) per person.

Note: *The excellence of this intense consommé depends upon the quality of the stock, which should be strong and fat-free.*

6 SERVINGS

The famed rock oysters of Australia—petite, buttery, plump—star in this pristine soup, here set on a background of black coral. Should you be in the country of the dish's origin when you're preparing it, use 3-year-old Sydney rock oysters, as chef Herbert Franceschini specifies (recipe appears on next page)

CHICKEN BROTH WITH CORIANDER DUMPLINGS

THAILAND

When Thailand's government undertook a programme of agricultural expansion in Chiang Mai, in the north of the country, the Hilton International Bangkok featured a herb promotion to familiarize Thais with Western herbs, and foreigners with the Eastern ones.

Sous-chef Martin Gerber developed this fresh first-course soup that he felt would be intriguing to both Oriental and Occidental diners. Light and clean, the pastel flurry of vegetable julienne contributes crunch and sweetness, the silky dumplings add a burst of assertive coriander (also known as Chinese or Mexican parsley) and an edge of red pepper hotness.

---

1 skinned and boned chicken breast
    half (about 100 g/4 oz), cleaned of
    all membrane and tendon
2 tablespoons sliced coriander leaves
1 teaspoon soya sauce
Salt, pepper, and grand red pepper
16 wonton wrappers, about 9 cm
    (3½ inches) square (see Note)
1 tablespoon plain flour blended with
    2 tablespoons water

1 small carrot
Trimmed pale green and white part
    of ½ small leek
1 medium tender inner stalk celery,
    strings removed
1 small turnip
1 litre (1¾ pints) chicken stock
Coriander sprigs for garnish

---

1. Cut the chicken breast into small pieces, then chop medium-fine with a cleaver or large knife. Combine in a bowl with the sliced coriander, soya sauce, and salt, pepper, and grand red pepper to taste.

2. Place about 1 teaspoon of the chicken mixture on each of the wonton skins. Paint the edges with the flour mixture and fold to form a neat triangle. Paint the 2 points of the triangle that are farthest apart, then paste together to form a bishop's hat shape.

3. Clean the carrot, leek, celery and turnip, then cut into fine julienne.

4. Drop the vegetables and dumplings into a large pot of boiling water. Cover and return to a boil on highest heat. Uncover and boil another minute or so, until just tender. Drain.

5. Meanwhile, bring the chicken stock to a boil. Divide the dumplings and vegetables into 4 soup bowls, then ladle in the stock. Decorate with the coriander sprigs.

Note: *Wonton skins this size are available in Oriental grocers.*
Serving/presentation: *If you prefer, simply pour the drained vegetables and dumplings into the hot broth, then serve in a tureen.*

4 SERVINGS AS A FIRST COURSE

THAI SOUP OF MIXED ORIENTAL VEGETABLES AND SHRIMP
(Gaeng Lieng)
THAILAND

Viboon Roongrojpanawan, who prepared this unusual soup, explained that it is well known to Thais, who relish it at home and in a few fine local restaurants, but that it seldom appears on a hotel menu. Happily, the Hilton International Bangkok, where Mr Roongrojpanawan is sous-chef, is an exception, and the light, mellow soup (neither oniony nor fishy, as one might expect from the ingredients) has become a popular round-the-clock item there. A colourful pick-me-up, the broth is at once salty, sweet, and peppery, the vegetables crisp and diverse, the shrimp barely poached and tender—and the whole subtle concoction takes just minutes to prepare.

75 g (3 oz) dried shrimp (see Note)
3 peeled whole small shallots
1 teaspoon white pepper
2 teaspoons fish paste (optional; see Note)
1 litre (1¾ pints) unsalted chicken broth
225 g (½ lb) hard orange-fleshed squash (such as acorn, sweet dumpling, pumpkin, butternut, *kabocha*), peeled, seeded, and cut into 1 cm (½-inch) dice
About 10 ears baby corn (see Note), cut into 2.5 cm (1-inch) lengths
150 g (6 oz) (1 medium) angled loofa (see Note), peeled and cut into 1 cm (½-inch) pieces

50–75 g (2–3 oz) small mushrooms, cut into 1 cm (½-inch) dice
50–75 g (2–3 oz) yardlong beans (see Note), cut into 5 cm (2-inch) lengths
2 tablespoons *nam plah* (see Note), or to taste
½ teaspoon sugar
About 75 g (3 oz) small-leafed spinach, stems removed and rinsed
8 medium raw prawns (150–175 g/ 6–7 oz), peeled and halved diagonally
1 large bunch basil, stems removed

1. Chop the dried shrimp to a medium texture in a food processor. With the motor running, add the shallots. Process to a medium purée. Add the white pepper, fish paste, and 100 ml (4 fl oz) chicken broth; continue processing for about 1 minute.

2. Add the purée to the remaining chicken broth in a large saucepan. Bring to a boil, skimming. Add the squash; boil for 1 minute, skimming. Add the corn, loofa, mushrooms and beans; boil until barely tender, 2–3 minutes.

3. Add the *nam plah* and sugar. Stir in the spinach, raw prawns, then the basil leaves. Remove from the heat at once and serve.

Note: *Dried, salted shrimp are available in almost any store that carries Oriental ingredients. Choose comparatively large ones.*

Shrimp paste, also called shrimp sauce, terasi, *or* balachan, *is a greyish-pink fermented purée of shrimp and salt, produced thoughout South-east Asia. Although strong-smelling, its effects are subtle.*

Baby ears of ready-to-eat corn are sold in jars and cans in Oriental groceries and many supermarkets. If fresh ears of baby corn are obtainable, cook them before adding to the soup.

Loofa, luffa, Chinese okra, or sze gwa *is a tapered, lightweight sharply ridged green vegetable 2.5–5 cm (1–2 inches) in diameter and 20–60 cm (8–24 inches) long. It is found in all Oriental vegetable markets and has a mild, grassy-fresh flavour. Peel the ribs before cutting up. Or substitute 100 g (4 oz) small courgettes.*

Yardlong beans are pencil-slim, flexible dark to medium-green beans (and yes, yard-long) available in most Oriental markets. If you cannot obtain them, substitute firm, thin string beans.

*Nam plah (*nuoc mam, *fish's gravy, fish sauce) is a thin, brown fermented fish sauce similar to light soya, but with a fishy taste.*

4 SERVINGS

RED BEAN SOUP WITH GINGER
(Sop Kacang Merah)
INDONESIA

Executive chef Detlef Skrobanek of the Jakarta Hilton International explained that in all regions of Indonesia red beans appear in salads, soups, and desserts. However, purées such as the following are not traditional; solid ingredients remain intact in soups, and are not removed from the liquid. The flavours here are typically betawi *(the adjective used to describe something from Jakarta) derived from the word Batavia, as the city was called by the conquering Dutch.*

A smooth, slightly thick consistency and rose-beige colour will invite the curious diner, but few will be prepared for the mysterious aroma and truly exotic taste of this silky purée which hints of frankincense and myrrh, ginger and chilli, coconut and cedar. The most powerful and unusual ingredient, galingale (see Note below), may seem a bit 'medicinal' to those not yet familiar with the cooking of South-east Asia. Do not overdo it—or the fiery peppers.

---

2 slices dried galingale (see Note)
1½ tablespoons peanut oil
75 g (3 oz) chopped onion
75 g (3 oz) chopped shallots
50 g (2 oz) chopped fresh ginger
2 teaspoons finely chopped garlic
400 g (14 oz) cooked, drained red kidney beans
825 ml (28 fl oz) chicken stock

100 ml (4 fl oz) unsweetened coconut milk (see Note)
Salt and pepper
1 tablespoon finest julienne of hot red chilli-pepper, seeded and deveined
1 tablespoon very fine fresh ginger julienne
4 sprigs coriander

---

1. Combine the galingale and 100 ml (4 fl oz) water in a small pan; simmer for 2 minutes. Cover; let stand for at least 15 minutes. Drain and reserve the liquid; chop the root.

2. Heat the peanut oil in a saucepan; add the onion, shallots, chopped ginger and garlic. Cook over low heat until soft, but not browned—10–15 minutes—stirring often. Add 300 g (10 oz) kidney beans to the saucepan; toss for 2 minutes. Add the stock, galingale, and reserved liquid.

3. Bring to a boil, then turn down heat and simmer, covered, until vegetables are very soft—about 15 minutes.

4. With a slotted spoon, transfer the solids from the saucepan to a blender or processor. Purée until smooth, gradually adding the liquid. Press through a sieve.

5. Return the soup to the saucepan; add the coconut milk and simmer for 5 minutes. Season with salt and pepper.

6. Distribute the remaining beans among 4 small bowls. Ladle in the soup. Sprinkle a few chilli and ginger julienne over each (serve the remainder separately in a small dish). Garnish each bowl with a coriander sprig.

Note: *Galingale, galangal, laos root,* lang uas *or* lengkuas *is a word used to describe several rhizomes of the ginger family that are popular in Asian cooking. It is available fresh in some Asian markets, but is more likely to be found in dried form (in powder or dried slices) in most Oriental markets. Its powerful and unusual flavour suggests ginger, camphor, and cardamom.*

Coconut milk is available in canned or bottled form in stores that carry ingredients from India. If you cannot buy it, make your own, following the directions on page 325.

Serving: *The potent bouquet of flavours is too intense to consider as a main course but serves brilliantly as a meal opener. Follow with grilled fish or poultry.*

Advance preparation: *The soup can be made ahead and reheated.*

4 SERVINGS

CLEAR PRAWN SOUP WITH LEMON GRASS
(Sop Pelangi Pagi)
INDONESIA

A sparkling example of chef Detlef Skrobanek's marriage of Asian ingredients to the techniques of European haute cuisine. The name of the soup in Bahasa, the primary Indonesian language, is 'rainbow of morning'—and a glance will tell you why: curled peach-coloured prawns, pearly lavender and green lemon grass stalks, pale yellow ears of baby corn, and sharp-cut tomato strips in a shining broth, the whole as bright and as natural as a bird-of-paradise. The flavours, while unfamiliar to some Western palates, are fresh and innocent, soft as a breeze.

225 g (½) lb medium-large raw
  prawns in the shell
450 g (1-lb) red snapper, filleted
  (bones and head reserved; see
  Note)
1 small carrot, peeled and cut into
  thick slices
1 very small leek, cleaned and cut
  into thick slices
2 medium garlic cloves, peeled
1 lemon grass stalk, upper leaves cut
  apart from bulb (see Note)

2 egg whites
1 bay leaf
About ¼ teaspoon Tabasco or other
  chilli-pepper sauce
2 teaspoons tamarind concentrate or
  paste (see Note)
Salt and pepper
4 ears baby corn (see Note)
2 medium tomatoes, peeled, seeded,
  and cut into thin strips or
  diamonds
12 basil leaves

1. Remove and reserve the prawn shells; devein the prawns. Clean any gills and innards from the fish bones. Rinse the bones, head, and prawn shells and combine in a pan with 1 litre (1¾ pints) water. Simmer gently, uncovered, for 20 minutes. Add the prawns; barely simmer for 1 minute. Remove the prawns and set aside for later; strain the stock. If there is more than 825 ml (26 fl oz), simmer to reduce. Chill.

2. Cut the fish into small pieces. With the motor running, drop the carrot, leek and garlic into a processor; chop to a coarse texture. Add the fish fillet; process to a medium-fine texture. Finely chop the upper part of the lemon grass; blend with the egg whites, bay leaf and Tabasco. Mix a few spoons of the cold stock with the tamarind; add this to the egg white mixture, then blend into the fish purée.

3. Whisk together the fish mixture and stock to blend. Bring to a simmer over low heat. Reduce the heat to its lowest point (no bubbles should rise) and cook until the 'crust' begins to crack and separate from the sides of the pan, 15–20 minutes.

4. Gently remove crust and ladle liquid through a muslin-lined sieve. Season with additional Tabasco and salt and pepper to taste. Reheat to boiling.

5. Trim the lemon grass bulb, then carefully quarter lengthwise. Cut the prawns and corn in diagonal 2 cm (¾-inch) slices. Arrange with the tomato and basil in 4 small, heated soup bowls. Pour in boiling liquid and serve at once, with the lemon grass.

Note: *Sea bass or another smallish, lean fish can be substituted for the red snapper, if desired.*

Long stalks of stiff, grey-green fresh lemon grass, found in South-east Asian markets and some supermarkets, add an inimitable lemony pungency. Although sliced, dried lemon grass (takrai or sereh) can be substituted for the chopped upper leaves (in approximately the same quantity as fresh), it is lighter and more tea-like in flavour. Add a bit of lemon zest and juice with the dried, if fresh is not obtainable.

Dark tamarind concentrate or paste, its flavour reminiscent of very sour apricots, is sold in Middle Eastern, South-east Asian, and some Caribbean shops, and can be added directly to foods. Other forms of the fruit must have pods, seeds, and fibres removed before being used. If solid or dry, the pulp must be mixed with a little boiling water to remove fibres and to soften to the texture of fruit butter.

Ready-to-eat ears of baby corn are sold in jars and cans in Oriental groceries and many supermarkets. If fresh ears of baby corn are obtainable, cook them before adding to the soup.

Presentation: *For a more elaborate look (although a bit difficult to eat tidily) arrange as in photograph.*

4 SERVINGS

Hilton International Bangkok:
The East Through Rose-Coloured Glasses

Vending snacks in the rural floating market of Damnoen Saduk, a half-day excursion outside of Bangkok

Outside: careening three-wheeled motorcycle-carriages called *tuc-tucs,* steaming air, a marketplace overflowing with vendors hawking edibles from snakes to lotus seeds, golden temples alongside shanties, bustling boulevards, clogged *klongs* (canals that comprise the secondary transportation system of Bangkok), sharply beeping high-pitched horns, miniature spirit houses alongside every building— even petrol stations, heavy pollution, a sprawling crazy-quilt of slums and palaces. Inside: a soft-toned dream of endless space; silence save for the gentlest plashing of waterfalls, the delicate jingle of a bell swinging from the sign carried by a handsome pastel-clad young page, alerting guests to phone calls as they sip tangerine juice in the marble lobby or exotic coolers in the cushioned lounge.

A five-storey architectural gala of soaring atriums and sunlit dining areas, two central halls the size of paddy fields, terraced interior pools shining with a rainbow of Oriental fish, the Hilton International Bangkok forms a crescent around manicured Nai Lert Park. A botanist's and hedonist's dream, this is a green oasis of frangipani, jasmine, weeping fig, papyrus, the Royal water lily (the world's largest), rose apple, mangosteen, and almost every other kind of fruit and flowering tree that will grow in the country. The scent of omnipresent orchids wafts through the cooled air of open corridors. The decor is modified Thai: subdued silks cover low banquettes; an airy teak *sala* (an ornately carved summerhouse with a peaked roof) occupies a corner of the lobby where one can relax to a chamber ensemble playing Bach, or stretch out to people-watch, for this luxurious space houses a rich cross-section of Eastern and Western faces.

This is a theatre of hospitality, a fulfilment of the fantasy that blossoms with the mere phrase 'the kingdom of Thailand', a place where one expects royal treatment. Here is the idealization of the East, a tamed version of the wild, an armchair traveller's hopes come to life. To keep the show in shape, a cast of 645 players tends to the 342 rooms and food and drink outlets (polishing the marble, cleaning the brass fittings on the silky teak banisters, and generally tidying the public areas requires a 24-hour staff of 20). One thousand roses are arranged each day, along with uncountable orchids. Twenty-odd ice carvings are fashioned in the same period of time, and 90 lb of fruit are turned into exquisite sculptures: Gardenias are made from watermelons, tulips from turnips, dragon boats from papaya. Pummelo segments arranged in spirals with petal-cut pineapple pieces overflow wooden baskets and banquet displays. Napkins are folded into pleated and swirled swans and angular artichokes that adorn the buffets and cradle the silver finger bowls in which rose petals float.

The food maintains the tone: muted Thai specialities, nippy with hot-pepper, aromatized with lemon grass, sweet with baby garlic and tender new ginger, are the rule in the tropical Suan Saranrom (garden restaurant) of the hotel, where water trickling down a wall of ferns forms a backdrop for the buffet of glistening-fresh dishes and sculpted fruits and vegetables. (In the outside world the food, sensational in another way, is most often breathtakingly chilli-laced and richly redolent of fermented fish sauce and healthy doses of raw garlic, onion and shallot.)

It is French cuisine that graces Ma Maison, a serene, stylized representation of an elegant Thai home. A glass wall abuts the garden, admitting moonlight through the tossing palms or a view of sun-struck butterflies—all hidden in this green enclave from the tumultuous city beyond. A taste of the untamed may sneak into the classical menu, such as a bevy of Thai game birds—wild pigeon broth with foie gras croûtons, wild duck with juniper brown sauce, or orange-braised hill doves—but the preparation will not jar the cultivated European palate. Asparagus arrives with velvety hollandaise or herbal vinaigrette—or a musky Thai sauce with undertones of smoky fish and pungent native lime leaves. The tart young green tamarind makes an appearance in subtly mellowed form, as ice cream.

Foods from both worlds are heaped in profusion alongside the free-form, palm-encircled garden pool for the nightly buffet. Torches flicker in the sultry dark; ice by the ton serves as a base for the display of some 18 barbecue candidates, from skewered local straw mushrooms and lobsters from the Gulf of Thailand to cervelat sausage and New Zealand lamb. A hot stand features spicy Thai soups and fragrant noodles dishes— as well as baked potatoes with all the trimmings. Condiments run the gamut from garlic toast, through Oriental pickles, to pummelo segments, while the salad bar ranges from Chinese cabbage to radicchio. Desserts, cooled by shining ice sculptures, may be as European as cream puffs or *Sachertorte,* or as Thai as *ruam mitr,* a popular sweet of vivid green and pink jellies and fruits swimming in coconut milk.

Chef Joseph Peter on the Chao Phraya River in Bangkok with a cargo of lemon grass

The two cultures are presented in refined essentials—discreet and luxurious—everywhere in the hotel . . . or almost everywhere. At a far corner of the compound, near the back entrance, is the shrine of a spirit goddess Tuptim (Pomegranate), who is visited daily by many of the hotel employees and others on whom she has bestowed favours, or who hope for the same. Here, in glorious Technicolour, are a jumble of offerings: heaps of rice, corn, dumplings, (even sandwiches), smoking incense, lotus buds, figurines, and hundreds—probably thousands—of giant male fertility symbols tied with shocking pink and chartreuse scarves. Stacked like logs in a woodpile amid the growth of tangled vines and jasmine wreaths, they contrast dramatically with the stream of white Mercedes that glide in and out of the parking lot alongside.

ASPARAGUS WITH THAI SAUCE

THAILAND

Chiang Mai is a centre for the arts—wood carving, painting, umbrella and parasol making—and for a developing agricultural programme. The asparagus from the area are green and delicate, like those available in Europe. The unusual sauce—meaty, fishy, buttery, citrusy, herbal, salty—is quite uncharacterizable. Although it looks creamy and innocently pale golden-brown, it is very concentrated and intense in flavour. Derived from a Thai sauce for steamed chicken, it was first altered by a Japanese chef, Otaki, then subsequently adapted by the kitchen staff of Ma Maison at the Hilton International Bangkok. There, the asparagus are offered with a choice of vinaigrette and hollandaise sauces, as well, for those with more traditional tastes.

450 ml (¾ pint) strong veal or chicken stock
5 dried kaffir lime leaves (see Note)
50 g (2 oz) finely grated fresh ginger
3½ tablespoons Vietnamese or Thai soya bean paste (see Note)

45 g (1½ oz) butter
50 ml (2 fl oz) lemon juice
1 teaspoon *nam plah* (see Note)
¼ teaspoon white pepper
700 g (1½ lb) slim asparagus (40 spears), trimmed and peeled

1. Boil the stock in a small saucepan to reduce to 100 ml (4 fl oz). Soak the lime leaves in warm water to cover. Meanwhile, blend together the ginger with 3 tablespoons water, pour into a sieve, then press hard with a spoon to extract the ginger juice (you should have 2 tablespoons).

2. Melt the butter in a small pan over low heat. Stir in the soya bean paste; set aside. Cut the lime leaves into thin strips and add them to the stock; then add the ginger juice, lemon juice, *nam plah*, and pepper. Simmer until reduced to 100 ml (4 fl oz). Remove from the heat. Stir in the butter mixture.

3. Cook the asparagus in a large pan of salted water until just tender. Drain, then spread on a towel to dry. Cut into 5–7.5 cm (2–3-inch) diagonals. (Do not chill.) Arrange on serving plates.

4. Pour the warm or room temperature sauce into a small dish or sauceboat. Pour very sparingly over the asparagus.

Note: *Strange and wildly aromatic kaffir lime leaves* (makrut, daun djeruk purut) *which are sold dried, in cellophane packets (or fresh, if you are very fortunate) can be obtained in stores that handle Asian products.*

Fermented soya bean paste from Thailand or Vietnam, a thick, but pourable salt-sweet brew, will be available in the same places as lime leaves, as will nam plah *(also called* nuoc mam, *fish sauce, or fish's gravy), which will also be found in any store that carries Oriental groceries.*

Serving and presentation: *In Bangkok, at Ma Maison, the asparagus are served in long spears with sauces ladled alongside, in traditional European fashion. However, we found it more practical to cut up the asparagus Oriental-style, which also alerts diners to their non-Western seasoning.*

4 SERVINGS AS A SALAD OR APPETIZER COURSE

STUFFED TOFU WITH PRAWNS

TAIWAN

Chefs Yu Wen-Shen and Huang Hsien of the Hilton International Taipei worked together on this version of a Chinese classic that is light and restrained—but releases a powerful perfume of ginger, chillis, and coriander as you spoon hot oil over the assembled ingredients. Although quick and easy to make, the visual impact is considerable: white tofu rectangles swimming in dark soya sauce are topped with balls of pink shrimp and shreds of red chilli, yellow ginger, spring onion, and frilly coriander leaves.

275 g (10 oz) small raw prawns in the shell
1 egg white
⅛ teaspoon salt
Pepper
450 g (1 lb) medium tofu in one block (see Note)
2 tablespoons Chinese dark soya sauce (see Note)

1 medium spring onion, cut into thin 5 cm (2-inch) strips
1 tablespoon very fine julienne-cut fresh ginger
1 teaspoon very fine julienne-cut hot red chilli-pepper, ribs and seeds removed
16 coriander sprigs
50 ml (2 fl oz) peanut oil

1. Peel the prawns and set aside 8 of them. Mince the remainder. Whisk the egg white lightly to break it up; measure one half of it, then discard the rest. Blend with the finely chopped prawns, salt, and pepper.

2. Cut the tofu into 8 rectangles by first halving the block lengthwise, then cutting in 4 crosswise. With a melon ball cutter or teaspoon, scoop a well in the centre of each piece to go about halfway through (see Options). Mound a heaped teaspoon of the prawn filling in each well. Set on a dish to fit on a steamer rack.

3. Place the dish in the steamer over boiling water. Cover and steam for 5 minutes. Set the whole prawns alongside the tofu; cook for 1–2 minutes longer, until pink. (Drain liquid from the plates if there seems to be an excess.)

4. Spoon the soya sauce onto a heated serving dish. Carefully transfer the tofu to the dish. Set a prawn on each. Sprinkle with the spring onion, ginger, and chilli; top with the coriander. Heat the oil in a small pan; pour evenly over all (beware of splatters).

Note: *The freshly made tofu blocks available in Oriental groceries will have more flavour and delicacy than the packaged varieties—although these will do nicely, as well.*

   Chinese dark, thick, or black soya sauce is available in all Oriental markets and many supermarkets.
Advance preparation: *The dish can be readied through Step 2 and the vegetables julienned, then all refrigerated until 10–15 minutes before serving time.*
Options: *The small balls scooped from the tofu can be steamed alongside the tofu blocks—or nibbled by the cook.*

SERVES 4 AS A MAIN COURSE; 8 AS AN APPETIZER

ROASTED ROOT VEGETABLE STRIPS WITH CARAWAY

AUSTRALIA

Although considerably simplified from chef Herbert Franceschini's original presentation in which a medley of shaped vegetables were set on a trellis of puff pastry, the flavours here are much the same. Colourful and earthy-sweet, this casual version of an elaborate dish is, nevertheless, attractive and unusual. The recipe was developed as an accompaniment to the Buffalo Fillets with Pumpkin Sauce and Goat Cheese (page 295), served at the Hilton International Brisbane.

4 medium-small beetroot (about 450 g/1 lb, weighed without leaves)	**2 medium potatoes (450 g/1 lb)**
1 small swede (about 450 g/1 lb), peeled	**Salt**
2 large carrots (about 300 g/10 oz), peeled	**25 g (1 oz) butter**
2 medium sweet potatoes (about 450 g/1 lb)	**1½ tablespoons vegetable oil**
	1 teaspoon coarse sea salt
	1 teaspoon caraway seeds
	½ teaspoon grated nutmeg
	About ¼ teaspoon pepper

1. Preheat the oven to 240°C/475°F (gas mark 9). Drop the beetroot into a pan of boiling, salted water. Boil until not quite tender, 15–20 minutes. Rinse in cool water; slip off the skins and trim.

2. Meanwhile, bring a very large pan of water to a boil. Cut the swede into strips about 5 cm (2-inches) long and 1 cm (½-inch) thick. Do the same to the carrots. Peel the sweet potatoes and cut to the same size. Do the same with the potatoes.

3. Add salt to the pan of boiling water; drop the vegetable strips in the water, cover, and return to a full boil. (The strips should be barely half-cooked, not tender; you'll need to cook more or less time, depending upon how effective your stove is.)

4. Drain the vegetables well. Heat a wide roasting pan (about 30 × 45 cm/12 × 18 inches) with the butter and 1 tablespoon vegetable oil. Add the vegetables, then sprinkle with the coarse salt, caraway, nutmeg and pepper. Toss to coat.

5. Place in the upper level of the hot oven. Bake for about 35 minutes, until browned and slightly crisp, tossing gently every 10 minutes or so. Meanwhile, cut the beetroot into strips the same size as the other vegetables. Combine them in a cake tin with the remaining ½ tablespoon oil. Bake about 15 minutes, until tender and lightly browned. Scoop the mixed vegetables onto a serving platter. Surround with the beetroot.

4–6 SERVINGS

Aromatic Rice with Nuts, Raisins and Shallots
(Nasi Beryani)
INDONESIA AND MALAYSIA

This traditional dish is a ceremonial one, served only at special banquets and on Fridays (the Muslim sabbath) at the Jakarta Hilton International and the Kuala Lumpur Hilton. For Malaysian and Indonesian dinners of importance, four or five dishes and soup are set out on the table, followed by the plates, onto which is spooned rice (nasi)—which may be plain white, or flavoured with coconut, tomato, turmeric, and a number of other variations, such as the following, of Indian Moghul origin. But the flowery incense that blooms forth from the bouquet of aromatics distinguishes the recipe as one transplanted to the Spice Islands.

100 g (4 oz) butter
150 g (5 oz) finely chopped onion
60 g (2½ oz) finely chopped shallots
60 g (2½ oz) finely chopped peeled
   fresh ginger
1 tablespoon finely chopped garlic
2 small cinnamon sticks, broken into
   tiny pieces
10 cardamom pods, crushed, seeds
   removed, and pods discarded
10 cloves
625 g (21 oz) long-grain white rice
1.5 litres (2½ pints) chicken stock

225 ml (8 fl oz) milk
About 2 teaspoons rose water
12 medium basil leaves (see Note)
1 teaspoon salt
75 g (3 oz) raisins
½ teaspoon saffron threads mixed
   with 3 tablespoons hot water
85 g (3½ oz) roasted *kemiri*
   (candlenuts), macadamia, or
   cashew nuts
Fried shallots (see recipe for
   Hainanese Chicken, page 302)

1. Heat the butter in a large heavy saucepan over moderate heat. Stir in the onion, shallots, ginger and garlic: cook until light brown, stirring often.

2. Add the cinnamon, cardamom seeds and cloves; toss for 2 minutes longer. Add the rice and stir for 1 minute. Add the chicken stock, milk, 2 teaspoons rose water, the basil and salt; bring to a boil, stirring.

3. Cover the pan and cook over lowest heat for 20 minutes. Remove from the heat and let stand, covered, for 10–20 minutes, as convenient. Toss together with the raisins in a warm serving dish. Let stand, covered, for 5 minutes. Drizzle the saffron water over the top. Add the nuts and fried shallots. Serve hot.

Note: *Basil leaves have been substituted for* pandanus *(screw pine). If the latter are available to you, use 6 of them instead.*

8 SERVINGS AS A SIDE DISH

FRIED EGG NOODLES WITH MIXED VEGETABLES
(Bakmi Goreng)
INDONESIA

Obviously influenced by the Chinese lo mein *stir-fries, this popular Javanese vegetable medley (accented with prawn and chicken) appears in many guises, all containing plenty of garlic. At the Jakarta Hilton International the dish is accompanied by cucumber, sliced tomato, a flower-cut red chilli-pepper, fried shallot flakes (see page 303), puffed prawn crackers (*krupuk *or* kroepek)*, and a side of* sambal oelek, *the omnipresent ground chilli condiment that fires Indonesian tastebuds.*

Although the following mix of vegetables is particularly colourful and crunchy, anything goes in this simple-to-make, one-dish meal that is comfortable, easy, but exotic.

225 g (½ lb) fine egg noodles
100 ml (4 fl oz) vegetable oil
2 eggs, beaten to blend
1 medium onion, halved and sliced
1½ tablespoons finely chopped garlic
175 g (6 oz) peeled raw prawns (10 medium), cut into 2.5 cm (1-inch) pieces
1 small boneless, skinless chicken breast (about 150 g/5 oz), cut into thin strips about 5 cm (2-inches) long
2 medium sticks celery, trimmed and cut into 5 cm (2-inch) julienne

100 g (4 oz) mangetout peas, strings removed and cut diagonally into 2–3 pieces
1 medium carrot, cut into 5 cm (2-inch) julienne
1 very small leek, cleaned and cut into 5 cm (2-inch) julienne
225 g (8 oz) small bok choy, leaves cut 2.5 cm (1-inch) wide, stems 1 cm (½-inch) wide
50 ml (2 fl oz) plus 1 tablespoon chicken stock
About 2 tablespoons *ketjap manis* (see Note)
Salt and pepper

1. Preheat the oven to its lowest setting. Drop the egg noodles into a pan of boiling salted water. Return to a boil and cook for a few minutes until just tender. Drain, rinse in cold water; drain again.

2. Heat a 20 cm (8-inch) non-stick pan with ½ tablespoon oil. Pour in half the egg and tip the pan to coat evenly. Cook over moderately low heat until no longer wet on the surface. With a thin, flexible spatula flip onto a chopping board surface. Repeat with the remaining egg and ½ tablespoon oil. Cut both pancakes into thin strips and reserve.

3. Heat a wok over high heat; pour 2 tablespoons oil around the rim. Add the onion and toss for a minute. Add the garlic, prawns, and chicken and toss until not quite done, about 1 minute. Scoop into a large serving dish and set in the warm oven.

4. Add 1½ tablespoons oil to the wok; add the celery, mangetout peas, and carrot. Toss over moderately high heat for 1½ minutes, until half-cooked. Add 1½ tablespoons more oil, the leek, and bok choy; toss a moment. Add 50 ml (2 fl oz) chicken stock and toss for about 1½ minutes, until just barely tender.

5. Meanwhile, blend together 2 tablespoons of the *ketjap manis* and the remaining 1 tablespoon stock. Raise the heat to high; add the remaining oil to the wok, then the noodles; toss. Add the prawn-chicken mixture, *ketjap manis,* and salt and pepper to taste, tossing vigorously and separating the noodle strands. Taste for additional *ketjap manis.*

6. Scoop into the heated dish. Sprinkle with the egg strips, toss lightly, and serve hot or at room temperature.

Note: Ketjap manis, *a thick, sweet, dark Indonesian soya sauce can be purchased at many Asian shops. If it is impossible to obtain, substitute half Chinese dark soya sauce and half molasses.*
Serving and presentation: *This makes a casual, but special hot main dish; or serve it with additional vegetables as a buffet pasta salad. Do not chill, or the special freshness and balance will be lost.*

4 SERVINGS

SPAGHETTI SAKURA

JAPAN

Sakura is the coffee shop in the Tokyo Hilton International that boasts fast-changing ethnic food promotions, beloved by the adventurous Japanese, who rapidly devour each new subject. A pasta week included this mild, slightly garlickly, creamy hybrid of Italian and Oriental (the shiitake *and* shimeji, *or oyster mushrooms) origin, which became a part of the regular menu in no time.*

150 g (5 oz) fresh *shiitake*
75 g (3 oz) small oyster mushrooms *(pleurottes)*
75 g (3 oz) small button mushrooms
50 g (2 oz) butter
60 g (2½ oz) finely chopped onion
1–1½ teaspoons finely chopped garlic
150 ml (¼ pint) very light dry white wine

225 ml (8 fl oz) double (or whipping) cream
2 tablespoons finely chopped parsley
2 teaspoons fresh thyme leaves
2 tablespoons finely chopped basil leaves
450 g (1 lb) spaghetti
Salt and pepper
Grated Parmesan cheese

1. Wipe the mushrooms clean with a damp towel. Remove the *shiitake* stems; trim the tips of the oyster mushrooms; reserve both for future stock-making. Cut the *shiitake* caps and button mushrooms in thin slices. If the oyster mushrooms are not small, cut them in small pieces.

2. Heat the butter in a wide frying pan over moderate heat. Add the onion and toss for a minute; add the garlic and toss a minute longer. Add all the mushrooms and toss over moderately high heat until some liquid is exuded, about 3 minutes. Turn the heat to high and toss until the juices have nearly evaporated.

3. Add the wine and boil until there are just a few spoonfuls left in the pan. Add the cream and boil until very slightly thickened. Stir in half the herbs, then remove from the heat.

4. Meanwhile, drop the spaghetti into a large pan of boiling salted water. Boil until just tender. Drain well.

5. Add the spaghetti to the frying pan; fold together with the sauce over low heat. Add salt and pepper to taste, then sprinkle with the remaining herbs. Serve with the cheese alongside.

4 SERVINGS

SPICED CHICK-PEAS WITH FRESH WHITE CHEESE
(Chana Pindi)
INDIA

Caraway and lime add new dimensions to warming chick-peas tinted tawny by tea. The fresh white cheese is quickly prepared, quite creamy and firm, and turns golden and soft when fried. While Sushil Chugh at the Hilton International Khartoum in the Sudan is the source of this recipe, it is a north Indian dish—which originated in Pindi, once in India, now in Pakistan. A popular street snack, the spicy mixture is served with deep-fried, thick pancake-type breads called bhaturas. *It also makes an unusual main course or side dish to a meat dinner.*

(continued)

Exuberant executive chef Detlef Skrobanek (right) in the Jakarta market

Like much of South-east Asia and the Pacific, Indonesia depends heavily upon rice (black and brick red, as well as white) and numerous rice flour products, coconut milk (the milk, cream and butter of the islands), fermented seafood pastes and sauces, chillis galore, and garlic. But a visit to the market in Jakarta, the capital, on the island of Java, reveals other distinctive mainstays: fresh, dried, pickled and sugared fruits of every colour, texture, and shape; peanuts; intensely sweet-sour tamarind (its sticky prunish flesh liquefied as a common cooking medium); oil-rich nuts that bind and thicken sauces; mountains of pearly-pink shallots; and of course, the wealth of spices from the Moluccas (the Spice Islands). But what most intrigues a curious cook is the unimaginable array of aromatics in the forms of roots, rhizomes, grasses and leaves. Citrusy, subtle lemon grass and bright ginger are paramount, but they are only the beginning. Bulbous yellow-orange turmeric and its leaves; *kentjur* and *lengkuas* (also called *laos* or galingale)—assertive members of the ginger clan; a half-dozen varieties of wild and cultivated limes, citrons, and their leaves; and the leaves of pomegranate, papaya and guava.

At a typical Indonesian meal, such as the one lavishly and lovingly prepared at the Jakarta Hilton International, all dishes (30, in this atypical instance) are offered together in serve-yourself fashion, to be eaten with spoon and fork only. Sauces are principal and omnipresent. They may be thin and fiery, thick and nutty, oily and spicy-sweet— or any combination of the above. Although ingredients reappear in many dishes, each final product is subtle and focused, not repetitious. Food may be hot, warm, or at room temperature, but is usually the latter. Condiments are a must, with soya sauce, chilli, shallot and seafood pastes the main ingredients of the compound sauces, plus a rainbow of raw and pickled fruits and vegetables. Rice, plain-cooked or fancified with aromatics and coconut, appears at all meals.

A few of the savoury specialities from this traditional array were *sayur bening*, a colourful soup of fragrant and bitter leaves stirred into a clean, hot stock with bits of sweet corn, tomato, shallot, and garlic; *sayur lodeh*, long beans, jakfruit (or jackfruit, an immense, fleshy tropical fruit), and aubergine braised in a spiced coconut sauce; *ayam tuturuga*, a hot-sweet, lime and chilli-sparked chicken stew; *gulai otak*, creamy brains in a thin curry sauce; *ayam goreng padang*, chicken marinated in chilli, crushed turmeric and ginger roots, and shallot, half-cooked in stock, then dried and deep-fried; *udang balado*, large chilli-marinated prawns sauced with tamarind, tomato, garlic and lemon leaves, grass and roots; *ayam kalio*, chicken simmered in a thick sauce of *laos* and ginger roots, lime leaves, cumin and coriander powders and coconut; and *nasi kuning*, a golden turmeric and ginger-scented rice.

As if these pleasures were not sufficient to entice even the most jaded palate, a new form of cooking is percolating at the Jakarta Hilton International, where a small team is refining dishes made from these evocative ingredients, honing the flavours, and streamlining the presentation for cosmopolitan connoisseurs. Surprisingly, in a country that appears to be even more nationalistically food-passionate than France or Italy, it is a German-Canadian chef trained in Switzerland, Detlef Skrobanek, who has managed to receive the culinary endorsement of the government through its foreign minister, Dr. Mochtar Kusumaatmadja. The minister, who sadly concedes that the dig-in buffet style of Indonesian meals is little suited to affairs of state and business dinners, but who wishes to present the fare of the country to visiting dignitaries, has encouraged the small revolution in the Hilton International's kitchen.

Nouvelle Indonesian cuisine, with executive chef Skrobanek and Sumatran sous-chef

S. Johan Darussalam in charge, is acquiring a quiet, but devoted audience. Skrobanek (a mastermind of organization and precision, who has systematically studied and deeply absorbed the culture) takes local ingredients and grafts onto them European techniques, without intruding foreign flavours or disturbing the intrinsic balance. He is not creating French menus with Indonesian fillips, but working with the precepts of the native cuisine and adjusting elements that are less desirable to Westerners. For example, foods usually served warm are now either hot or cold. Dishes that have traditionally been over-cooked by Western standards are now cooked *à point*. Dishes that are normally heavily sauced and extremely rich and oily have been lightened. (But the sauces and seasonings that are the roots of the Indonesian cuisine are little touched. Skrobanek is intrigued by the use of leaves, nuts, large quantities of spices and grated coconut flesh and coconut milk as thickeners; no starches are introduced. He is in awe of the brilliant way in which Indonesian cooks invariably balance the complicated mixtures.) Presentation that is festive, but hodge-podge, has been replaced with a personal visual aesthetic that is in keeping with the food, and as graceful as Balinese wood carving or the exquisite and fleeting Javanese fresh palm leaf decoration *(janur)* that decorates the dining areas.

A team of eight has also created new dishes using Indonesian ingredients, pure inventions in the style of the country—which are either accepted or rejected summarily by the locals ('fortunately, they are most outspoken,' says Skrobanek, 'you know at once what they like.'). For most Indonesians, the deliberate presentation and comparatively small quantities are reason for hesitation; for Westerners, the mysterious flavours engender ambivalence (What is this? What am I eating?). For those lucky enough to fit somewhere in-between, there may be a taste of paradise in their future— such as this exemplary meal of innovative and traditionally based dishes, served in small portions, in the Nouvelle style, and embellished with a centrepiece of weeping jasmine and roses:

—Warm Duck Breast Salad: hot-smoked, spice-marinated duck with a toss of bean sprouts, Chinese black mushrooms, yardlong beans, and tomatoes in a light vinaigrette;

—Bird's Nest Soup with Quail Eggs: clarified amber chicken broth made with the world's premiere birds' nests, from Java; the bite of chilli and perfume of lemon grass and coriander dominate, as a confetti of diced carrots, green pepper diamonds, celery strands, and transparent, chewy bird's nest supply textural counterpoints;

—Fillets of Sole with Sour Turmeric Sauce: thin fillets sandwiching basil and finely chopped fresh red chilli served on a thick, mustard-yellow sweet-sour turmeric sauce, garnished with vegetables and basil leaves;

—Cucumber Granita: a bracing *intermezzo* of icy shredded cucumber, ginger slivers, and lime juice;

—Beef Tenderloin with Vegetables in Peanut Sauce: beef is marinated in spices, garlic, and shallots, briefly simmered, then roasted until crusty on the outside and cool-rare on the inside; accompanied by a light, hot-sweet sauce and a salad of chilli, cucumber, bean sprouts, lime leaves, and baby aubergine with peanut and tamarind dressing served in a nest of braided yardlong beans;

—Fruits with Fermented Rice and Cinnamon Sauce: melons, pineapple, and papaya macerated in palm wine, with rough grains of black rice softened and fermented in wine, topped with coconut ice cream, then cloaked in a light sabayon sauce and burnt-glazed under intense heat.

PRAWNS IN COCONUT-CHILLI SAUCE
(Sambal Goreng Udang)
INDONESIA

A beginner's guide to the tastes of Indonesia (specifically Sumatra, in this case): Fresh hot red chilli-pepper, lemon grass, garlic, shallot and coconut milk are among the most common flavours and textures to be found, but by no means common in their blending. At the Peacock Café in the Jakarta Hilton International, where this popular (and speedily prepared) dish is featured, it is served with rice topped with fried shallots (see recipe for Hainanese Chicken, page 302) and a dish of bean sprouts.

Because there is tremendous variation in the pungency of lemon grass and chillis, the seasoning may need some adjustment. Stir additional chilli into the sauce at the end, if necessary. Coconut milk varies as well, and may be very thick. In Indonesia the sauce is quite thin, but Westerners usually prefer a richer consistency, such as the following. Do not be surprised when the sauce separates slightly, which coconut will do.

(continued)

2 medium stalks lemon grass
  (see Note)
2 tablespoons vegetable oil
1 tablespoon finely chopped garlic
50 g (2 oz) finely chopped shallots
2–3 teaspoons thinly slivered very
  hot red chilli-pepper, seeds and
  ribs removed

2 bay leaves (see Note)
450 ml (¾ pint) unsweetened coconut milk (see Note)
About ¾ teaspoon salt
700 g (1½ lb) shelled medium
  prawns (about 900 g/2 lb unpeeled)

1. Cut the heavy, dry upper leaves from the lemon grass and trim off the heavy tip of the base. Unwrap several layers of the coarse leaves. Halve the inner stalks lengthwise. Cut into the very finest slices possible, to equal 3 tablespoons.

2. Heat the oil in a saucepan; stir in the garlic, shallots, 2 teaspoons chilli-pepper, bay leaves and lemon grass; stir for a minute. Cover and cook over lowest heat for 5 minutes.

3. Add the coconut milk and salt; bring to a simmer. Add the prawns and poach at under a simmer until just warmed through, about 1 minute. Scoop into a wide, heated dish.

Note: *Long stalks of greyish-green fresh lemon grass can be found in some stores that carry foods from South-east Asia and in some supermarkets. They add a subtle, inimitable lemon pungency.*
  Salam leaves are used in Indonesia instead of bay leaves; substitute these, if they are available to you.
  Coconut milk is available in bottles or cans in stores that carry ingredients from India and Asia. If you cannot buy it, make your own, following the directions on page 325.
Serving: *This is unquestionably a dish to serve with fluffy, white rice, plenty of it.*
Options: *While testing, we added a sprinkling of fine fresh ginger julienne, which was delicious, if untraditional.*

4 SERVINGS

Prawns in Papaya Sauce

SINGAPORE

The sensitive touch of the chefs at the Hilton International Singapore is evident in this beautiful, simple dish from the Harbour Grill. Lightly sweet, fruity, with a touch of heat, the effect is tropical, but tempered. The deliriously sunset pink papaya of Asia is difficult to come by outside of Hawaii and California, but the easily obtained small, apricot-coloured variety will do as nicely—provided you choose one that is yellow-ripe.

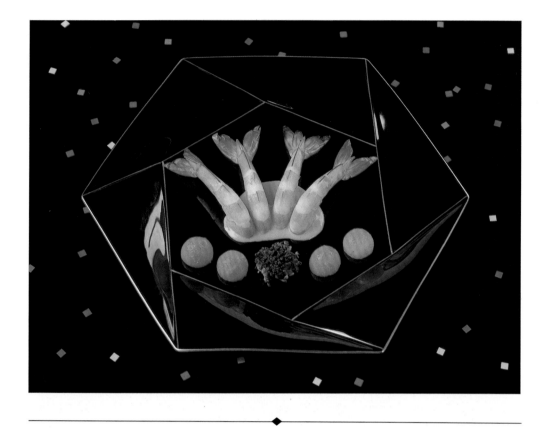

1 ripe papaya (about 450 g/1 lb), halved and seeded
20 medium-large prawns, peeled (about 900 g/2 lb in the shell)
50 ml (2 fl oz) fish stock (see page 326)
2 tablespoons double cream

¼–1 teaspoon finely chopped hot red chilli-pepper (seeded, veins removed)
Lemon juice
Salt, pepper, and sugar
30 g (generous 1 oz) butter

1. Preheat the oven to its lowest setting. With a 2.5 cm (1-inch) melon ball cutter, scoop 20 balls of papaya; set aside in a heatproof, shallow serving dish in the warm oven. Scrape the remaining flesh into the container of a blender or processor; purée.

2. Set the prawns on a steaming rack over boiling water; cover and steam for about 1½ minutes, until just heated through.

3. Meanwhile, combine the papaya purée, fish stock and cream in a non-aluminium saucepan and bring to a boil, stirring. Simmer for a minute, then remove from the heat. With an electric hand mixer beat in the chilli and lemon juice, and salt, pepper, and sugar to taste. Gradually beat in the butter.

4. Arrange the prawns and papaya balls, pour over the sauce, and serve at once.

4 SERVINGS

POMFRET WITH GINGER FRAGRANCE

SINGAPORE

When Peter Knipp (now executive chef of the Shanghai Hilton International) was sous-chef in the Harbour Grill of the Hilton International Singapore, he developed this balanced dish, one that still suits his taste: 'It's a fine example of ingredients that fit together with no pushing.' A garnish of multicoloured, fine vegetable julienne with twirls of spring onion decorates the snowy, smooth-grained pomfret. The sharply gingered cooking stock is much reduced, then considerably mellowed with butter to create the pale yellow 'East meets West' sauce that surrounds the fish.

1.6 kilo (3¼-lb) pomfret, filleted and skinned, bones and head reserved
100 g (4 oz) coarsely chopped fresh ginger
1 medium carrot, sliced
1 stick celery, sliced
2 tablespoons parsley stalks
2 tablespoons coriander leaves and stems, sliced
2 medium spring onions, sliced
1 teaspoon white peppercorns, crushed
½ teaspoon dried thyme leaves

100 ml (4 fl oz) dry white wine or dry vermouth
750 ml (1¼ pints) fish stock (see page 326)
Salt and pepper
Vegetable garnish (see Note)
60 g (2½ oz) very fine fresh ginger julienne
50 g (2 oz) fine celery julienne
50 g (2 oz) fine carrot julienne
50 g (2 oz) thin sliced spring onion
100 g (4 oz) butter, chilled
Salt and white pepper

---

1. Remove and discard the gills and innards from the fish skeleton. Rinse the bones and head well and combine in a non-aluminium pan with the chopped ginger, sliced carrot, celery, parsley stalks, coriander, spring onions, peppercorns, thyme, white wine and fish stock. Barely simmer, uncovered, for 25 minutes. Strain through a muslin-lined sieve. Boil briefly to reduce to 175 ml (6 fl oz).

2. Preheat the oven to 190°C/375°F (gas mark 5). Halve each pomfret fillet crosswise; season with salt and pepper. Place in a single layer in a buttered baking dish. Spoon over 2 tablespoons of the stock, distributing evenly. Cover with foil; set in the upper level of the preheated oven until the fish is no longer translucent in the centre—about 12 minutes.

3. Meanwhile, spread the julienned vegetables in a 23 cm (9-inch) frying pan or sauce-pan. Pour over the remaining stock. Boil for 2 minutes, until barely tender. On lowest heat, add the butter, a little at a time, stirring vigorously. Season with salt and pepper. Keep over low heat.

4. Transfer the fish to a warmed serving platter. Spoon over the vegetables and sauce.

Note: *It is important to cut the finest julienne of vegetables. The vivid lemony ginger, herbal celery, and sweet carrot should blend, not remain distinct.*

4 SERVINGS

FANCY-CUT SQUID STIR-FRIED WITH ASPARAGUS

TAIWAN

Of Cantonese origin, this light dish hails from the Hilton International Taipei. Scoring the squid tenderizes the flesh and transforms the pieces into patterned twists that look appealing with the orange carrot ovals and diagonally cut jade asparagus. The flavours are natural and unaffected, clear and individualized.

Although cutting the ingredients is comparatively time-consuming, the cooking takes only minutes. Do not skip the squid-blanching, which prevents liquid from seeping into the crisp vegetables.

---

700 g (1½ lb) cleaned squid
450 g (1 lb) medium asparagus
2 medium-large carrots, peeled and cut into thin diagonal slices
4 medium spring onions, cleaned and cut into 2.5 cm (1-inch) diagonal slices
1–2 tablespoons finely chopped garlic

3 tablespoons fine julienne-cut fresh ginger
1 teaspoon cornflour
2 tablespoons rice wine
2 teaspoons rice vinegar
1 teaspoon sesame oil
About 5 tablespoons peanut oil
Salt and pepper

---

1. Slit the cleaned squid mantles so that they lie flat. With a sharp knife score halfway through the flesh in as small a criss-cross pattern as you can manage, covering the entire surface. Cut the scored squid into bite-size rectangles, triangles, or squares, as convenient. Drop the pieces into a large pot of boiling salted water. Return to a boil over highest heat; drain.

2. Break the woody base from the asparagus. Peel the asparagus, then cut into long diagonal slices about 2 mm (¹⁄₁₆ inch) thick. Prepare the remaining vegetables as indicated. Blend together the cornflour, rice wine, rice vinegar, and sesame oil in a cup.

3. Heat a wok over high heat; pour 2 tablespoons peanut oil around the rim. Add the carrots and asparagus and toss for 3–4 minutes, until almost cooked through. Transfer to a plate.

4. Add another tablespoon of oil to the wok. Add the squid and toss for about 1 minute. Scoop onto the plate with the vegetables.

5. Add the remaining peanut oil to the wok. Toss the spring onions, garlic, and ginger for 1 minute. Add the squid and vegetables to the wok and toss for 1 minute. Lower the heat, then stir in the cornflour mixture. Toss for another minute. Add salt and pepper to taste, then transfer to a heated dish.

Advance preparation: Although the wok-cooking cannot be done until the last minute, all the cutting can be accomplished ahead of time and the squid scored and blanched.

4 SERVINGS

The Best of Both Worlds:
Chef Peter Knipp

'I don't consider myself Western or Asian,' says German-born executive chef Peter Knipp, 'just plain fortunate.' Although barely into his thirties, Mr Knipp, a 16-year veteran of Hilton International, has worked in the kitchens of West Germany, Canada, Switzerland, Malaysia, Indonesia (where he married his Chinese wife in the Jakarta Hilton), Australia, Japan, Singapore, Taiwan, and now China. 'My cooking has evolved as a natural consequence of the audience I wish to please.' At first, a lack of Western produce forced Knipp and his colleagues in Asian countries to fashion local ingredients into forms suitable for a multinational clientele, but now such combinations are sought after. Knipp predicts that during the next 10 years Asian foods will become household words all over the West: 'A union of exotic ingredients and European culinary styles is the marriage of the future.'

Such an alliance was exemplified in a cross-cultural meal recently created by Knipp:

—A lacquer-skinned tiny *ballottine* of warm, lightly smoked chicken stuffed with minced chicken and pine nuts, sliced into rounds and set on greens in basil vinaigrette;

—Pomfret fillets wrapped around blanched spring onions, steamed, and served with a ginger butter sauce, slices of luffa gourd stuffed with a purée of fish and chilli-peppers, and fennel boats heaped with turmeric rice;

—A palate cleanser of barely sugared ginger sorbet;

—Rectangles of silken tofu topped with finely chopped veal and *shiitake* drenched with herbal cream sauce and accompanied by baby corn and a fan of *al dente* carrot strips;

—Guava compote contained in deep-fried wonton wrappers—hot, crunchy and sugar-dusted—set between 'waves' of custard-soft furled mango slices and a violet sauce of blueberry tofu cream.

Knipp has always felt an affinity with Asian food and culture and is gratified that work as a chef has permitted him to travel in the countries he wished to explore. Despite his remarkable height and youth, his composure, basso voice and Oriental Vandyke give the impression of an implacable and ageless mandarin. He has learned several Asian languages sufficiently well to communicate in the kitchen and beyond. 'Food has a different meaning here, and if you are willing and able to absorb the messages, understanding follows. Food maintains cultural practices and enforces important parts of the life cycle, particularly in Chinese society.'

Knipp, whose dedication to Chinese aesthetics is apparent in his work (including photography, his other love), has gathered, through his artistic creations, a bouquet of medals and honours for Hilton International and for the national teams he has headed in Singapore and Taipei. In fact, he may be the one responsible for putting the East on the map of culinary competitions. As sous-chef in Singapore, Knipp won the overall

Chef Peter Knipp, fish in hand

Stuffed Tofu with Prawns (see page 264 for recipe)

gold medal in the individual category and the grand prize trophy of the World Culinary Contest (held every 10 years, that time in Osaka) in which 140 European and Japanese chefs participated. Consecutive years of medals followed, including the 1984 gold medal at the prestigious culinary Olympics in Frankfurt. With Knipp leading a team of eight chefs from Singapore in a competition of 1,000 professionals, the group culled eight gold medals in as many categories that ran from 'pure' Eastern to 'pure' Western. Few had even given a thought to an Asian team in the midst of European stars.

Yet no one who knows this chef would be surprised, for he is an inspiring teacher who develops extensive, individualized training programmes in each kitchen he oversees, energizing the staff. 'Medals are temporary,' he declares, 'but the stimulating, exhilarating effects of the competition last. These are the most exciting places for cultural exchanges to take place.' For many Asian chefs it is a first exposure to the work of their Asian peers and to Western chefs—and for the latter, it can be a stunning eye-opener that leads to awe for the work done in Asia, and to the inclusion of Oriental ingredients and presentation techniques in their food.

At the 1986 Salon Culinaire of Food & Hotel Asia, the panel of judges awarded eight gold and two silver medals to the Taipei International Culinary Team headed by Knipp, whose personal East-West mastery was demonstrated in two entries that stunned the judges. One extravaganza, Eight Divine Diagrams, interpreted the symbols of an octagram devised by Fu-Shi, a primary Chinese saint: earth, heaven, wind, thunder, mountain, fire, water and swamp were expressed in personal food combinations. In another presentation, tofu, chameleon of the Eastern kitchen, was the medium of the Eight Mythologies, each bearing the name of a god, each perfect as a jewel—and eminently edible. For one mythology, tofu was smoked, then filled with herbs and salmon eggs; for another, it was layered in small cakes with puréed vegetables and black sesame seeds; it appeared rolled with Chinese trout in *nori* and smoked salmon, as a terrine with seaweed, as a canapé with crab mousse and black beans, and enclosed in duck breast with young leeks in a vegetable broth with chillis. Finally, cut in the shapes of ancient Chinese coins, tofu was served on dark bread with a garnish of papaya and herbs. Neither strictly traditional nor culturally or culinarily jarring, the creations might be considered ideograms in a new vocabulary.

A selection of Chinese tidbits (dim sum) in bamboo steamer baskets

BEEF STEAKS WITH MUSTARD CREAM

JAPAN

The exquisite beef from Matsuzaka and Kobe that is offered by executive chef Siegfried Jaeger in the elegant Imari restaurant of the Tokyo Hilton International needs little accompaniment. The lustrous mahogany-hued sauce that surrounds the steak is a meaty classic of reduced veal stock sharpened with mustard, but the dish is given a unique contemporary tone with the addition of a dollop of cold whipped cream enriched with whole-grain mustard. Fresh egg noodles are a must.

1.8 kilos (4 lb) veal bones, cut or
   sawed into small pieces
1 large onion, cut into chunks
2 medium carrots, cut into chunks
1 celery stick, sliced
90 ml (3½ fl oz) double (or whipping) cream
40 g (1½ oz) butter

1 teaspoon Dijon mustard
1 teaspoon coarse (whole grain)
   mustard
1 tablespoon vegetable oil
Salt and pepper
4 boneless beef steaks (about
    175 g/6 oz each; see Option)

1. Prepare the veal stock: Preheat the oven to 230°C/450°F (gas mark 8). Spread the bones in a large roasting pan in a single layer. Set in the hot oven until well browned, about 30 minutes, stirring once. Add the onion, carrots, and celery. Reduce the heat to 200°C/400°F (gas mark 6) and roast for 10 minutes. Stir and roast for 10 minutes longer. Remove from the oven; tip the pan so the fat runs to one side; let stand briefly. Pour off fat. Transfer the contents of the pan into a stockpot; add 3 litres (5 pints) water. Bring to a boil, skimming. Meanwhile, add 450 ml (16 fl oz) water to the roasting pan. Stir over moderate heat to loosen the brown bits. Add to the stockpot. Keep at a bare simmer for 2 hours, or until reduced to about 900 ml (32 fl oz).

2. Strain the stock into a saucepan; boil gently until reduced to about 100 ml (4 fl oz). Add 2 tablespoons of the cream and bring to a boil. Add two-thirds of the butter and the Dijon mustard and whisk to just barely blend. Remove from the heat.

3. Combine the remaining cream with the whole grain mustard in a small, narrow bowl or measuring cup; beat to form firm peaks. Cover and refrigerate (can be left for at least an hour).

4. Heat the remaining butter and the oil in a 25 cm (10-inch) frying pan. Salt and pepper both sides of the steak and cook to the desired doneness. Place on 4 heated plates.

5. Warm the sauce and divide over the steaks. Scoop neat ovals of the mustard cream with a teaspoon and set one on each steak. Serve at once.

Note: *If you have a supply of veal stock, Step 1 can be skipped.*
Advance preparation: *The sauce can be prepared days ahead and heated. The mustard cream can be made an hour or so ahead.*
Option: *Although fillet is the cut served in Tokyo, other tender, boneless steaks—such as sirloin—are fine.*

4 SERVINGS

Buffalo Fillets with Pumpkin Sauce and Goat Cheese

AUSTRALIA

This most unusual combination of tender, juicy buffalo fillet topped with tart goat cheese set in a pool of sweet pumpkin sauce is adapted from an elaborate presentation devised by chef Herbert Franceschini of the Hilton International Brisbane. As served in the hotel, the buffalo (which is water buffalo in Australia, not bison, and which hails from Kangaroo Island, off the southern coast of Australia) is placed on a caraway-speckled puff pastry trellis and served with shaped beetroots, carrots, potatoes, rutabaga, and sweet potatoes on sautéed spinach leaves. A simplified version of these flavourful roots and tubers (see page 265) complements colourfully.

25 g (1 oz) butter
1 medium onion, sliced thin
450 g (1 lb) pumpkin or any hard, orange-fleshed squash, such as butternut or acorn; peeled, seeded, and cut into 2.5 cm (1-inch) pieces
1 teaspoon sliced garlic
225 ml (8 fl oz) veal or beef stock
¼ teaspoon dried thyme
1 tablespoon honey

100 g (4 fl oz) sweet or semisweet white wine or white port
About 50 ml (2 fl oz) double (or whipping) cream
Salt and pepper
1 tablespoon vegetable oil
4 buffalo fillets, cut about 5 cm (2-inches) thick (175 g/6 oz each)
60 g (2½-oz) cylinder fresh goat cheese, cut into 4 slices

1. Melt the butter in a medium saucepan over moderately low heat. Add the onion; stir occasionally until browned, about 10 minutes.

2. Add the pumpkin and garlic; stir for about 2 minutes. Add the stock, thyme, honey and wine. Bring to a boil. Cover, lower the heat, then simmer until very tender (timing can vary from 15–25 minutes, depending upon the variety of squash).

3. Pour the contents of the saucepan into the container of a blender. Purée until very smooth. Add the cream, adjusting to the desired consistency. Add salt and pepper to taste. Scoop into a saucepan.

4. Heat a medium-large frying pan over moderate heat. Add the vegetable oil, then the fillets. Brown deeply on both sides, cooking until done to taste—about 8 minutes for rare. (Buffalo needs slightly longer cooking than beef and is particularly luscious when rare.) Just as the meat reaches the desired degree of doneness, place a slice of cheese on top. Remove the pan from the heat.

5. Heat the sauce to simmering. Pour onto a heated serving dish (or onto 4 plates). Set the steaks on top and serve at once.

Advance preparation: *The sauce can be made ahead and reheated.*

4 SERVINGS

SMOKED DUCK BREAST SALAD, JAVANESE-STYLE
(Bebek Asap Lalaban)
INDONESIA

This spicy, beguiling combination, another illustration of the Indonesian nouvelle cuisine of Detlef Skrobanek and his team at the Jakarta Hilton International, was the opener for a spectacular dinner that they developed for the United Nations in New York. It has since become a best-seller at the hotel, although neither smoking, nor duck (with a few exceptions in Sumatra and Bali), is popular in Indonesia.

An adaptation of the dramatically smoky duck breast is surprisingly easy to accomplish at home without a smoker. The mahogany-edged slices are offered with crunchy vegetables in a light vinaigrette and a sweet-hot-sour peanut sauce.

Breasts from two 2.25 kilo (5-lb) ducks
1 teaspoon ground coriander
1 teaspoon ground cumin
1 teaspoon ground cloves
1 teaspoon ground turmeric
2½ teaspoons finely chopped shallot
2 tablespoons vegetable oil
50 g (2 oz) roasted unsalted peanuts
45 g (1¾ oz) soft brown sugar
About 2 teaspoons finely chopped very hot red chilli-pepper, seeds removed
About 60 ml (2½ fl oz) lemon juice (see Note)

Salt and pepper
3 tablespoons whole mixed pickling spices
10 dried black Oriental mushrooms (*shiitake*, forest mushrooms, Chinese mushrooms)
4 tablespoons peanut oil
175 g (6 oz) string beans, cut into 4 cm (1½-inch) pieces (see Note)
2 tablespoons distilled white vinegar
About 175 g (6 oz) mung bean sprouts
Optional: 4 ears baby corn, 4 fresh bay leaves (see Note)

1. Bone the breasts; trim each neatly. Combine the coriander, cumin, cloves, turmeric, 1½ teaspoons shallot and the vegetable oil. Rub over the duck (wear rubber gloves if you will be bothered by a curry-coloured temporary stain). Wrap tightly in clingfilm and refrigerate for about 24 hours. (The marinating may be omitted, if you prefer; simply rub the breasts with the spice mixture; let stand at room temperature as you proceed.)

2. Prepare the sauce: Combine the peanuts, brown sugar, and 1 teaspoon chilli-pepper in a blender or processor. Blend to a medium-fine texture. Add the lemon juice and process to a fine texture. Add salt, pepper, additional chilli and lemon juice to taste.

3. Combine the pickling spices in a small dish with water to cover. Combine the mushrooms, 225 ml (8 fl oz) water, and 1 tablespoon peanut oil in a small pan. Bring to a boil. Cover and let stand for at least 30 minutes. Trim off the stems (reserve for

(continued)

future stock-making). Cut the caps into thin slices. Boil the beans in salted water until they just lose their raw taste. Drain, refresh in cold water, then pat dry.

4. Blend together the vinegar with the remaining 1 teaspoon shallot, salt to taste, and about ½ teaspoon chilli-pepper. Blend in the remaining peanut oil. Pour over the mushrooms, beans, and bean sprouts. Toss gently, then taste and add salt and/or chilli to taste. Cover; refrigerate and chill for at least 30 minutes.

5. Heat a very heavy large cast-iron casserole or Dutch oven over moderate heat until very hot, about 10 minutes. Meanwhile, cook the duck breasts, fat side down, in a wide frying pan over moderate heat until nicely browned, pouring off the fat as it accumulates. Sear the other side of the breasts to brown.

6. Place the duck breasts, skin side up, on a round cake rack about 23 cm (9-inches) in diameter. Drain the pickling spices and sprinkle quickly and evenly in the cast-iron pot. Immediately set the rack with the duck over the spices; cover at once. Cook for 8 minutes (still over moderate heat). Turn off the heat and let stand 2 minutes longer. Open the pot, remove the ducks directly (quickly pour some water into the pot and cover; the drippings will soak off easily this way). Let the ducks cool on a cutting board for 5–20 minutes before serving.

7. Portion the vegetables onto 4 large serving dishes. Divide the sauce in neat pools alongside. Cut the breasts in thin, lengthwise slices and arrange neatly over the sauce. Sprinkle with the remaining ½ teaspoon or so of finely chopped chilli. Garnish, if desired, with the baby corn and bay leaves.

Note: *Mr Skrobanek uses tamarind juice instead of lemon and yardlong beans for the green beans. If these are available to you, do the same, adding the tamarind juice gradually to taste. Cook the beans slightly longer than string beans until tender throughout.*

Ready-to-eat ears of baby corn are sold in jars and cans in Oriental groceries and many supermarkets. If fresh ears of baby corn are obtainable, blanch them.

4 SERVINGS AS LUNCH OR LIGHT SUPPER

Pork Loin with Quince

AUSTRALIA

Chef Gerard Taye of the Hilton International Adelaide created a deep-flavoured course of wild boar steeped in brandy, quince, and ginger (a dish that hails back to ancient Rome) for the lavish Ultimate Dinner that is staged annually by the Hilton International Hotels in Australia in conjunction with Penfolds, notable vintners. Because wild boar is extremely difficult to obtain in many areas, pork has been substituted, and the techniques have been simplified for home cooks. The result, an easy-to-prepare melding of tender fruit and meat, is no compromise in taste.

1½ teaspoons peppercorns, crushed
1 medium onion, chopped
About 1 teaspoon salt
100 ml (4 fl oz) brandy
50 g (2 oz) peeled, thin-sliced
  fresh ginger
2 kilo (4½-lb) pork loin roast, boned
  (will equal about 1.3 kilos/3 lb);
  bones and trimmings reserved

1 tablespoon vegetable oil
1 tablespoon tomato purée
225 ml (8 fl oz) chicken stock
225 ml (8 fl oz) port
3 quinces (about 675 g/1½ lb), quartered, peeled, and cored
25 g (1 oz) pine nuts (pignolia)
Pepper

1. Combine the peppercorns, onion, salt, brandy, and ginger in a non-aluminium dish large enough to hold the meat. Add the pork; turn to coat. Cover and refrigerate for about 24 hours, turning as convenient.

2. Preheat the oven to 170°C/325°F (gas mark 3). Remove the meat and pat dry; reserve the marinade. Heat the vegetable oil in a heavy 5 litre (1 gallon) casserole or Dutch oven (preferably oval, not made of unlined iron or aluminium, which will discolour the quinces). Brown the meat well over high heat, then transfer to a dish. Add the reserved pork bones and trimmings to the pot; brown well. Pour off excessive fat, if necessary.

3. Strain and reserve the liquid from the marinade; add the solids to the pot. Cook over high heat for 5 minutes, stirring occasionally. Add the tomato purée; stir for 1 minute. Add the marinating liquid and 100 ml (4 fl oz) each of chicken stock and port.

4. Set the pork on this. Arrange the quinces closely around the pork (set on top of the bones, not immersed in liquid). Roast until the meat is cooked—1¼–1½ hours, depending on its thickness. Baste the quinces with the cooking liquid every 20 minutes or so during roasting.

5. Meanwhile, spread the pine nuts in a small pan and roast in the oven with the pork for about 10 minutes, until pale golden. Cool.

6. Transfer the meat to a cutting board and cover lightly with foil. Arrange the quince quarters around a platter; set in the turned-off oven. Add the remaining chicken stock and port to the pot. Bring to a boil, stirring to loosen all the brown bits; simmer for 2 minutes. Strain the juices from the pot. Skim off some of the fat. Season to taste with salt, pepper, brandy, and extra port.

7. Slice the meat; arrange with the quinces. Spoon over a little sauce; serve the rest separately. Sprinkle with pine nuts.

6 SERVINGS

STIR-FRIED PORK AND CASHEW NUTS
(Moo Pad Mamoung Himapan)
THAILAND

This attractive, casual Thai dish (almost Chinese, so direct is the influence) has the quintessential stir-fry look: brown-glazed cashew crescents, onion strips, and pork chunks sprinkled with slivers of red and green chilli-peppers. Although the oyster sauce offers a complex undertone, the combination is frankly garlicky, salty, hot, and satisfying.

2 medium onions
450 g (1 lb) boned pork loin
2 tablespoons vegetable oil
2 tablespoons sliced garlic
1 teaspoon sugar
100 g (4 oz) roasted unsalted cashew nuts

60 ml (2½ fl oz) oyster sauce (see Note)
1 large spring onion stalk (green part), cut into fine julienne
About 1 tablespoon *each* very fine julienne of hot red and green chilli-pepper, seeds and ribs removed

1. Cut the onions into 1 cm (½-inch) squares, separating the layers. Cut the pork crosswise into 1 cm (½-inch) slices. Cut each slice into strips about 2 cm (¾-inch) wide.

2. Heat a wok over moderate heat; pour 1 tablespoon oil around the rim. Toss the onions over moderate heat until lightly browned; add the garlic and toss for a minute. Transfer to a dish.

3. Pour the remaining 1 tablespoon of oil into the heated wok. Add the pork, spreading it out and up the sides in a single layer. Cook over high heat without turning until browned, a few minutes. Sprinkle with the sugar and toss for a minute or so, until browned all over.

4. Add the onion and garlic, cashews, and oyster sauce. Toss for about 2 minutes, until some of the liquid has evaporated and the meat is tender. Scoop into a heated serving dish; sprinkle with the spring onion and chilli-peppers to taste. Serve at once.

Note: *Bottled oyster sauce, a staple in the East, is available in all stores that carry Oriental ingredients and in many supermarkets.*

4 SERVINGS

HAINANESE CHICKEN-RICE DINNER

SINGAPORE/CHINA/TAIWAN

A traditional speciality of Singapore, this ideal party meal of exotic soup, ginger-flavoured rice, poached chicken, three intense sauces, and fried shallot garnish originates in the Hainan Islands of China. When chef Peter Knipp worked at the Singapore Hilton International, he added this version to the coffee shop menu, where it quickly became a fast favourite. When transferred to the Hilton International Taipei, he did the same—with equal success.

While the description and steps appear lengthy, the labour is minimal—and rewards are considerable, with an entire meal the result, not just a single dish.

1.75 litres (3 pints) homemade, unsalted chicken broth
3 medium spring onions, cleaned
  and trimmed
100–150 g (4–5 oz) fresh ginger
1.6 kilo (3½-lb) chicken
225 ml (8 fl oz) plus 1 tablespoon
  vegetable oil
8 medium shallots, peeled and sliced
1 tablespoon plain flour
250 g (9 oz) long-grain white rice
3 medium hot red chilli-peppers
1 teaspoon finely chopped garlic
50 ml (2 fl oz) lime juice

1 tablespoon packed brown sugar
2 teaspoons light soya sauce
2 teaspoons Chinese rice wine or
  dry sherry
2 teaspoons Oriental (dark) sesame
  oil
6–8 cos lettuce leaves
2 small cucumbers, peeled, seeded,
  and cut into 5–7.5 cm (2–3-inch)
  strips about 5 mm (¼ inch) thick
4 teaspoons coarsely chopped
  preserved Chinese vegetable
  (see Note)
60 ml (2½ fl oz) dark soya sauce
  (see Note)

1. Combine the chicken broth, 2 of the spring onions, and 4 ginger rounds cut about 1 cm (½ inch) thick in a pot just large enough to hold the chicken. Bring to a boil. Add the chicken; cover, and maintain just below a simmer for 25 minutes.

2. Meanwhile, heat 225 ml (8 fl oz) of the vegetable oil in a small saucepan over moderate heat. Toss the shallots with the flour. Add to the oil gradually, being careful of bubbling oil; fry until crisp and golden, stirring occasionally, 5–6 minutes. Drain and set aside on kitchen paper.

3. Carefully transfer the chicken to a platter and cover with wet muslin. When cool enough to handle, cut the leg-thigh sections from the bird and gently twist and cut out the bones. Halve the breast meat and lift from the carcass in 2 sections. Place in a close-fitting frying pan and pour over 225 ml (8 fl oz) of the broth. Cover with muslin. Refrigerate if not eating within an hour.

4. Combine the rice with 600 ml (1¼ pints) of the stock and 4 thin ginger slices in a 2 litre (3 pint) saucepan. Bring to a boil; turn the heat to its lowest point. Cover and cook for 20 minutes; remove from the heat and let stand for 15–30 minutes, covered. Fluff into a warm serving dish. Meanwhile, boil the remaining stock to reduce to 600 ml (1 pint).

5. Drop the chillis into boiling water; return to a boil. Remove them and chop finely (do not seed). Heat the remaining 1 tablespoon oil in a small pan. Add the chillis and toss for 1 minute over moderate heat. Add the finely chopped garlic, lime juice, and brown sugar; stir for a minute. Set aside.

6. Finely grate enough peeled ginger to equal 3 tablespoons; blend with 4 tablespoons cold water and salt to taste. Blend the light soya, rice wine and sesame oil. Arrange the lettuce and cucumbers on a platter.

7. Reheat the chicken on low heat. Transfer to a work surface; cut diagonal slices

(continued)

about 2.5 cm (1-inch) wide. Arrange on the cucumbers. Brush generously with the sesame oil mixture.

8. Slice the remaining spring onion into thin rounds. Divide the hot stock into small soup bowls; sprinkle with the spring onion, a teaspoon or so of fried shallots, and pickled vegetable. Serve the soup and rice along with tiny dishes of the grated ginger, the chilli dip, and the dark soya sauce for each diner.

Note: *Tianjin (Tientsin) pickled vegetable or Sichuanese (Szechuan) preserved mustard greens are among the several tangy members of the cabbage clan available in crocks, bottles, cans, and even sealed in plastic. They can be found in just about all Oriental markets.*

Chinese dark, thick, or black soya sauce is available in all Oriental groceries and many supermarkets.
Serving and presentation: *As much fun to make and serve as a fondue or firepot meal, the progression of dishes begs for company—and all the trimmings: chopsticks, miniature trios of sauceplates for each guest, individual Chinese rice bowls and soup bowls. Also desirable is a sense of play to mix and match the simple but intensely flavourful ingredients, so harmoniously balanced. The usual sequence is to dip a piece of chicken into a sauce, then soup, varying the dips, and drinking the intense brew that results.*
Advance preparation: *Although the chicken will not be just-poached perfect, it is delicious made in advance (but cook only 20 minutes), as is the entire meal. The soup and chilli and ginger sauces can be made a day ahead, cooled, and refrigerated. The shallots can be prepared days in advance, then closed in a tightly sealed jar. Cucumbers and lettuce can be cleaned and cut, then refrigerated in plastic.*

4 SERVINGS

CHICKEN TERRINE WITH COCONUT-CHILLI SAUCE
(Sambal Goreng Hati Ayam)
INDONESIA

From the Jakarta Hilton International, another beautiful example of exotic Eastern ingredients fashioned to fit a European mode (but beware of the innocent-looking sauce). The firm, tofu-lightened chicken loaf with its centre medallion of cabbage-wrapped liver is complemented by a wildly pungent purée redolent of chillis, garlic, ginger, and citrus, enriched with coconut. The use of cream (which seldom appears in Asian cooking) is due to an Indonesian cook's attendance of a European terrine demonstration. Much impressed, he employed the techniques for creating such a dish, incorporating local ingredients for the main part and adapting the flavours to fit the clientele.

Terrine

450 g (1 lb) boneless, skinless chicken breasts

¾ teaspoon salt

¼ teaspoon white pepper

1 egg

100 ml (4 fl oz) double (or whipping) cream

275 g (10 oz) firm tofu, well drained and cut into 2 cm (¾-inch) dice

1 tablespoon peanut oil

100 g (4 oz) chicken livers, cleaned and halved (see Option)

3 large, smooth Chinese cabbage leaves, about 30 cm (12 inches) long (choose the narrow, upright kind of cabbage rather than the rounded)

Sauce

1 tablespoon peanut oil

1½ tablespoons finely chopped garlic

1½ tablespoons finely chopped shallots

1 bay leaf

2 tablespoons chopped peeled fresh ginger

1 small stalk lemon grass, halved lengthwise, then cut in 10 cm (4-inch) lengths, or 10 cm (4-inch) strip lemon zest (see Note)

1 teaspoon tamarind paste, or 1 tablespoon lemon juice (see Note)

1 teaspoon brown sugar

1 tomato, peeled, cored, and coarsely chopped

3 tablespoons roasted macadamia nuts (or, preferably, candlenuts if available), crushed with a knife, meat pounder, or heavy pot

1 tablespoon or more Chinese chilli sauce (see Note)

225 ml (8 fl oz) unsweetened coconut milk (see Note)

Garnish: 1 tomato, peeled, seeded, and cut into small dice; a few feathery-cut Chinese cabbage leaf tips

1. Preheat the oven to 180°C/350°F (gas mark 4). Remove and discard all tendons and membranes from the chicken; cut the meat into 2.5 cm (1-inch) dice. Combine in a processor with the salt and pepper. Work to a smooth paste. Add the egg and cream and process just to blend. Scrape into a bowl and mix gently with the tofu.

2. Heat the peanut oil in a small frying pan; salt and pepper the livers lightly, then sauté just until they lose their raw look. Drop the Chinese cabbage leaves into boiling salted water; return to a boil. Refresh in cold water, drain; pat dry. Arrange the livers in a single file along the centre of 1 leaf, then enclose with 1 or 2 others to form a neat cylinder. Wrap in a towel to dry and firm.

3. Line a 1 litre (36 fl oz) rectangular terrine mould about 8 × 30 cm (3½ × 11-inches) with greaseproof paper. Spread half the chicken mixture in this. Set the cabbage cylinder on this, then fill with the remaining chicken mixture, packing it tightly against and over the roll so no air holes are left. Bang the terrine against the table a few times to eliminate any other holes. Fold over the greaseproof paper.   *(continued)*

4. Set the terrine on a folded tea towel in a roasting pan; half-fill witn boiling water. Set in the centre of the oven. Bake for 30 minutes. Remove from the water and set on a rack to cool. Chill for 6–24 hours before serving.

5. Make the sauce: Heat the oil in a small saucepan. Add the garlic, shallots, bay leaf, and ginger and stir over low heat until softened, about 3 minutes. Add the lemon grass, tamarind, brown sugar, tomato, macadamia nuts and 1 tablespoon chilli sauce. Stir for 5 minutes over moderately low heat. Add the coconut milk (and lemon juice, if you have not used tamarind). Simmer for 5 minutes, until slightly thickened.

6. Remove the bay leaf and lemon grass (or zest). Purée the sauce in a processor or blender to a fine texture. Season, adding salt, pepper and chilli sauce to taste. Cool, then chill several hours or more.

7. To serve, place 3 tablespoons of sauce (or half this amount, for an appetizer) in the centre of each plate. Arrange the garnishes alongside, then place 1 or 2 slices of the terrine on this.

Note: *Lemon grass and tamarind paste (see Clear Prawn Soup with Lemon Grass for both, page 258) will give the sauce an intense aroma and sweet-tart finish. Substituting lemon zest and juice will result in a delicious, if less concentrated and perfumed mixture.*

Canned or bottled Chinese chilli sauce is available in varying thicknesses and pungencies in some supermarkets and in all Oriental groceries. It should contain primarily chilli-peppers, garlic, sugar, vinegar, and salt.

Coconut milk can be found in Caribbean and Asian groceries. Or make your own following the instructions on page 325.

Serving and presentation: *Mr. Skrobanek serves the terrine with a palette of colourful, texturally contrasting, decorative garnishes: marbled quail eggs (for this follow any recipe for tea eggs in a Chinese cookbook, but cut down the cooking and steeping time considerably); yardlong beans cut in small pieces and blanched, and diamond-cut red papaya, water chestnuts, red chilli-peppers, and turnips—all blanched and chilled.*

Option: *For a pretty, delicate (non-Indonesian) alternative to the liver, substitute 9 medium, shelled prawns. Simply season the raw prawns with salt and pepper and wrap tightly in the cabbage cylinder. Proceed as directed for the livers.*

8 SERVINGS AS A LIGHT SUPPER OR LUNCH; 16 AS AN APPETIZER

CHICKEN STIR-FRIED WITH TREE EARS AND GINGER JULIENNE
(Gai Pad Khing Hed Hoo Noo)
THAILAND

You get an astonishing amount of taste and texture for little effort in this very popular Chinese-influenced dish that was demonstrated by sous-chef Viboon Roongrojpanawan in the busy Thai kitchen of the Hilton International Bangkok. The fresh and bright dish, which is served in the sunlit garden restaurant, Suan Saranrom, is composed of tender white chicken, crisp spring onion pieces, a very large quantity of tingly ginger strips, brisk red chilli-pepper, and black, crunchy mushrooms—lightly sauced with a bit of garlic and a touch of sweetness.

---

6 large or 10 medium dried tree ears (see Note)
450 g (1 lb) boneless chicken breast (3 large breast halves)
3 tablespoons vegetable oil
2 teaspoons finely chopped garlic
1 medium-large Spanish onion, quartered and sliced 5 mm (¼ inch) thick
60 g (2½ oz) peeled julienne-cut fresh ginger

1 red chili-pepper (10–12 cm/4–5 inches long, cut into 3 cm (1½-inch) diagonal slices
50 g (2 fl oz) oyster sauce (see Note)
50 g (2 fl oz) chicken stock
1½ teaspoons sugar
4 small spring onions, cut into 2.5 cm (1-inch) lengths
1 tablespoon distilled white vinegar
6 g (¼ oz) coriander leaves

---

1. Soak the tree ears in about 450 ml (¾ pint) warm water until supple, about 15 minutes. Drain and rinse. Cut into 5 cm (2-inch) pieces, trimming off any knotty bits.

2. Trim skin and any tendons or membrane from the chicken. Cut into strips about 5 cm (2-inches) long and 1 cm (½-inch) wide.

3. Have all the other ingredients measured and ready. Heat a wok over moderate heat. Pour the oil around the rim; toss the garlic for a moment until light golden. Add the onion and toss for 30 seconds.

4. Add the chicken and raise the heat to its highest point. Stir-fry until half-cooked, about 1½ minutes. Add the ginger, mushrooms, and chilli. Toss for 1 minute.

5. Add the oyster sauce and toss for 30 seconds. Add the stock and toss a moment. Add the sugar and spring onions; toss for 15 seconds. Add the vinegar and toss.

6. Transfer to a hot dish. Sprinkle with the coriander.

Note: *Tree ears, also known as cloud ears, wood ears,* mo-ehr, *black fungus, are readily obtained in most Oriental groceries in many different sizes.*

   Bottled oyster sauce, a staple in the East, can be found in all Oriental groceries and many supermarkets.
Serving: *If you are not passionate chilli-lovers, pick out the peppers and place as garnish; or warn diners not to crunch the pods.*

4 SERVINGS

OVERLEAF: Chicken Stir-Fried with Tree Ears and Ginger Julienne

CHICKEN AND CASHEWS WITH CHINESE MUSTARD GREENS

TAIWAN

Yu Wen-Shen and Huang Hsien developed this version of a fine Chinese dish served at the Hilton International Taipei. Simple, attractive, and accessible, it appeals to both Eastern and Western guests. The Chinese mustard greens, furled and channelled like giant seashells, have a radish-cabbage flavour, bitter and cleansing, that is balanced by the sweetness of cashews and tender chicken. Although boldly flavoured with garlic and fresh chilli-pepper, the egg binding mellows the sauce, making it creamier than most dishes of this kind.

8 medium chicken thighs (about
    700 g/1½ lb)
2 tablespoons soya sauce
2¼ teaspoons cornflour
1 egg
1 medium head Chinese mustard
    greens (Swatow mustard cabbage,
    dai gai choi; see Note)
4 tablespoons peanut oil
Salt and pepper

1 tablespoon slivered hot red chilli-
    pepper, seeds and ribs removed
2 tablespoons Chinese rice wine or
    dry sherry
1 tablespoon distilled white vinegar
2 large spring onions, trimmed and
    cut into 5 cm (2-inch) lengths
4 medium-large garlic cloves, sliced
60 g (2½ oz) roasted cashew nuts,
    preferably unsalted

1. Preheat the oven to its lowest setting. Remove the skin and bones from the chicken; cut the meat into 1 cm (½-inch) cubes. Stir together 1 tablespoon soya sauce and 2 teaspoons cornflour. Add the egg and blend. Add the chicken pieces. Cover and let marinate for ½–1 hour.

2. Meanwhile, select 8 of the firmest, prettiest mustard green leaves; trim off most of the ruffly leaf tips and wash the broad ribs. Drop into boiling, salted water; boil for 2–3 minutes, until crisp-tender. Drain, run under cold water. Spread on a towel.

3. Drain the chicken in a sieve, tossing to drip off the excess liquid. Heat a wok over moderate heat. Pour 2 tablespoons peanut oil around the rim. Toss the blanched greens in the oil to heat through. Sprinkle with salt and pepper. Arrange in a heatproof serving dish as a base for the chicken. Set in the low oven.

4. Combine the chilli-pepper, rice wine, vinegar, the remaining 1 tablespoon soya sauce, and the remaining ¼ teaspoon cornflour. Pour the remaining 2 tablespoons oil into the wok. Add the chicken and toss to not quite cook through. With a slotted spoon transfer to a dish.

5. Add the spring onions and garlic to the wok; toss until soft. Add the chicken and the rice wine mixture to the pan; toss for a minute. Add the cashews and toss.

6. Scoop into the warm platter lined with the greens. Serve hot.

Note: *Several cultivars of this mustard family member can be found in most Oriental shops. Some are rounded and fairly tightly furled, others long-leafed and loosely bunched. All have pale green midribs with shallow channels or furrows and darker leaf tips (which may be removed). Vaguely resembling a head of long-leafed lettuce, the innocent-seeming vegetable packs a big, bitter, radishy punch, which is softened by the blanching.*

4 SERVINGS

BRAISED AND GRILLED CHICKEN IN COCONUT AND JAVANESE SPICES
(Ayam Sakang)
INDONESIA

The popular Peacock Café at the Jakarta Hilton International is warmly rose-beige and pink, spacious—and superb for people-watching around the clock. Whether it is 15 French teenagers enjoying a full rijstaffel *buffet, a group of Chinese businessmen downing a mountain of croissants and Danish pastry before an early morning flight, a superbly painted Vietnamese actress and her hairdresser nibbling a salty rice porridge after a night of discos, or the Indonesian family of eight—all members of which were happily eating the following dish—the place is always hopping.*

This informal, curryish Javanese chicken is braised in a rich sauce of coconut milk, ginger, coriander, lemon grass, and chilli, thickened and sweetened with roasted nuts and brown sugar, then briefly browned and crisped under the grill.

6 medium leg-thigh chicken pieces (about 1.4 kilos/3¼ lb)
3 tablespoons vegetable oil
2 stalks lemon grass (see Note)
4 medium shallots
4 medium-large garlic cloves
7 cm (2½-inch) chunk peeled fresh ginger
3 tablespoons ground coriander
2 teaspoons ground turmeric

4 bay leaves
¾ teaspoon salt
350 ml (12 fl oz) unsweetened coconut milk (see Note)
50 ml (2 fl oz) Chinese chilli sauce (see Note)
3 tablespoons brown sugar
50 g (2 oz) roasted macadamia nuts, chopped fine
Basil leaves for garnish

1. Trim loose fat from the chicken, then cut apart the legs and thighs.

2. Heat 2 tablespoons of the oil in a 25 cm (10-inch) frying pan over moderate heat. Add the chicken pieces and brown well on both sides. Remove from the pan and set aside. Pour out all but 2 tablespoons fat from the pan and reserve.

3. Cut the heavy upper leaves from the lemon grass; unwrap the dry green layers until you get to the pale core. Halve lengthwise; cut into 2.5–5 cm (1–2-inch) slices. With the motor running, drop the lemon grass into a food processor. Add the shallots, garlic and ginger, and grind to a fine texture to make a seasoning paste.

4. Heat the reserved fat over moderately low heat. Scoop in the seasoning paste; stir constantly for 2 minutes. Add the coriander, turmeric, bay leaves and salt; stir for 1 minute. Add the coconut milk; stir to blend. Add the chilli sauce, brown sugar, and macadamia nuts; stir for another minute.

5. Add the chicken; press into the thick sauce. Cook over low heat for 20 minutes, stirring often and moving the chicken around in the pan to cook evenly and prevent sticking.

6. Preheat the grill. Transfer the chicken pieces to a grill pan, skin side up. Remove all the fat from the sauce along with the bay leaves. Simmer the sauce, stirring, for about 5 minutes, or until it is pasty. Spoon off any remaining fat. Brush the chicken pieces generously with the sauce (if some remains, save it to use as the base of a curry-type braise).

7. Set the chicken pieces in the middle level of a preheated grill. Cook until crisped, about 10 minutes.

Note: *Long stalks of greyish-green fresh lemon grass can be found in Asian groceries and some supermarkets. They add a subtle, inimitable lemon pungency.*

Coconut milk is available in canned or bottled form in stores that carry ingredients from India and Asia. If you cannot buy it, make your own, following the directions on page 325.

Chinese chilli sauce (easily obtained in Oriental markets and many other stores) has varying pungencies, densities, and flavourings. As long as it is fairly thick but pourable, and contains primarily chilli, garlic, salt, sugar, and vinegar, it will do. The bite is considerably tamed by the other ingredients and cooking procedures.

4 SERVINGS

1. Sprinkle the gelatine over the orange juice in a small non-aluminium saucepan. Add the sugar. Let stand a few minutes to soften.

2. Meanwhile, slice enough berries into crosswise rounds to line the bottom and sides of six 100 ml (4 fl oz) timbale (dariole) moulds (see Note). Do not overlap the slices. Cut remaining berries into tiny dice.

3. Bring the gelatine mixture to a simmer over low heat, stirring. Add the diced strawberries and stir; remove from the heat.

4. Set the saucepan in iced water. Cool, stirring occasionally, until thickened and partly set. Whisk the yogurt in a mixing bowl to liquefy. Whip the cream in a small bowl to form soft peaks. Pour the gelatine-berry mixture over the yogurt; add the rum. Blend thoroughly with a rubber spatula. Fold in the cream, mixing until few blobs remain visible.

5. Spoon the mixture into the prepared moulds. Cover with clingfilm and refrigerate for 3 hours or longer.

6. While the desserts chill, prepare the sauce: Combine the orange juice and sugar in a small non-aluminium saucepan; bring to a boil to dissolve the sugar. Cool. Add the Grand Marnier and mint to taste. Refrigerate until serving time.

7. Remove all skin and pith from the oranges. Sliver off the membrane, then cut between the partitions to section the oranges closely. Chill.

8. To serve, dip each timbale into warm water for a few seconds; gently unmould onto an individual serving plate (leaving plenty of room for the sauce and fruit). Spoon the sauce onto the plate, arrange 6 orange slices alongside, then garnish with the mint sprigs. Repeat with all the desserts.

Note: *The neat timbale shape looks very stylish and trim, but you can substitute ramekins or any other small forms from which the dessert will unmould easily.*

6 SERVINGS

GUAVA FRITTERS AND MANGO WITH BLUEBERRY TOFU CREAM

TAIWAN

Chef Peter Knipp's cross-cultural creations are never predictable. This festive dessert, served at the Hilton International Taipei, looks wild and gaudy: tart, violet sauce and sweet orange mango are tucked around easy-to-make, extremely delicate fried packets of guava.

(continued)

225 g (8 oz) tender ripe guava (or use canned, see Note)
1 tablespoon granulated sugar
1 star anise, broken into 2 sections
¼ teaspoon ground cinnamon
1 lemon slice
Sauce
1 tablespoon granulated sugar
75 g (3 oz) fresh blueberries
100 g (4 oz) silken or soft tofu (see Note)

About 2 tablespoons single cream
About 1 tablespoon lime juice
Final assembly
16 wonton skins, 8.5 cm (3½-inches) square (see Note)
1 egg yolk blended with 1 teaspoon water
2 medium mangos
Vegetable oil for deep frying
Icing sugar
Sprigs of mint for garnish (optional)

1. Peel, quarter, and seed the guava; cut into small dice. Combine 50 ml (2 fl oz) water, the granulated sugar, star anise, cinnamon and lemon in a small non-aluminium saucepan and bring to a simmer. Add the fruit; stir and cover. Cook over low heat until tender—5–15 minutes. Uncover; simmer to evaporate any liquid, if necessary. Remove the lemon and star anise. Cool.

2. Prepare the sauce: Combine the granulated sugar, 2 tablespoons water, and the blueberries in a small non-aluminium saucepan. Bring to a boil, stirring. Boil for 30 seconds. Press through a sieve. Chill the purée. Beat the tofu with a whisk to liquefy it. Whisk in the blueberry purée, then the cream, adjusting to the desired consistency. Add the lime juice. Refrigerate.

3. Assembly: Spread the wonton skins on a dry work surface. Place about 1 heaped teaspoon of the guava compote on each; brush the edges with the egg yolk. Fold to form neat triangles.

4. Peel the mangos; cut into thin slices. Arrange on 4 large plates.

5. Pour oil into a deep-fat fryer or electric frying pan to a depth of about 5 cm (2 inches). Heat to 180°C/350°F. Drop in the wontons, 8 at a time, and fry until light golden, ½–1 minute. Drain on paper towels while you fry the remainder.

6. Spoon blueberry cream onto each plate. Dust icing sugar over the fritters; arrange alongside. Serve warm, garnished with mint.

Note: *If fresh guava is not available to you, substitute a 450 g (1 lb) can of guava shells in syrup. Drain and rinse the fruit; cut the correct weight into tiny dice. Add 2 tablespoons lime juice and ¼ teaspoon cinnamon. Proceed to Step 2.*

Silken tofu is more delicate and custard-like than soft tofu which may, however, be substituted.

Wonton skins this size are available in all Oriental grocery stores and in many supermarkets, as is the silken tofu.

Advance preparation: *The blueberry sauce improves if made a day in advance. Dumplings made with canned guava can be tightly wrapped in a single layer and refrigerated for 24 hours before frying; ones made from the fresh should wait no longer than 4 hours before being fried.*

Serving and presentation: *Mr Knipp cuts the mangos in thinnest lengthwise slices and folds them to overlap, like waves. If you have custard-soft, fibreless mangos, do the same.*

4 SERVINGS

A Sip of Australian Wine Country:
The Grange at the
Hilton International Adelaide

Adelaide, in South Australia, a broad, open city that blends aspects of Victorian, Wild West, and state-of-the-art contemporary architecture, is a peaceful place, except during the Grand Prix, which zooms through it. Settled primarily by English, Scottish and Irish, who had done well in banking, real estate and mining, the grapevines were first planted in 1838—and 60 per cent of the country's wines are now produced there. The Hilton International Adelaide is home to The Grange, an esteemed restaurant named in honour of the Grange Hermitage of Penfolds, one of Australia's most celebrated wines (itself named after the original Grange cottage built by the founder of the vineyard in the mid-nineteenth century). The hotel is within an hour's drive of 120 registered wineries and offers (from a unique walk-in cellar and tasting room) an award-winning wine list of 400 wines, 80 per cent of which come from the area.

For a dinner that showcased local foods and wine, Gerard Taye, executive chef, began with Marinated Tasmanian Salmon Roses, a presentation of subtly marinated slices of richly coloured raw fish furled into rose forms and served with a piquant and fresh peppercorn sauce. The Atlantic salmon featured has been, until recently, a species found only in northern climes, but is being farmed successfully in Tasmania for the first time. The dish was accompanied by a long-finishing 1984 Orlando St Hillary Chardonnay, tinged with tropical fruit flavours. There followed an intense consommé of wild Coorong stubble quail which held tiny quenelles—each containing a creamy-soft poached quail egg that burst on the tongue. Matched with the deep amber essence was a like-coloured, brilliant special-blend sherry, reminiscent of both amontillado and amoroso, the work of the legendary Master Winemaker of Penfolds, Max Schubert. Smoked loin of kangaroo (surprisingly bland, lean, and tender—and permissible as restaurant fare only in this part of the country) was embellished with blackcurrant sauce, a tiny potato galette, baby carrots and turnips, and perfectly paired with a deeply cassis-flavoured Penfolds Bin 389 1982. The complex Gippsland blue cheese and buttery Tasmanian Camembert were complemented by celery bread, pillowy-fat dried muscat raisins, celery sprigs, and the namesake wine of the restaurant, 1980 vintage. Passion fruit, mango, and strawberry sherbets with passion fruit sauce left a clean perfume in the mouth—or one could move on to the multitude of dessert wines offered, if one possibly could survive.

The Hilton International chefs responsible for the annual Ultimate Dinner (from left to right): Jean-Yves Meraud of Sydney; Herbert Franceschini of Brisbane; Gerard Taye of Adelaide; Anton Muhlbock of Perth; Heiner Volkens of Sydney Airport; and Patrick Biddlecomb, of Melbourne. In the centre is Max Schubert, the creator of Grange Hermitage, the most celebrated of the wines of Penfolds, the event's co-sponsor.

The Ultimate Dinner

Since 1984, the executive chefs of Hilton International's Australian hotels and the distinguished winery, Penfolds, have created an annual gala known as The Ultimate Dinner, a celebration of native ingredients in elaborate and fanciful guises. In 1986 the event, which took place at the Hilton International Adelaide, progressed from an aspic of hare and kangaroo with a creamy sauce of puréed artichoke bottoms, through pigeon broth garnished with quail eggs and flakes of gold leaf, to a trio of local shellfish (Sydney rock oysters, South Australian green king prawns, Western Australian scallops) with sauces of lobster and mud crabs, to a roast loin of wild boar in quince sauce (see adaptation, page 298), through a cheese course, to a finale of cream-puff pelicans filled with mango and strawberry bavarian creams set in swirled fruit sauce 'paintings'.

DRIED FRUIT BREAD

AUSTRALIA

Although many of the dishes from The Ultimate Dinner are not ones that can be duplicated at home (unless you live in Australia and have a kitchen staff of vast proportions), part of the meal can be successfully made by the amateur cook. The course dubbed 'Cheeses from the Pastoral Lands' was offered with two simple baked goods (both recipes follow): long, egg-glazed loaves packed with dried fruits, and pale biscuit-like rounds—both unusual complements for the rich cheeses. Outside of Australia, a double cream cheese can be substituted for the King Island cheese, a creamy blue for the Gippsland blue, and Brie for the Jindivick. The three cheeses and two breads were served along with dried muscat grapes or figs and a garnish of celery leaves.

---

6 g (¼-oz) packet of active dry yeast
2 tablespoons warm water
2 tablespoons sugar
350 ml (12 fl oz) warm milk
460 g (17½ oz) bread flour, plus
    about 100 g (4 oz) for kneading
100 g (4 oz) dried currants
75 g (3 oz) raisins
75 g (3 oz) sultanas

100 g (4 oz) mixed glacéed fruit peel,
    chopped small
250 g (9 oz) dried apples, coarse-
    chopped
1 egg, beaten
1 teaspoon ground nutmeg
2 teaspoons salt
25 g (1 oz) softened butter
1 egg beaten with 1 tablespoon milk
    for glaze

---

1. Stir together the yeast, warm water and a pinch of the sugar. Let stand 5 minutes, until slightly fluffy. (If the mixture does not puff, begin again with fresh ingredients.) Add the remaining sugar and half the warm milk. Stir in 100 g (4 oz) flour to make a fairly smooth mixture. Sprinkle over 50 g (2 oz) more flour to coat evenly. Cover with a damp cloth. Let stand until the top has cracked in a marbled pattern, about ½ hour.

2. Meanwhile, combine the currants, raisins, sultanas, peel, and apples in a bowl. Pour over boiling water to cover.

3. When the dough 'sponge' is ready, stir in the flour on top, then beat in the remaining milk, the egg, nutmeg, salt, and remaining flour. Knead in the soft butter, folding and stirring the dough in the bowl.

4. Spread the kneading flour on a working surface. Scrape the dough onto this and knead until shiny and supple, about 5 minutes, incorporating only as much flour as needed to prevent the dough from sticking.

5. Drain the fruit thoroughly, then dry on a towel. Gradually knead into the dough, incorporating flour from the board as needed. Cover and let stand for 10 minutes.

(continued)

Dried Fruit Bread (left) and Dampers (right) from the cheese course served at The Ultimate Dinner

6. Cut the dough in half. Roll each piece under your palms to form a cylinder about 38 cm (15 inches) long. With the side of your hand, press a trench lengthwise, down the centre of the loaf. Follow this mark to pinch the sides of the dough together and close the seam. Repeat. Turn seam side down and roll to form an even cylinder.

7. With a long spatula gently set the soft loaves well apart on a non-stick or parchment-covered baking sheet. Cover with a towel and let rise until doubled in bulk, about 1½ hours. Preheat the oven to 180°C/350°F (gas mark 4).

8. Brush the loaves with the egg glaze. Set in the centre of the oven and bake until the bread is evenly golden brown and sounds hollow when picked up and rapped on the bottom—about 45 minutes.

9. Cool completely on racks.

Advance preparation: *Loaves may be prepared several days ahead and cooled completely, then wrapped in clingfilm. Unwrap and warm for 10 minutes in a 180°C/350°F (gas mark 4) oven before serving.*

2 LOAVES, EACH ABOUT 20 SLICES

DAMPERS

AUSTRALIA

Damper *is a word used in the Australian outback for a primitive pancake made of flour and water that is baked in the coals of a campfire and consumed hot. Although it may be leavened, more often than not it is flat, unseasoned, and tough. By contrast the following so-called dampers are soft-spoken companions for the luxurious cheeses served at the Ultimate Dinner. They are pale, puffy, salty-sweet rounds somewhere between milk crackers and beaten biscuits and are decidedly not campfire fare. Paired with the Dried Fruit Bread (preceding recipe) and cheeses, they make an interesting dessert course. Or serve alongside soups and stews, or for a cheese and wine party.*

500 g (18 oz) bread flour, plus 50 g (2 oz) for rolling
1 tablespoon sugar
1 teaspoon salt

2 tablespoons baking powder
15 g (½ oz) butter
60 ml (2½ fl oz) double (or whipping) cream

1. Place the main quantity of flour, the sugar, salt and baking powder in a mixing bowl. Add 400 ml (14 fl oz) water and mix on low speed for 3 minutes. Add the butter and cream. Mix on medium speed for 3 minutes longer.

2. Cover and let stand for 5–10 minutes. (The dough will be *very* soft and sticky.)

3. Preheat the oven to 190°C/375°F (gas mark 5). Spread half of the extra flour on a working surface. Scoop the soft dough onto this. Using a dough scraper or stiff pancake turner, knead the dough briefly to incorporate most of the flour. Sprinkle half the remainder on the board, then pat the dough to form a rectangle. Sprinkle the remaining flour over this, then pat to form an even rectangle about 45 × 30 cm (18 × 12 inches).

4. Using a 17.5 cm (3-inch) round cutter, cut about 20 circles. Lifting carefully with the long side of a spatula, set 14 rounds on one baking sheet, 6 on another. Roll out the remaining dough and cut about 8 more. Place these on the second baking sheet.

5. Set the baking sheets in the middle and lower positions of the oven. Bake for 10 minutes, then switch positions. Bake for about 7 minutes longer, or until the tops are dry and firm and the undersides are lightly golden. Do not bake until browned. Serve freshly baked.

Advance preparation: *Although these soft, doughy dampers are at their best if served warm and fresh, they can be wrapped and stored for a day or so. To revive them, mist with a little water, then reheat for about 5 minutes in a 180°C/350°F (gas mark 4) oven.*

ABOUT 28

ABOUT THE INGREDIENTS

Most uncommon ingredients are described within the recipes.

Butter is unsalted.

Chilli-peppers' heat and intensity are so variable, even within the same variety, that it is impossible to give more than a vague general idea of how much to use. Add gradually, and to taste; remove ribs and seeds for most dishes, but leave in the ribs for passionate heat-lovers.

Eggs are size 1.

Flour is plain, unless otherwise specified.

Gelatine is the powdered, unflavoured type most commonly sold in packets.

Mussels that are cultivated, generally meatier and cleaner than wild, are available in fine fishmongers and some supermarkets. They are well worth the slightly higher price, as there is little waste. To clean, simply rinse the mussels in ice cold water. If any are open, test their freshness by sliding the shells in opposite directions. If there is considerable resistance, and the mussel either closes up or almost closes, keep it. If it stays open, or the shells slide apart, discard it. Remove the byssus threads ('beard').

Soya sauce refers to what is sometimes called 'thin' or 'regular' soya, such as the Kikkoman brand that is widely available. This is neither as salty as the Chinese soya, nor as sweet as most Japanese brands. If you use either of these others, cut down slightly on the quantity.

Squid cleaning is simple—more so than writing the directions: Holding the body (mantle) with one hand and tentacle part with the other, pull to separate the two: the viscera and ink sac will come out attached to the tentacle section. Cut the tentacle section from the head part and discard the latter. Squeeze the bony beak from the centre of tentacles; it will pop out. Cut tentacles into small sections. Pull out the clear plastic-like pen or sword from the mantle section and discard. Peel the purplish membrane from this section, working under running water. Carefully wash the mantle inside and out, emptying it of any remaining material.

Tomatoes, 'peeled, seeded, and diced', are treated slightly differently in hotels than most home kitchens. The skin is removed by blanching in the traditional manner; or, as we prefer for small quantities, by holding a tomato on a long-handled fork directly in a flame for a few seconds to blister the skin which is easily slipped off. The tomato is then quartered, and the entire soft, seedy section is cut out and discarded, leaving only the firm shell, which is cut into small squares. This presents a more attractive, less unpredictably watery dish (although it wastes the pulp).

COCONUT MILK

1 coconut

1. Preheat the oven to 190°C/375°F (gas mark 5). With clean nail or pick, tap holes in two 'eyes' of the coconut; drain and reserve the liquid.

2. Bake for 10 minutes. Holding with a towel, hit around the middle with a hammer until cracked all around. Pry out the flesh and cut into chunks.

3. Add enough water to the reserved coconut juice to make 450 ml ($^4/_5$ pint); bring to a boil. Combine half the boiling liquid with half the coconut flesh in a blender or processor; grind as fine as possible. Pour into a sieve lined with dampened muslin and let drain. Repeat, using the remaining coconut and liquid. Press and twist the cloth to extract all liquid from the coconut shreds.

Note: *For a thinner coconut milk, repeat the process with the ground coconut and an additional 1 cup boiling water. Store for only a day or two in the refrigerator, or for months in the freezer.*

MAKES 600 ML (1 PINT)

BASIC FISH STOCK

For most stocks, the bones of lean-fleshed, mild fish are preferable, as oily or strong fish may yield an undesirably aggressive flavour. Gauge the oiliness (or assertiveness of taste) by previous eating and cooking experience. Mackerel, herring and tuna will be too potent or fatty for most sauces or soups. Fish that contain large quantities of gelatine, such as halibut or cod, should be used in moderation, unless the finished dish will be one with considerable body and some stickiness—such as chowder. Fish that are considered prime candidates for the stockpot might be all types of plaice and sole, whiting, pike, pomfret, perch, red snapper and sea bass. Before putting any fish into the stockpot, be sure it is completly free of gills and viscera.

---

2 kilos (4 lb) fish bones and heads, with no innards or gills
2 small onions, quartered
2 sticks celery with leaves, sliced

1 large carrot, sliced
1 bay leaf
Small handful parsley stems

---

1. Wash the fish heads and bones well in cold water. Combine in a stockpot with 4 litres (7 pints) water, the onions, celery, carrot, bay leaf, and parsley stems. Bring to a simmer, skimming.

2. Simmer very gently for 20 minutes, skimming as needed. Ladle through a fine sieve.

3. Cool, cover, then refrigerate or freeze until needed.

MAKES ABOUT 2.75 LITRES (5 PINTS)

INDEX